5.00
11/

EVERYMAN, I will go with thee,

and be thy guide,

In thy most need to go by thy side

PLATO

Born at Athens, 428–427 B.C. After the death
of Socrates (399) he travelled in Greece, Egypt
and Italy. About 387 he returned to Athens
and founded the Academy, over which he
presided for the remainder of his life, except for
two visits to Sicily on political business (367
and 361). He died in 348–347 B.C.

PLATO

Parmenides · Theaitetos
The Sophist · The Statesman

TRANSLATED WITH AN INTRODUCTION BY
JOHN WARRINGTON

DENT: LONDON
EVERYMAN'S LIBRARY
DUTTON: NEW YORK

NO. 456

SBN: 460 00456 5

CONTENTS

▼

INTRODUCTION

THE dialogues printed in this volume form a single group, and internal evidence shows that Plato intended them to be read in the order here observed. *Theaitetos* is closely related to *Parmenides*;[1] it contains a reference to the great Eleatic's supposed visit to Athens, which is represented as the occasion of *Parmenides*. *The Sophist* and *The Statesman* are professed sequels to the conversation begun in *Theaitetos*.

Although these four dialogues were not intended as a systematic treatise on epistemology, they do in fact give us a fair picture of the author's theory of knowledge and scientific method, and are consequently of great importance in the history of human thought. They represent Plato's critical reconstruction of the Ideal theory, which had been foreshadowed in the early dialogues and explicitly set out in the *Phaedo* and *Republic*. These latter tell us only that a sensible thing is a temporary meeting-point of a plurality of Forms, but such a thing is obviously more than an agglomeration of universal predicates; clearly the relation between a thing and a Form, which Plato described as 'participation', needed further elucidation. Plato was also aware that the simple formula that 'knowledge is confined to Forms and their relations, while we can have only shifting opinions about temporal facts' did less than justice to our scientific knowledge of the natural world. Again, he saw that if Forms constitute a rationally ordered system, there must be definite principles of interrelation between Forms themselves as well as between Forms and sensibles, and that those principles called for investigation. Finally, he was moved to undertake this reappraisal by his interest in the Eleatic philosophy. *Parmenides* and *The Sophist* in particular reveal his anxiety to show that, despite some important divergences, he, and not the Megarian school, was the true spiritual heir of Parmenides.

Since these four great dialogues are extremely difficult—they

[1] *Parmenides*, in the original, is written in straight narrative form. I have rendered it here as a dialogue for the sake of clarity.

would have been incomprehensible to any but the most advanced students of the Academy—a short summary of their teaching will not be out of place here.

Parmenides consists of two parts. In the first Plato reproduces the Megarian criticisms of the doctrine which he himself had ascribed to Socrates. The youthful Socrates expounds the doctrine of the 'participation' of sensibles in Forms to the Eleatic philosophers Zeno and Parmenides, as the solution of the problem of the One and the Many. Parmenides then raises what appear to be insuperable objections[1] to the doctrine of participation, though he admits that dialectic would be impossible if the existence of Forms were denied. He suggests that Socrates' inability to refute his criticism is due to inadequate training in logic.

Parmenides' objections then are directed not against the existence of Forms, but against the possibility of sensibles 'participating' in them. He argues first that the Ideal theory fails to reconcile unity and plurality, leading only to an infinite regress. According to it the many things which have a common predicate 'participate' in a single Form. But since the Form itself admits of a common predicate there must be a second Form 'participated' both by the sensibles and by the first Form, and so on *ad infinitum*. It is no use urging that the Form exists in the mind alone; if it did, a Form would be simply a thought, and sensibles would consist of thoughts. This in turn would mean either that everything thinks, or that there are such things as unthinking thoughts, and both those propositions are manifestly absurd. Again, says Parmenides, if there is a world of Forms and another world of sensibles, the relations between Forms belong to the world of Forms, and those between sensibles to the world of sensibles. But we men, and therefore our knowledge, belong to the latter, so that we can have no knowledge of true realities (the Forms). If anyone knows them it is God; but since his knowledge is of realities it will not reach to the world of sensibles.

In the second and longer part of the dialogue Parmenides offers some examples of the kind of logical training he recommends. Taking his own celebrated thesis 'the One is', he propounds eight antinomies after the manner of Zeno, seeming to

[1] The reasoning is fallacious. *See* A. E. Taylor, 'Parmenides, Zeno and Socrates', in *Transactions of the Aristotelian Society*, N.S., xvi, 234 ff.

prove that whether you affirm or deny the thesis you are in either case obliged to affirm simultaneously or to deny simultaneously a series of contradictory predicates, alike of the 'One' and of the 'Many'. The purpose of these antinomies has been much disputed. The most probable opinion seems to be that they are nothing but parody, the object being to show that the Megarians employ logical methods more harmful to their own system than to the Platonic doctrine of 'participation'.

Theaitetos, apart from a noble panegyric on the contemplative life (pp. 105–10), is a discussion of the question 'How are we to define knowledge?' Each of the three suggested definitions is shown to be unacceptable, but the dialogue remains to this day the most valuable introduction to the problem of knowledge.

The first definition put forward is 'Knowledge is perception', which is very much like saying with Protagoras that 'Man is the measure of all things'. This doctrine of the relativity of all knowledge might be based on the Heraclitean theory that the only reality is motion. But (1) (*a*) even the followers of Protagoras do not maintain that a man is the sole 'measure' of his *future* perceptions; (*b*) a man's own opinion of what will be good for him often proves to be wrong; (*c*) to say that 'knowledge is perception' is to ignore the distinction between sense-data and those things which are perceived without the intervention of bodily organs, e.g. number, sameness, good, bad, right. Consequently knowledge is to be looked for not in sensations, but in the mind's judgment upon them.

(2) Knowledge is then declared to be 'true judgment'. This definition implies, of course, that we know the meaning of 'false judgment', i.e. error. This, however, is not so. It is important not to confuse error with mere false recognition, that is to say, with the misinterpretation of present sensation, for there are purely intellectual errors, whose nature we find ourselves unable to explain. And, in fact, it is clear that rhetoric may produce in the hearer judgments which are true, but which cannot possibly be described as knowledge.

(3) It is finally suggested that 'knowledge is true judgment accompanied by discourse', i.e. judgment for which we can give grounds. Such a definition distinguishes knowledge from simple apprehension, and agrees with the theory of those who maintain that knowledge is invariably of compounds and never of the

simple elements. Now this theory itself presents certain difficulties; and furthermore, if we claim that knowledge is true
judgment with discourse, the 'discourse' can only be a statement of the logical *differentia* of the object known. The suggested
definition, therefore, amounts to saying that knowledge is true
judgment about an object together with *knowledge* of its
differentia.

The Sophist and *The Statesman* are both ostensibly concerned
with a problem of definition, in which a *genus* is repeatedly subdivided until the thing to be defined emerges as a subspecies.
The real purpose of *The Sophist*, however, is to explain the
nature of negative predication and thus to refute the Eleatic
thesis that the temporal and sensible world, because it contains
a negative moment, is mere illusion. The true object of *The
Statesman* is to examine the respective merits of personal
government and constitutionalism. It decides in favour of the
second in the form of limited monarchy. *The Sophist* is the root
of all subsequent logic, *The Statesman* that of all constitutionalism. Both dialogues incidentally seek to emphasize the
importance of careful classification as a basis of scientific
definition.

In *The Sophist* Plato begins by defining the sophist as an
illusionist, one who, by abuse of logic, produces the illusion that
all nature is full of insoluble contradictions.[1] The sophist would
answer that the definition is absurd; for there can be no such
thing as a false statement or a false impression. The false means
'what is not', and 'what is not', being nothing at all, is not
susceptible of utterance or thought. In order to refute him it is
necessary to show that which is not, in some sense also is and
vice versa. In other words we have to explain the meaning of a
significant negative proposition. A right theory of 'being' must
dispose first of the corporealists, who maintain that the real
'what is' is nothing other than visible and tangible body. These
people are refuted by the simple reminder that they themselves
cannot deny the reality of force, which is not a body. Secondly,
our theory of 'being' must meet the 'friends of Forms',[2] who

[1] The persons attacked under the name 'sophist' are the Megarians, who
abuse the dialectic of Zeno and Socrates. Here again, as in *Parmenides*, Plato
is claiming that he and not the Megarian school is the true heir of Parmenides.
[2] Probably Italian Pythagoreans.

hold that the real is a multitude of incorporeal Forms, who deny that sense-perception allows us any apprehension of it, and who consider force or activity as belonging to the unreal world of 'becoming'. To them Plato replies that knowing is itself an activity and that we cannot deny intelligence and knowledge to the supreme reality. This is equivalent to saying that the supreme reality possesses a soul and is alive. Now if life is real, movement and repose must likewise be real.

We are therefore left to deal with the monism of Parmenides by distinguishing between absolute and relative 'non-being'. To say that X is not Y does not signify that X is nothing, but that X is other than Y. The true business of dialectic is to study the various possible combinations of the universal 'categories' (being, identity, difference, motion, rest), each of which is other than every other. The Forms are thus made to appear as an interrelated system, with relations of compatibility and incompatibility among themselves. And since negation is a moment in the system of intelligible reality, its presence in the world of sensibles does not render that world illusory.

The main conclusion of *The Statesman* is that government by a benevolent dictator is unsuited to the conditions of human life, since the dictator is inevitably a fallible man and not a god. In any human society the substitute for personal rule by a god is the impersonal supremacy of inviolable law. Where such a law prevails, monarchy will be the best type of constitution, democracy the least satisfactory. But where there is no fundamental law this situation is reversed; a sovereign democracy is better than an irresponsible autocrat.

JOHN WARRINGTON.

1961.

The Stephanus numbers are placed in square brackets in the text.

SELECT BIBLIOGRAPHY

EDITIONS. Complete Works: A. P. Manutius and M. Musurus (Aldine Ed.), Venice, 1513; H. Stephanus and J. Serranus, Paris, 1578; G. Stalbaum, 1850; C. F. Hermann, 1851–3; I. Bekker, 10 vols. (Greek and Latin), 1816–1823; J. G. Baiter, J. C. Orelli and A. G. Winckelmann, 21 vols., 1839–41; R. B. Hirschig and C. E. C. Schneider, 1856–73; M. Schanz, 12 vols., 1875–1879; J. Burnet, 5 vols., 1899–1907.

TRANSLATIONS. F. Sydenham, 1759, 1776; T. Taylor and F. Sydenham, 1804; H. Cary and H. Davis, 1848–52, 1900; W. Whewell (Dialogues), 3 vols., 1859–61; B. Jowett (Dialogues), 3rd ed., 1892; H. N. Fowler, W. R. Lamb, R. G. Bury and P. Shorey, 12 vols. (Loeb Library), with text, 1919–1937.

GENUINE WORKS. *Hippias Major, Hippias Minor, Jon, Menexenus, Charmides, Laches, Lysis, Cratylus, Euthydemus, Gorgias, Meno, Protagoras, Euthyphro, Apology, Crito, Phaedo, Symposium, Phaedrus, Republic, Parmenides, Theaetetus, Sophistes, Politicus, Philebus, Timaeus, Critias, Laws.* Separate editions and translations of the foregoing dialogues are numerous. Opinion is divided as to the authenticity of *Epinomis.* It is safe to admit the *Epistles* as genuine, with the exception of I and XII which are undoubtedly spurious. Plato's will (Diogenes Laertius III. 41–3) is certainly authentic; but the great majority, if not all, of the 32 epigrams attributed to him in the *Greek Anthology* are by other hands.

CRITICAL. F. Zeller, *History of Greek Philosophy*, 1881; W. Pater, *Plato and Platonism*, 1893; E. Parker, *Greek Political Theory : Plato and his Predecessors*, 1918; P. E. More, *The Religion of Plato*, 1921; A. E. Taylor, *Platonism and its Influence*, 1925; *Plato, the Man and his Work*, 1926; R. C. Lodge, *Plato's Theory of Logic*, 1928; C. Ritter, *The Essence of Plato's Philosophy* (trans. E. Alles), 1933; F. H. Anderson, *The Argument of Plato*, 1935; R. L. Nettleship, *The Theory of Education in Plato's Republic*, 1935; R. Demos, *The Philosophy of Plato*, 1939; *Plato's Academy : the Birth of the Idea and its Rediscovery*, 1939; J. Wild, *Plato's Theory of Man*, 1946; G. C. Field, *The Philosophy of Plato*, 1949; N. R. Murphy, *The Interpretation of Plato's Republic*, 1951; Sir W. D. Ross, *Plato's Theory of Ideas*, 1951; R. C. Lodge, *Philosophy of Plato*, 1956; R. S. Brumbaugh, *Plato on the One*, 1961; I. M. Crombie, *Examination of Plato's Doctrine*, 1962–3; R. L. Patterson, *Plato on Immortality*, 1966.

PARMENIDES

PERSONS OF THE DIALOGUE

Cephalos, the immediate narrator.
Adeimantos, Glaucon, brothers of Plato.
Antiphon, half-brother of Plato.
Pythodoros, the original narrator.

Socrates.
Zeno, a disciple of Parmenides.
Parmenides, founder of the Eleatic school.
Aristoteles, friend of Pythodoros.

[126] *Cephalos.* On arrival at Athens from Clazomenai, our home, we came across Adeimantos and Glaucon in the Agora. The former took my hand. 'Welcome, Cephalos!' he said; 'let us know if there is anything we can do for you here.'

'As a matter of fact', I replied, 'that is exactly the purpose of my visit. There is something I want to ask the two of you.'

'Ask then,' he said.

'I've forgotten the name of your half-brother,' said I. 'What was it now? He was only a child when I was last here, and that's a very long time ago. Let me see, wasn't his father called Pyrilampes?'

'That's right,' said Adeimantos; 'and the son's name is Antiphon. But why do you ask?'

'These gentlemen', I told him, 'are fellow citizens of mine. They are students of philosophy, and have heard that Antiphon, as you say his name is, was well acquainted with Pythodoros, Zeno's associate, and that he clearly remembers an account given him by Pythodoros of a conversation between Socrates, Zeno and Parmenides.'

'Yes, that's true,' said he.

'Well,' I replied, 'it is that conversation we are anxious to hear.'

'Simple enough,' he answered. 'When Antiphon was a lad he made a prolonged and careful study of its subject-matter; though now, like his grandfather and namesake, he spends most of his time riding horses. However, if you insist, let us go and see him. He left the Agora only a few minutes ago, but it's no distance to his house in Melite.'

1

With that we began our walk, [127] and found Antiphon at home; he was ordering a bridle, or some such apparatus, from a smith. When the fellow had gone his brothers explained the purpose of our call. Antiphon remembered me from my previous visit, and made me welcome. When we asked him to tell us about that conversation he showed some reluctance; it would take so long, he explained. But eventually he let us have the story as follows.

According to Pythodoros, Zeno and Parmenides once came to Athens for the Great Panathenaea. Parmenides was already well on in years; but although sixty-five and almost white, he was a fine-looking old man. Zeno was about forty at the time. He was tall and graceful, and was said to have been a particular favourite of Parmenides. They lodged, said Antiphon, at Pythodoros' house in the Cerameicos, outside the walls; and there they were visited by Socrates with a few companions, who were all anxious to hear a treatise by Zeno, which he and Parmenides had brought to Athens for the first time. Socrates was still a very young man.

Well, Parmenides was out, and Zeno read them the treatise on his own. He had almost finished when Pythodoros (as he said) returned in company with Parmenides and Aristoteles, who was afterwards one of the Thirty; so they did not hear much of the contents—excepting of course Pythodoros, who had heard Zeno read it once before.

Socrates listened, and then requested him to repeat the first thesis of the first Book. That done, he asked: 'Zeno, what exactly are you getting at there? Do you mean that if reality is a "many", many things must be at once like and unlike—which is absolutely impossible, because the unlike can never be like, nor the like unlike?'

'I do,' replied Zeno.

Soc. Ah! Since unlike cannot be like, or like unlike, it must also be impossible that reality should be many, because if it were it would have these irreconcilable characters. Am I right then in saying that your arguments have no other purpose than to maintain, against all contrary assertions, that reality is not many? Do you believe that each of those arguments proves this one point, and that you yourself, accordingly, are offering as many proofs that reality is not many as you have put forward arguments? [128] Is that what you mean; or have I misunderstood you?

ZENO. No, you have a perfect grasp of my theory as a whole.

SOC. I realize, Parmenides, that our friend Zeno here is resolved to identify himself with you in writing as well as in affection. His position in this treatise is closely akin to your own, though he tries to create an illusion of difference by altering the form. You say in your poem that 'reality is one', and you bring forward an impressive array of evidence in support of your thesis. Zeno, on the other hand, declares that 'reality is not many'; and he too advances a mass of weighty arguments. Now when you, Parmenides, say 'one' and Zeno says 'not many', in such a way that neither appears to repeat the other at any point, though both are in effect saying the same thing—that is where your pronouncements baffle us.

ZENO. Exactly, Socrates; which means that you have not fully grasped the real nature of my treatise, although you have picked up the scent of its argument in a way that reminds me of a Laconian bracket! In the first place you overlook the fact that my work does not exactly boast of being written for the purpose you mention, while cleverly concealing that purpose from mankind! No, you were referring to an incidental effect of my treatise, which in point of fact was composed in *support* of Parmenides' doctrine against those who try to make a fool of him by maintaining that if reality is one, many absurdities are involved which contradict the argument itself. My treatise, then, is directed against those who assert a plurality. It pays them in their own coin with a vengeance; and it is meant to show that their hypothesis ('Reality is Many'), when closely examined, involves yet greater absurdities than our assumption of the One. I wrote it in my young days as a controversial piece, and someone made an unauthorized copy; so I never had a chance to consider whether or not it should be published. That, Socrates, is where you are mistaken. You imagine the essay to have proceeded from the ambition of maturity, not from the controversial zeal of youth. However, as I was saying, your surmise was not a bad one.

SOC. Thank you; I accept what you say. But tell me this: Do you not agree that there is a Form of likeness, i.e. Likeness itself, [129] and another, opposite Form, Unlikeness, in both of which you and I and everything else we include in the term 'many' participate? And do you not agree further that things which partake of Likeness become alike in the same respect and to the same extent in which they partake of it, whereas things which partake of Unlikeness become unlike, and those which partake of both, both? And even if *all* things partake of both opposite Forms, and, by virtue of their participation in both, are simultaneously like and unlike one another, what wonder? It would of course be astonishing to discover *absolute* likes becoming unlike, or *absolute* unlikes becoming like. But if things which merely *partake* of both Forms are found to possess both characters—well, Zeno, I see nothing extraordinary about that, any more than I do if all things are shown to be *one* by virtue of their participation in plurality. I shall be flabbergasted if (but *only* if) someone demonstrates that what is *in itself* one is many, and conversely that the many are one. So too in all other cases. It would certainly be surprising if the kinds, or Forms, were shown to have these opposite characters in themselves; but there is surely nothing to be surprised at if somebody shows *me*, for instance, to be simultaneously one and many. In order to prove that I am *many*, he can point to my right side as different from my left, my front from my back, my upper from my lower parts; naturally, because I partake of *plurality*. When he wishes to show that I am *one*, he will say that I am one of the seven of us here together, thus partaking of unity also. In this way both assertions will be proved true. We may therefore conclude that if a man sets out to demonstrate that such things as stones, bits of wood, etc., are simultaneously many and one, we shall say he proves that some *thing* is both many and one, not that unity is plurality or vice versa. We shall find nothing extraordinary in what he says, which is after all a mere commonplace. If, on the other hand, having clearly discriminated the Forms, to which I just now referred—e.g. Likeness and Unlikeness, Plurality and Unity, Rest and Motion, etc.—he goes on to prove that these can alternately merge into and separate from one another, then, Zeno, I shall be dumbfounded. I think you have put up a fine show in handling the subject; but, as I say, I would be far more surprised if it were possible to show that the same difficulty arises, in its manifold complexity, among the Forms

themselves, which are apprehended by the intellect, [130] as
you two have traced it in objects of vision.

(While Socrates was speaking, Pythodoros expected Parmenides and Zeno to resent his words. On the contrary, they
listened most attentively and frequently exchanged glances indicative of their admiration; and when he had finished:)

PAR. Well, well, Socrates, your ardour in debate is altogether
praiseworthy. Tell me then, is this distinction your own—
the distinction, I mean, between the Forms and the things
which participate in them? Do you actually hold that there is
a Form of likeness quite distinct from any likeness apparent
in ourselves, and so too of unity, plurality, etc., of which you
have just heard Zeno discourse?

SOC. I do, indeed.

PAR. And how about such cases as these: are there Forms of
right, beautiful, good, etc.?

SOC. Yes.

PAR. What, and a Form of man distinct from ourselves here and
others like us, a Form of man, or of fire, or again of water?

SOC. As a matter of fact, Parmenides, I have often felt uncertain
whether or not to say the same in these cases as in the others
you have mentioned.

PAR. Then, Socrates, take certain instances which might seem
ridiculous—hair, for example, or mud, or dirt, or anything
else particularly worthless or particularly valuable. Have you
any doubt as to whether there are Forms of such things,
distinct from the specimens we can handle?

SOC. Oh no, things of this sort are just what we see them to be.
It would perhaps be going too far to posit Forms of such
things. On the other hand, there have been times when I have
had a niggling suspicion that what is true in one case may be
true in all. But I stop short on the brink and take to my heels
for fear of falling headlong into an abyss of nonsense and
losing myself altogether. I therefore content myself with the
things we have just referred to as definitely having Forms, and
devote my time to them.

PAR. Ah, that is because you are still young, and philosophy has
not yet enthralled you as I think she will do some day. When
that time comes you will lay aside all this indifference; but at
present, because of your age, you keep an eye on popular

opinion. However, there is one question I would like to ask
you. You have told us you believe there are certain Forms in
which the things of our world participate, and from which
accordingly they take their denominations; [131] e.g. by
participation in likeness they become alike, by participation
in magnitude large, by participation in beauty or justice just
or beautiful. Is that correct?

Soc. Perfectly.

PAR. Very good then, I take it you will agree that whatever
participates in a Form must participate in the whole or in part
of it. Is there any other possible mode of participation?

Soc. Why, of course not.

PAR. Then do you consider that the Form is present as a whole
in each and every one of the particulars, while remaining a
unity, or how?

Soc. What prevents its being so present?

PAR. In that case, though one and the same, it will be simultaneously present in many distinct things, and must therefore
be distinct from itself.

Soc. Not necessarily; not if each Form, one and the selfsame,
were present in them all, just as the one and selfsame daylight
is in several places at once without thereby becoming any the
more distinct from itself.

PAR. Surely, Socrates, that is a queer way of making one and
the same thing present in several places at once! You might as
well spread a single sail over a group of men and then say that
the one sail as a whole was stretched over many. Don't you
accept that as a fair comparison?

Soc. Maybe it is.

PAR. Very well, what would be over each of them, the sail as a
whole or a different part of it?

Soc. A different part.

PAR. These Forms of yours then are divisible, and the things
that participate in them will do so only in a part of them; and
what is present in each will never be the Form as a whole, but
only a part thereof.

Soc. Yes, I suppose so.

PAR. Right, Socrates; are you prepared to agree that our Form,
which you describe as *one*, is in fact divisible? If it is, will it
still be one?

Soc. Certainly not.

Par. Look now, suppose you split up Magnitude itself and say that every large thing is large by virtue of a *part* of Magnitude, which is less than Magnitude itself; won't your statement appear rather silly?

Soc. It will indeed.

Par. Again, suppose each thing gets a small *portion* of equality, will that thing possess anything by virtue of which it will be equal to something else—equal by virtue of what is less than equality itself?

Soc. Impossible.

Par. Moreover, one of us will have a portion of Smallness, and Smallness will be larger than this portion which is a mere fraction of it. Smallness itself, therefore, will be larger; but if the remainder be added to anything, the latter will become smaller instead of larger than it was.

Soc. That is something absolutely impossible.

Par. How then, Socrates, will other things participate in your Forms, seeing they can partake of them neither wholly nor in part?

Soc. Sure, that is no easy problem to solve.

Par. There's another point too.

Soc. What is that?

Par. I think I know why [132] you imagine these unitary Forms exist. When you have decided that a number of individual things are large, you probably cast your eye over the lot of them, notice that they present one and the same distinctive character, or pattern, and accordingly pronounce the Large to be one thing.

Soc. Quite right.

Par. But now take the Form Largeness and particular large things. When you cast your mind's eye over them in the same way, surely you must likewise conceive the notion of a single large Something by virtue of which they all seem large.

Soc. Granted.

Par. So here we have *another* Form of Largeness, distinct both from Largeness itself and from all things which partake thereof; and yet another by virtue of which all *these* will be large; so that none of your Forms will any longer be one, but an indefinite plurality.

SOC. Come, Parmenides, may not each of these Forms be a *thought*, properly located nowhere but in our *minds*? Looked at in this way, each of them would be one, and exempt from the consequences to which you just referred.

PAR. What, is each of them one of our thoughts, but a thought of nothing?

SOC. No, that is impossible.

PAR. A thought of something then?

SOC. Yes.

PAR. Of something that is, or of something that is not?

SOC. Of something that is.

PAR. Of *one* something, you mean, which that thought thinks here and now as one distinctive character, or pattern, in all the particulars?

SOC. Yes.

PAR. Then it will be this which is thought of as one and is in every case the same for all the particulars, which will be a Form. Do you not agree?

SOC. Once again, the conclusion seems unavoidable.

PAR. Well then, if other things participate in the Forms, as you say they do, must you not admit that each of these things is composed of thoughts, and so they all think, or else they are thoughts but unthinking thoughts?

SOC. That too is devoid of sense. Here is the view which most appeals to me. These Forms may be described as fixed patterns in nature; other things resemble them, i.e. are copies of them, and the so-called participation of those things in Forms is nothing else but resemblance to the Forms.

PAR. Then if anything is like the Form, must not the Form be like its likeness, in so far as the likeness was copied from it? Is it at all possible that A should not be like B when B is like A?

SOC. Indeed no.

PAR. And is it not absolutely inevitable that two likes must participate in one and the same Form?

SOC. It is.

PAR. And must not that by partaking whereof like things are alike be the Form itself?

SOC. Certainly.

PAR. It is accordingly impossible that anything should be like the Form, or the Form like anything else. Otherwise a second Form will invariably make its appearance in addition to the first, and then a third [133] if the second is like anything; and so fresh forms will appear *ad infinitum* if the Form is allowed to resemble that which partakes of it.

Soc. You are perfectly right.

Par. It follows that things do not participate in Forms by resembling them; no, we must look for some other means of participation.

Soc. So it seems.

Par. Now do you understand, Socrates, the extent of the problem created by your doctrine of independent Forms?

Soc. I certainly do.

Par. Mark my words, you have as yet little or no appreciation of the difficulty involved in postulating a single distinct Form for each class of things.

Soc. How is that?

Par. Well, the greatest difficulty, apart from many others, is this. If the Forms are as we say they must be, and someone denies that they can actually be known, it would be impossible to convince such an opponent of his error, unless he were a man of great experience and considerable attainments, and unless he were willing to follow the demonstration through a long and abstruse course of reasoning, without which the man who insists that the Forms are unknowable would remain unconvinced.

Soc. But why, Parmenides?

Par. Because, Socrates, you or anyone else who postulates the existence of any such 'reality in itself' will surely allow from the start that there are no such realities in this world round about us.

Soc. Of course not; if there were, how could they be 'realities *in themselves*'?

Par. You've hit the nail right on the head. Consequently those of your 'distinctive characters', or 'patterns', which are of their nature relative, exist in relation to one another, not in relation to their 'copies' or what not in our world, from participation in which we get various denominations. But things in the world about us which bear the same names are in point of fact relative to one another, not to the Forms; and when they have correlative names, those names have reference to one another rather than to the Forms.

Soc. How do you mean?

Par. Suppose, for example, one of us is the owner or the slave of another: he is not of course the slave of that owner simply as owner, or (if he is the owner) owner of the slave simply as slave; in each case the relation is one of man to man. Ownership *as such*, on the other hand, is correlative to servitude *as such*, and vice versa. The significance of terms in our world is quite unrelated to those of the world of Forms, as they are to us; as I say, they belong to their own world and are relative to [134] one another, and the same applies to the terms of our world. Do you follow me?

Soc. I see exactly what you mean.

Par. Now must not knowledge as such be knowledge of reality as such?

Soc. Certainly.

Par. And will you agree further that each distinct branch of knowledge as such must be knowledge of some department of being as such?

Soc. Yes, I will.

Par. But knowledge in our world must be knowledge of the reality in our world; moreover, each branch of knowledge in our world must be knowledge of some department of being in our world. Is not that so?

Soc. Of course.

Par. But again, as you yourself admit, we have no access to the Forms themselves, which cannot possibly belong to our world.

Soc. No, they cannot.

Par. Presumably the several Forms are known by the Form of knowledge?

Soc. Yes.

Par. But we do not possess this Form.

Soc. No, we don't.

Par. Consequently we know none of the Forms, because we have not the Form of knowledge.

Soc. Apparently.

Par. Therefore the Form of beauty, of good and so forth are unknowable for us.

Soc. I am afraid so.

PAR. Now consider an even graver consequence.

SOC. What is that?

PAR. You will no doubt agree that if there is a Form of knowledge, it is far superior to the knowledge in our world, and that the same is true of beauty, etc.

SOC. Yes.

PAR. Now if anything possesses the Form of knowledge, will you not grant that such perfect knowledge belongs to the divine nature rather than to any other?

SOC. Naturally.

PAR. Well, if the divine nature has the Form of knowledge, can it possibly know things in our world?

SOC. Why ever not?

PAR. Because it is agreed between us, Socrates, that the significance of those Forms has no relation to the things in our world, nor these latter to them; the contents of each world are relative only to one another.

SOC. Yes, we are agreed on that point.

PAR. Well then, if the ownership and knowledge belonging to the divine nature is this most perfect ownership and knowledge, the gods' ownership can never be ownership of us, nor their knowledge knowledge of us or of anything else in our world. Just as our dominion is not dominion over them, nor our knowledge knowledge of anything appertaining to the divine nature, it follows likewise that they, in spite of their divinity, neither own us nor know anything of human affairs.

SOC. It would surely be paradoxical to deny knowledge to the divine nature.

PAR. It would indeed, Socrates; but these and other difficulties [135] are inevitable if one postulates Forms which are the distinctive characters, or patterns, of things, and assumes an independent Form for everything. Hence a hearer will be perplexed and question the existence of such Forms, or else maintain that, in spite of their reality, they must of necessity be beyond the scope of human knowledge. He will make much more of these assertions, and, as I was saying, it will be extraordinarily difficult to change his mind. Only a man of very high intelligence will be able to understand that there is an independent Form of everything; and a man of even higher intelligence will be required to discover that Form and reveal what he has found to another who has made a careful study of all these difficulties.

Soc. You are quite right, Parmenides; you have taken the words out of my mouth.

Par. On the other hand, Socrates, if the contemplation of these and similar difficulties prevents our believing in Forms of things, if one declines to recognize a Form for each particular, one will have no object of thought, so long as one refuses to allow an unchanging Idea for every individual thing. Thus one will utterly destroy the procedure of dialectic. However, I believe you are fully conscious of that peril.

Soc. True enough.

Par. Then what about your career as a philosopher? What path will you follow while these problems remain unsolved?

Soc. I confess myself to be as yet somewhat in the dark.

Par. The reason is, Socrates, that you attempt prematurely, that is to say without previous training, to establish forms of Beauty, Justice, Goodness and so on. I made a mental note of that some days ago when listening to your conversation in this very house with our friend Aristoteles. Believe me, it is a splendid, nay a godlike urge that drives you to argument. But while you are still young you really must discipline yourself by taking more exercise in the supposedly futile procedure commonly known as Disputation; otherwise you will never catch up with truth.

Soc. How does one take this exercise, Parmenides?

Par. Zeno has given an example in your hearing. I must admit, on the other hand, that I was vastly impressed by one thing you said to him; I mean your insistence upon not limiting the discussion to visible particulars or to the visible world, instead of allowing it to range over those objects which are most specially apprehended by discourse and most readily considered as Forms.

Soc. Quite so; unless that is done it is fairly easy to prove that things are both like and unlike, or have any other character you please to name.

Par. Splendid! But there is one further point: if you intend to take a thorough course of exercise, you must not only assume for the sake of argument that 'X *is*', and then go on to examine the consequences of your assumption; [136] you must also assume likewise that 'X *is not*'.

Soc. What exactly do you mean?

Par. Well, take, if you like, the example of Zeno's hypothesis that 'reality is many'. First inquire what will be its consequences for (*a*) the many in relation to (i) one another and (ii) the one, and for (*b*) the one in relation to (i) itself and (ii) the many. Next, ask yourself what will be the consequences if reality is *not* many, as regards (*a*) the one and (*b*) the many, relatively (i) to themselves and (ii) to each other. Again, if you assume that 'there is similarity', or 'there is no similarity', you must ask yourself what follows, in either case, with regard (*a*) to the actual subjects of the assumption and (*b*) to other things, relatively both to themselves and to each other, The same rule will hold good of unlikeness, motion, rest, coming into being and perishing, yes, and even of being and not-being. In fact, when you postulate that anything is, or is not, or that it has any character you choose to name, you must, if you hope to attain a perfect vision of truth by thorough self-training, consider the consequences to that thing, or to any others you may choose, both severally, in groups, and altogether; moreover, you must study these 'others' as related among themselves as well as towards the particular 'other' you select in each case, whether your assumption is that the assumed thing *is* or that it *is not*.

Soc. That, Parmenides, is a stupendous task, and one which I do not fully understand. Why have you yourself not made some such assumption and gone through the process for my benefit?

Par. That, Socrates, is asking a great deal of a man as old as I am.

Soc. Well then, Zeno, what about you? Why have not *you* done what I suggest?

Zeno (*laughing*). Let us ask Parmenides himself to shoulder the business that he has in mind; it is no light burden, I can tell you. Do you not realize the magnitude of the task you would impose? If there were more of us here, it would not be right to expect it of him. The subject we have in mind is not for discussion before a large company, particularly by a man of his years; few men realize that without this circuitous and

comprehensive inquiry one can never meet with and understand the truth. Therefore, Parmenides, I join Socrates in his
request, and look forward myself to hearing you again after
all this time.

(I learned from Antiphon, who had it from Pythodoros, that
when Zeno had finished speaking he (Pythodoros), Aristoteles
and the rest, begged and implored Parmenides to explain what
he meant. The conversation then continued as follows.)

[137] PAR. I must do as you ask; all the same I feel rather like
the aged horse in Ibycus' poem, quivering with fear born of
experience as it waits to start in the chariot-race. The poet
compares himself to such an animal because of his reluctance
at being driven into love in his old age; in the same way, when
my memory stirs, I begin to dread the necessity of a voyage at
my time of life through so formidable a sea of words. However,
I must do my best to satisfy you, considering, as Zeno says, we
are alone together. Where, then, shall we begin? I mean what
is our initial postulate to be? Since we have bound ourselves
to play this energetic game may I suggest that we begin
with myself and my own hypothesis? Shall I assume (a) the
existence, and (b) the non-existence of my 'One', and examine
the consequences in each case?

ZENO. Do so by all means.

PAR. Who then will answer my questions? How about the
youngest of you? He would raise the fewest difficulties, and
would be most likely to reply exactly as he thinks. In any case,
his answers would give me a breather.

ARIST. The 'youngest of you' obviously refers to me, and I am
quite ready to accept your invitation, Parmenides. Ask, then I
will supply the answers.

[*The First Antinomy* [1]]

PAR. Right. Now if the One is, does it not follow that that One
is not many?

ARIST. Of course it does.

PAR. Therefore it can neither have parts, nor be a whole.

ARIST. Why not?

---

[1] If the One is, i.e. if all that exists is a single undifferentiated unity, we can
assert nothing about it.

PAR. Well, a part is surely part of a whole.

ARIST. Yes.

PAR. And what is a whole? Is it not that whereof no part is lacking?

ARIST. Certainly.

PAR. In either case, then, the One will be composed of parts, whether it is a whole or has parts?

ARIST. Inevitably.

PAR. Accordingly, and again in each case, the One will be not one but many.

ARIST. True.

PAR. But *ex hypothesi* it *is* one, and *not* many.

ARIST. It is.

PAR. Consequently, if the One is to be one, it can neither be a whole nor have any parts.

ARIST. Clearly not.

PAR. Well then, if it has no parts, it can have neither beginning, end, nor middle; for such qualifications would immediately be parts of it.

ARIST. Correct.

PAR. Furthermore, the end and beginning of anything are its limits.

ARIST. Certainly.

PAR. The One is therefore limitless, if it has neither beginning nor end.

ARIST. Agreed.

PAR. And consequently shapeless, for it can be neither round nor straight.

ARIST. How do you make that out?

PAR. Well, 'round' is surely that whereof the extremities are everywhere equidistant from its centre.

ARIST. Yes.

PAR. And 'straight', again, is that whereof the middle is in front of both extremities.

ARIST. Quite right.

PAR. Therefore, if the One could have shape, either straight or round, it would have parts and accordingly be many.

ARIST. Indeed it would.

PAR. Consequently it is neither straight nor round, [138] since it has no parts.

ARIST. True enough.

PAR. Furthermore, because it is such as we have just described, it cannot be anywhere; for it can neither be in another nor in itself.

ARIST. Why not?

PAR. If the One were in another it would be enclosed by that wherein it lay, and would have numerous contacts therewith at many points. But since it has no parts and no circularity, nothing can possibly touch its circumference at many points.

ARIST. Of course not.

PAR. Again, if it were in itself, it would by that very fact enclose itself within itself, because nothing can be *in* anything without being enclosed thereby.

ARIST. No, that is quite impossible.

PAR. Thus the envelope as such would be one thing, and that which is enclosed another; the same thing cannot as a whole perform both functions (enclosing and being enclosed) at the same time. Hence the One would no longer be one, but two.

ARIST. Undoubtedly.

PAR. If the One then can be neither in itself nor in anything else, it is nowhere at all.

ARIST. That is the inevitable conclusion.

PAR. Go on, now, from there and ask whether it can be at rest or in motion.

ARIST. Why shouldn't it be?

PAR. Well, if it were in motion it would be changing in respect either of position or of quality; there is no other kind of motion.

ARIST. Agreed.

PAR. But if the One is changing in respect of its quality it cannot in fact be one.

ARIST. No, it cannot.

PAR. Therefore it cannot be subject to motion in this sense.

ARIST. Apparently not.

PAR. Then what about local motion?

ARIST. It may perhaps have that.

PAR. Suppose it has: it must either revolve in one and the same place or be transferred from one place to another.

ARIST. Yes, it must.

PAR. Well, if it revolves, its movement must be about a centre; and the parts of it which turn around that centre must be other than itself. But how can a thing to which no centre or parts can be attributed revolve about its centre?

ARIST. It just cannot do so.

PAR. Maybe, then, it can move in the sense of altering its position, of being now in one place and now in another.

ARIST. It must do that if it moves at all.

PAR. But have we not just proved that the One can never *be in* anything?

ARIST. Yes.

PAR. Well, how much more impossible that it should *come into* anything.

ARIST. I do not follow your argument.

PAR. Why, surely if X is *coming into* Y, it cannot, so long as the process continues, *be* in Y, nor yet wholly outside it, because it is actually *coming into* Y.

ARIST. Agreed.

PAR. Consequently this can happen only to a thing which has parts; one part of X will be *in* and another part *outside* Y, at one and the same time. But that which is devoid of parts cannot possibly, as a whole and simultaneously, be inside or outside anything else.

ARIST. True.

PAR. And if X neither has parts nor is a whole, how much more impossible for it to *come into* Y, seeing that it can do so neither part by part nor as a whole.

ARIST. Evidently.

PAR. [139] Thus it cannot alter its position by going anywhere and *coming into* anything, nor by revolving about a centre, nor by changing in respect of quality.

ARIST. It would seem not.

PAR. The One, therefore, is incapable of moving, in any sense of the word 'motion'.

ARIST. It is.

PAR. But we also maintain, do we not, that the One cannot *be in* anything?

ARIST. We do.

PAR. Then it is never in the same state.

ARIST. How on earth do you make that out?

PAR. Because if it were, it would immediately be *in* that self-same state wherein it is.

ARIST. True enough.

PAR. But we have agreed that it cannot be *in* anything at all, either in itself or in another.

ARIST. We have.

PAR. Very well then, the One can never be in the same state.

ARIST. Yes, I see that.

PAR. But what is never in the same state is not at rest, or stationary.

ARIST. No, it cannot be.

PAR. It would appear then that the One is neither stationary nor in motion.

ARIST. It would certainly appear so.

PAR. Again, it cannot be the *same as* itself or as anything else, or *other than* itself or anything else.

ARIST. Why not?

PAR. If it were other than itself it would clearly be other than one, i.e. *not* one.

ARIST. True.

PAR. And if it were the same as something else, it would *be* that thing, i.e. not itself; so that here again it would not be what it is, viz. *one*, but *other than* one.

ARIST. Yes, of course it would.

PAR. In that case it can neither be the same as something else, nor other than itself.

ARIST. Granted.

PAR. Nor, so long as it is one, can it be other than something else; for to be other than something else is characteristic not of the One but only of that which is 'other than' another, and of nothing else.

ARIST. Correct.

PAR. So you will doubtless agree that it cannot be an 'other' by virtue of being one.

ARIST. Certainly I agree.

PAR. In other words, it cannot be an 'other' by virtue of being itself, and therefore not *as* itself; and if *as* itself it is in no sense 'other', it cannot be other than anything.

ARIST. Right again.

PAR. Nor indeed can it be the same as itself.

ARIST. Why not?

PAR. Well, I think you will admit that the nature of unity is one thing, and that of sameness another.

ARIST. Why?

PAR. Because a thing does not always become one when it becomes the same as something.

ARIST. But why not?

PAR. If it becomes the same as the many, it must thereby become many and not one.

ARIST. True.

PAR. On the other hand, if there were no difference between unity and sameness, whenever a thing became the same it would always become one, and vice versa.

ARIST. Certainly.

PAR. Therefore if the One is to be the same as itself, it will not be *one* with itself; so it will be one and yet not one, which is impossible. Hence, it is impossible for the One to be (*a*) other than something else, *or* (*b*) the same with itself.

ARIST. Quite impossible.

PAR. So it comes to this, that the One cannot be other than, or the same with, itself or something else.

ARIST. No, it cannot.

PAR. Nor again can it be either like or unlike itself or anything else.

ARIST. How so?

PAR. Well, the 'like' is presumably something which has an identical character.

ARIST. Yes.

PAR. But we have already seen that the character of sameness is quite distinct from that of unity.

ARIST. We have.

PAR. [140] But if the One has any character apart from that of being one, it must be that of being more than one, which is impossible.

ARIST. Yes.

PAR. Therefore the One cannot possibly have an identical character with anything else or with itself.

ARIST. Apparently not.

PAR. Accordingly, the One cannot be 'like' another thing or 'like' itself.

ARIST. So it would seem.

PAR. At the same time it cannot have the character of being different; otherwise it would again have the character of being more than one.

ARIST. Yes, it would.

PAR. But if the 'like' is that which has an identical character, then the 'unlike' is that which has a difference in character from itself or from something else.

ARIST. Correct.

PAR. But since the One appears to have no differences in character, it is in no way unlike either itself or anything else.

ARIST. No, it cannot be.

PAR. So it amounts to this, that the One cannot be like *or* unlike either itself or anything else.

ARIST. Apparently not.

PAR. In which case it can be neither equal nor unequal to itself or to anything else.

ARIST. How do you account for that?

PAR. If it is equal it must be of the same measures as that to which it is equal.

ARIST. Yes.

PAR. Then if it is greater or less, it will have more measures than the things that are less than itself, and fewer than the things that are greater than itself, presuming in each case that those things are commensurable with it.

ARIST. Yes.

PAR. Where, on the other hand, they are *not* commensurable with it, it will have smaller measures in the one case and larger in the other.

ARIST. Inevitably.

PAR. But is it not absolutely impossible that a thing which has no trace of sameness should 'be of the same' measures—or 'of the same' anything, for that matter?

ARIST. Quite impossible.

PAR. We may conclude, then, that since the One is not 'of the same measures', it cannot be equal to itself or to anything else.

ARIST. That would seem to be the obvious inference.

PAR. Again, if it were of more or fewer measures, it would have as many parts as it had measures.

ARIST. Yes, it would.

PAR. And if it were of one measure only, it would be found to be equal to that measure, despite our having proved that it can never be equal to anything.

ARIST. We certainly proved that.

PAR. Well then, since it has neither one measure, nor many, nor few, and has no trace whatsoever of sameness, it can surely not be equal to, or greater or less than, itself or anything else.

ARIST. That is perfectly true.

PAR. What think you, next, about the possibility of the One being older or younger than, or the same age as, anything?

ARIST. Why shouldn't it be?

PAR. Why, because if it is of the same age as itself or anything else, it will have the character of equality or similarity of duration; but we said just now that the One has no part in equality or similarity.

ARIST. Yes, we did.

PAR. We said also that it has no part in dissimilarity or in-equality.

ARIST. We did indeed.

PAR. [141] How then can it possibly be older or younger than, or the same age as, anything?

ARIST. Quite impossible.

PAR. Therefore it cannot be younger or older than, or the same age as, itself or anything else.

ARIST. Apparently not.

PAR. I suggest then that the One, being such as we have found it to be, cannot be in time at all. If a thing is in time, must it not constantly be becoming older than itself? [1]

ARIST. Obviously it must.

PAR. Is it not also true that whatever is older is older than some-thing younger?

ARIST. Of course.

PAR. And so anything which is becoming *older* than itself is at the same time becoming *younger* than itself, because there must be something *than which* it is becoming older.

ARIST. How do you mean?

PAR. Let me explain. If A is *already* different from B, it cannot be in process of becoming different therefrom. It differs *here and now* from what is different from itself; it has become different from what has become different from it; and it will

[1] i.e. older than it was the instant before.

become different from what will become different from it. As regards that which *is becoming* different from it, it can neither *have become*, nor *be about to become*, nor here and now *be* different therefrom; it can only *be in process of becoming* different.

ARIST. Naturally.

PAR. Again, the difference implied by the word 'older' is nothing more nor less than a difference from something younger.

ARIST. That is so.

PAR. Which means to say that a thing becoming older than itself must by that very fact be in process of becoming.

ARIST. Undoubtedly.

PAR. Furthermore, no stage of becoming can endure for a longer or a shorter time than the term of its fulfilment; a thing must be becoming, or be, or have become, or be about to become, for exactly the time (neither more nor less) during which it is in any of these states.

ARIST. That also is absolutely certain.

PAR. It would consequently appear that each and every one of the things which are in time, i.e. are temporal, is at once of the same age as itself, and becoming younger as well as older than itself.

ARIST. The conclusion seems inevitable.

PAR. But we agreed that no such character belongs to the One.

ARIST. We did.

PAR. The One, therefore, is unrelated to time; there is no time at which it is.

ARIST. In the light of your argument, certainly there is not.

PAR. Now 'was', 'has become', 'was becoming' are considered to denote relation to *past* time.

ARIST. Of course.

PAR. And 'will be', 'will become', relation to *future* time.

ARIST. Yes.

PAR. And 'is', 'is becoming', relation to *present* time.

ARIST. Certainly.

PAR. Therefore, if the One is wholly unrelated to time, it has never become, never was becoming, and never was; it is never true to say that it has now become, is now becoming, or now is, or that it will become, or be, in the future.

ARIST. Absolutely true.

PAR. Now is there any way in which a thing can have a share in being, other than those I have enumerated?

ARIST. No.

PAR. The One, therefore, has no share in being.

ARIST. I don't see how it can have.

PAR. Consequently the One just *is not*.

ARIST. That is apparent.

PAR. And therefore it has not even sufficient being to be *one*; otherwise it would here and now exist, and so have a share in being; whereas, if our argument is reliable, the one neither is one nor is at all.

ARIST. I cannot deny that.

PAR. [142] Well, if A is non-existent, does not its very nonentity rule out the possibility of B standing in any relation to it whatsoever?

ARIST. Undoubtedly.

PAR. Therefore A cannot even have a name, cannot be spoken of, cannot be the object of any science, perception or judgment.

ARIST. Apparently.

PAR. Therefore it is never named, never spoken of, never thought of or known and never perceived by anyone.

ARIST. It would seem not.

PAR. But can all this really be true of the One?

ARIST. No, I don't think it can.

[*The Second Antinomy* [1]]

PAR. Would you care, then, to reconsider the whole question from the very beginning? By doing so we may perhaps reach a different conclusion.

ARIST. Yes, I should be delighted.

PAR. Well, on the assumption that the One is, what we have to do is to find out the sort of conditions to which it will be subject. That, I think, is what we agreed.

ARIST. We did.

PAR. Back we go then to the start. If the One is, can that One *be* and at the same time *have no share in* being?

[1] If the One is, i.e. if there is unity which is something real, we can both affirm and deny all kinds of predicates of it.

ARIST. Of course not.

PAR. Then the One itself and the *being* of the One cannot be identical, otherwise being would not *belong to* it, and it (the One) would not share in that being; to say 'one is' would be equivalent to saying 'one is one', whereas we are now trying to discover what must follow, not 'if one is one', but 'if the One is'. Am I right?

ARIST. Perfectly.

PAR. Which shows, does it not, that *is* means something quite different from *one*?

ARIST. Certainly.

PAR. In fact, if we combine the two words and say 'the One *is*', we mean simply that the One *has being*.

ARIST. Exactly.

PAR. Then let us inquire again: if the One is, what will follow? Ask yourself whether this postulate does not imply that the One is such that it has parts.

ARIST. How do you prove that?

PAR. I will tell you. Since (*a*) *is* is predicated of a *One* that exists, and *one* of an *existent* One, and (*b*) existence and unity are not the same thing, whereas the subject of the postulate (i.e. the existent one) is identical with itself, must it not be as a whole the existent One, with unity and existence as its parts?

ARIST. That must be so.

PAR. Shall we then allude to each of these parts simply as a part? Must we not rather speak of the part as part of a whole?

ARIST. Yes, as part of the whole.

PAR. Therefore anything that is one is a whole, and also has a part.

ARIST. Certainly.

PAR. Well now, what about each part (unity and existence) of the existent One: is the one part (unity) devoid of the other (existence), or vice versa?

ARIST. Indeed no.

PAR. So once again, each of the parts contains both unity and being; each is found to be composed, in its turn, of at least two parts. And no matter what part we come upon, the same reasoning will invariably show that it contains these two parts; the unity always contains existence, and the existence unity. The part must therefore always be two [143] and can never be one.

ARIST. That is absolutely correct.

PAR. And therefore the existent One must be an indefinite plurality.

ARIST. Apparently it must.

PAR. Here is another point for your consideration.

ARIST. What is that?

PAR. We established that the One has being, which accounts for its existence.

ARIST. Yes.

PAR. And for this very reason the existent One was found to be a plurality.

ARIST. It was.

PAR. But what about the One itself, which, as we say, *has* existence? Suppose we think of it in complete isolation from this existence: will it then appear only as one, or also as many?

ARIST. As one, I imagine.

PAR. Think again. Its *being* must surely be distinct from its *self*, since we agreed that the One *is* not being, but *has* being—as a unit.

ARIST. True enough.

PAR. Thus if being is one thing and the One another, the One is not other than being by virtue of its *unity*, nor is being other than the One by virtue of its being *being*; no, they differ from each other by virtue of *otherness*, or *difference*.

ARIST. Certainly.

PAR. Therefore otherness is not the same thing either as unity or as being.

ARIST. Naturally not.

PAR. Well, let us choose any two of these terms you like—being and otherness, being and unity, or unity and otherness. Am I not right when I say that in each case we are choosing certain things which can truthfully be referred to as 'both'?

ARIST. I'm not sure that I follow you.

PAR. I will explain. It is possible to speak of being?

ARIST. Yes.

PAR. And also of unity?

ARIST. Again yes.

PAR. Each of them has now been named, has it not?

ARIST. It has.

PAR. But when I say 'being *and* unity', have I not referred to *both*?

ARIST. Certainly.

PAR. So too if I say 'being and otherness', or 'otherness and unity', do not those phrases also undoubtedly refer to *both*?

ARIST. They do.

PAR. And can any pair of things which is rightly described as *both* possibly be 'both' without being two?

ARIST. Of course they cannot.

PAR. And is it conceivable that each of two things should not be *one*?

ARIST. Quite inconceivable.

PAR. Therefore, since each of the above-mentioned pairs is two-fold, either of its members must be one.

ARIST. Obviously.

PAR. And if each member is one, when any such unit is combined with any of the said pairs, the sum total of them must, of course, amount to three?

ARIST. Yes.

PAR. And three are odd, and two even?

ARIST. Of course.

PAR. Well then, if there are two there must be a 'twice', and if there are three there must be a 'thrice', since two is the product of one and two, three the product of one and three. Is that not so?

ARIST. Assuredly.

PAR. And if there are two and twice, three and thrice, must there not also be twice two and thrice three?

ARIST. There must indeed.

PAR. And if there are three and twice, two and thrice, must there not also be twice three and thrice two?

ARIST. Why, certainly.

PAR. That being so, there will be even multiples of even numbers, odd multiples of odd numbers, [144] even multiples of odd, and odd multiples of even.

ARIST. There will.

PAR. If that is the case, can you think of any number that will be left over whose existence can be disputed?

ARIST. None at all.

PAR. Consequently, if there is *one*, there must also be *number*.

ARIST. There must.

PAR. Right, then, if there is number, reality will be many, indefinitely numerous; number, in fact, emerges as unlimited and having existence.

ARIST. Indeed it does.

PAR. Therefore, if number as a whole has existence, each part of it must also have existence.

ARIST. Yes.

PAR. Existence then is distributed over all the numerous existents; it belongs to the greatest as well as to the least of them. Indeed, there is no sense in the remark, for how can existence *not* belong to an existing thing?

ARIST. Of course it cannot.

PAR. So existence is shared out in fractions small and great and of every possible kind; it is subdivided to a greater degree than anything else—without limit, in fact.

ARIST. That is so.

PAR. Existence therefore has an enormous number of parts.

ARIST. It has.

PAR. Now, is there any one of those parts which is a part of existence and yet no part?

ARIST. That would be quite impossible.

PAR. I take it that, since the part exists, it must (so long as it continues to exist) be some one part; it cannot be nothing.

ARIST. No, it cannot.

PAR. Unity therefore belongs to each and every part of existence, omitting neither greater nor smaller, nor indeed any part whatsoever.

ARIST. True.

PAR. Now ask yourself whether it can be simultaneously one and whole throughout the whole range of this manifold.

ARIST. Let me think—— No, I see the impossibility.

PAR. If it is not whole it must be split up into fractions; there is absolutely no way, other than by being split up, in which it can be present in all the parts of existence at once.

ARIST. I quite agree.

PAR. Furthermore, what is split up must certainly be as many things as the parts into which it is split.

ARIST. It must.

PAR. We were therefore inaccurate in saying just now that

existence is subdivided to a greater degree than anything else. Its parts, we now discover, are not more numerous than, but just as many as, those of unity; existence is never absent from unity, nor unity from existence; the two correspond always and everywhere.

ARIST. That would certainly appear to be the case.

PAR. Therefore unity itself is split up by existence into an indefinitely numerous manifold.

ARIST. Apparently so.

PAR. Thus not only is the existent One many, but the One itself is obviously subdivided by existence.

ARIST. No doubt whatever about that.

PAR. Next, since its parts are parts of a whole, the unity must be bounded by the wholeness—unless of course we are going to deny that the parts of a whole are not contained by it.

ARIST. Naturally they are.

PAR. [145] And that which contains must be a boundary.

ARIST. It must.

PAR. The One then is presumably both one and many, both whole and parts, bounded and yet limitless in number.

ARIST. So it appears.

PAR. Well, if it is bounded it must also have limits, must it not?

ARIST. Certainly.

PAR. And if it is a whole it must surely have a beginning, a middle and an end. I mean, can anything be a whole without these three, or will it be any longer a whole if any of them is removed?

ARIST. It will not.

PAR. Apparently, therefore, the one must have a beginning, an end and a middle.

ARIST. It must have.

PAR. Now the middle is by definition equidistant from the two extremes.

ARIST. Yes.

PAR. It would seem therefore that the One, being what it is, has some kind of shape, straight or round, or a combination of both.

ARIST. Quite so.

PAR. In that case, will not the One be in itself and also in something else?

ARIST. Why?

PAR. We may take it, I suppose, that each of its parts is in the whole and none of them outside the whole.

ARIST. True.

PAR. And all the parts are contained by the whole.

ARIST. Yes.

PAR. Furthermore, the sum total of all its parts, neither more nor less, *is* the One.

ARIST. Agreed.

PAR. Is not then the whole also the One?

ARIST. Certainly.

PAR. Therefore, since (*a*) all the parts are in the whole, and (*b*) their sum total and the whole are equally the One, and (*c*) the sum total of the parts is contained by the whole, it follows (*d*) that the One is contained by the One, so that (*e*) the One is in the One.

ARIST. Manifestly.

PAR. On the other hand, the whole is not in its parts, collectively or individually. If it is in all it must likewise be in any given one; if it were not in any given one, it could certainly not be in *all*. But if the One is one of the all, and the whole is not in it, how can it still be in all?

ARIST. It cannot.

PAR. Nor can the whole be in some only of its parts; otherwise the greater would be in the less, which is impossible.

ARIST. Quite impossible.

PAR. Then if the One is neither in several of its parts, nor in any one, nor in all of them together, must it not be either in some other thing or else nowhere?

ARIST. Granted.

PAR. If it were nowhere, it would be nothing; but it is actually a whole and, therefore, since it is not in itself, it must surely be in something else.

ARIST. That much is certain.

PAR. Therefore, inasmuch as it is a whole, the One is in something else; as the sum total of its parts it is in itself. So the One is necessarily in itself *and* in something else.

ARIST. It must be.

PAR. That being its nature, must not the One be also at rest *and* in motion?

ARIST. Why? [146]

PAR. Well, seeing that it is in itself, it is presumably at rest. It is
in one thing (itself), from which it never removes, and is
consequently in the same place.

ARIST. Yes, it is.

PAR. And that which is always in the same place must be always
at rest.

ARIST. Undoubtedly.

PAR. Contrariwise, that which is always in a different thing is
never in the same place, and therefore not at rest, and therefore again in motion. Am I right?

ARIST. You are.

PAR. The One then being always in itself and always in something different, must be permanently at rest and permanently
in motion.

ARIST. Evidently.

PAR. Further, in view of the properties we have found it to
possess, the One must be at once the same as and different
from both itself and the Many.

ARIST. Why?

PAR. One of the following relations must be taken to hold good
of any two terms: they are either identical or different, or, if
neither, one must be a part of the other, or a whole of which
the other is part.

ARIST. Clear enough.

PAR. Well now, is the One part of itself?

ARIST. Certainly not.

PAR. It cannot, therefore, stand to itself as a whole of which it is
itself a part.

ARIST. No, it cannot.

PAR. Next, is the One different from the One?

ARIST. Of course not.

PAR. Then it cannot be other than itself.

ARIST. No indeed.

PAR. Very good; then, since it is neither other than itself, nor
stands in relation to itself as a whole to its part, or as part to
whole, clearly it must be identical with itself.

ARIST. Clearly.

PAR. But what is elsewhere than itself—than itself which is in
the same place as itself—must surely, since it is elsewhere, be
also different from itself.

ARIST. I agree.

PAR. Now we saw that this is so with the One; it is at once in itself and in something other than itself.

ARIST. We did.

PAR. It would seem, then, that the One must accordingly be different from itself.

ARIST. So it does.

PAR. Next, if A is other than B, B must be other than A.

ARIST. Naturally.

PAR. From which it follows that whatever is not one is other than the One, and the One other than it.

ARIST. Inevitably.

PAR. Therefore the One is different from the Many.

ARIST. It is.

PAR. But consider this point: 'same' and 'different' are contraries, are they not?

ARIST. Certainly.

PAR. Then can the same ever be in the different, or vice versa?

ARIST. Never.

PAR. Well, if there is no room for difference within the same, there is absolutely nothing in which difference is present for any length of time whatsoever; were it to be so present even for a moment, there would for that moment be difference within the same. Do you agree?

ARIST. I do.

PAR. And since there never is difference within the same, there never is difference in anything at all.

ARIST. True.

PAR. Consequently there never can be difference in what is not one, *or* in the One.

ARIST. No, there cannot.

PAR. Hence it cannot be by virtue of the presence of difference that the One differs from what is not one, or what is not one from the One.

ARIST. No.

PAR. Nor can they differ by virtue of their own internal character, which has nothing to do with difference. [147]

ARIST. Of course not.

PAR. But if they differ neither by virtue of their own internal character nor by virtue of the presence of difference, surely the very possibility of their differing at all flies out at the window.

ARIST. It does.

PAR. Furthermore, what is not one has no unity; otherwise it would cease to be not-one, and would be in some sense one.

ARIST. True.

PAR. And so what is not one cannot even be a number; otherwise, it would once again cease to be entirely not-one.

ARIST. Yes, it would.

PAR. How say you then: can things that are not one be parts of the One? Even if they were, would they not partake of unity?

ARIST. Yes, they would.

PAR. Thus if the One is wholly and entirely one, and the not-one absolutely not one, the One can neither be a part of the not-one, nor a whole of which the latter are parts; and conversely, the not-one can neither be parts of the One, nor wholes of which the One is a part.

ARIST. Of course not.

PAR. But we agreed that things which stand to each other in the relation neither of parts nor of wholes, and which do not differ from one another, must be identical.

ARIST. We did.

PAR. So we are driven to agree also that since this is the case as between the One and the not-one, they must be identical.

ARIST. We are.

PAR. It would seem then that the One is different both from the Many and from itself, and also identical with the Many and with itself.

ARIST. That is the inescapable consequence of your reasoning.

PAR. Next we may ask whether it is simultaneously like and unlike itself and the Many.

ARIST. It may be.

PAR. You will at any rate allow that since it has been proved different from the Many, the latter must also be different from it.

ARIST. Of course.

PAR. Therefore it must differ from the Many to exactly the same extent as the latter differs from it, neither more nor less.

ARIST. Granted.

PAR. Consequently, to the extent that the One has the character of difference from the Many, and they of a corresponding difference from it, to that extent also the One and the Many must have the character of sameness.

ARIST. How do you mean?

PAR. Let me explain. I take it that whenever you use a word you are referring to some *thing*.

ARIST. Indeed I am.

PAR. Good. And you can use the same word more than once?

ARIST. I can.

PAR. The question therefore arises whether, when you use it once, you are speaking of that which it denotes, but not if you use it several times. Is it not perfectly clear that whether you utter the same word once or time and again, you are always referring to the same thing?

ARIST. Of course.

PAR. Now, is not 'different' a word that has reference to something?

ARIST. Certainly.

PAR. Therefore, whenever you utter that word, whether once or many times, you do so with reference to, or by way of naming, that which it denotes, and nothing else.

ARIST. Sure.

PAR. Accordingly, when we say 'the Many are *different* from the One, and the One is *different* from the Many', despite the fact that we use the same word twice, we do so in each case with reference to nothing else than the very character which it denotes.

ARIST. Agreed.

PAR. Therefore, precisely *because* the One is different from the Many, and the Many from the One, [148] by virtue of the very character of difference between them the One has the character of *identity with*, not *difference from*, the Many; and you will presumably admit that what has the character of identity is like.

ARIST. Yes, I admit that.

PAR. So, precisely because the One has the character of *difference* from the Many, it must, as a whole, be *like* them as wholes; for the one whole, *qua* whole, is different from the other wholes.

ARIST. Your conclusion appears to follow.

PAR. Again, like is the contrary of unlike.

ARIST. Yes.

PAR. And different is the contrary of identical.

ARIST. It is.

PAR. But this also has at any rate been proved, namely that the One is identical with other things.

ARIST. It has.

PAR. And the character of being identical with other things is the contrary of being different from them.

ARIST. Certainly.

PAR. And the One has been shown to be like other things inasmuch as it is different from them.

ARIST. Yes.

PAR. Therefore, inasmuch as it is identical with them and thus has a character contrary to the character which gives rise to their likeness, it will be unlike them. But it was their difference that gave rise to their likeness.

ARIST. Yes.

PAR. And therefore their identity will give rise to their unlikeness; otherwise we shall be driven to conclude that identity is not the contrary of difference.

ARIST. So it seems.

PAR. Therefore the One is both like and unlike the Many: like inasmuch as it is different from them, and unlike inasmuch as it is identical with them.

ARIST. Your reasoning certainly appears valid.

PAR. So is another line of argument.

ARIST. What is that?

PAR. Well, inasmuch as the One has an identical character it has not a different character; as not having the latter, it is not unlike; and being not unlike, it must be like.

ARIST. You are perfectly correct.

PAR. Therefore, since the One is identical with *and* different from other things, for both reasons together and for either of them separately, it must be simultaneously like and unlike those other things.

ARIST. Quite right.

PAR. So too as regards its self: we have seen that it is different from *and* identical with itself; so again, for both reasons together and for either of them separately, it will be found to be both like and unlike itself.

ARIST. Undoubtedly.

PAR. Here now is the next point for your consideration, I mean the possibility of contact or non-contact of the One with itself and with other things.

ARIST. Go ahead.

PAR. Well, it has been shown that the One is in itself as in a whole.

ARIST. Correct.

PAR. And is not the One also in other things?

ARIST. Yes.

PAR. Therefore, as being *in* other things, it must surely be in *contact* with them. As being, on the other hand, in itself, it must be barred from contact with other things, but, being *in* itself, must be in *contact* with itself.

Arist. Obviously.

PAR. So the one must be in contact both with itself and with other things.

ARIST. It must.

PAR. But look now: is it not a fact that anything which is to be in contact with anything else must lie immediately next to that with which it is to be in contact, i.e. must occupy a space adjacent to that of the thing it touches?

ARIST. That is certainly true.

PAR. Therefore, if the One is to be in contact with itself, it must lie immediately next to itself, i.e. it must occupy the space adjacent to that in which itself is.

ARIST. Of course.

PAR. Now if the One were two, it might do [149] just that, i.e. occupy two spaces at once; but it cannot do so while it remains one.

ARIST. Certainly not.

PAR. Then the very same necessity which prevents the One being two rules out the possibility of its having contact with itself.

ARIST. The very same.

PAR. Nor indeed will it be in contact with other things.

ARIST. Why not?

PAR. Because, as we agreed, that which is to have contact with a thing, though distinct from the latter, must be *adjacent* to it, i.e. without any third entity between them.

ARIST. True.

PAR. Therefore, if there is to be contact, there must be two things at the very least.

ARIST. There must.

PAR. And if a third becomes adjacent to the original two, they will together form a trio, and there will be two contacts.

ARIST. Yes.

PAR. Thus, as often as we add a fresh term, there will be one more contact, so that the contacts will be fewer by one than the sum total of the numbers. In other words, the same numerical excess revealed by the first two terms in comparison with the contacts will appear from a comparison of the total number of terms with their contacts; for at every subsequent stage one is added to their number, and there is likewise an addition of one contact.

ARIST. Quite right.

PAR. Therefore, no matter how many terms there are, the number of their contacts is always less by one.

ARIST. Exactly.

PAR. And if there is only one, and not two things, there can be no contact.

ARIST. Of course not.

PAR. Now we admit that things other than the One are not one, and therefore have no share in the One.

ARIST. None at all.

PAR. Consequently there is no number in things other than the one because there is no unit in them.

ARIST. Certainly not.

PAR. Therefore the Many are neither one, nor two, nor of any recognizable number.

ARIST. No.

PAR. The One alone, therefore, is, and there can be no two.

ARIST. Apparently not.

PAR. Therefore, since there is no two, there is no such thing as contact.

ARIST. No, there isn't.

PAR. Well, since there is no such thing as contact, the One is not in contact with the Many, nor the Many with the One.

ARIST. No.

PAR. There you are then; all these facts go to prove that the One *is* in contact, and also *is not* in contact, with itself and with the Many.

ARIST. So it appears.

PAR. Is it then equal and unequal both to itself and to other things?

ARIST. What is your view?

PAR. If the One were greater or less than the Many, or they than the One, neither could be so by virtue of these specific characters themselves (i.e. that the One is one and the Many other than the one). But if, in addition to the said characters, each possessed equality, they would be equal to one another, while if the One possessed (*a*) relatively great and the Many (*b*) relatively small size (or vice versa), the entity to which the additional character (*a*) belonged would be the greater, and that which had (*b*) would be the less.

ARIST. Inevitably.

PAR. Now these two entities, relative greatness and relative smallness, undoubtedly exist; if they did not they could not of course be contraries and manifest themselves in existing things.

ARIST. True enough.

PAR. [150] Then if smallness manifests itself in the One, it will reside therein as in a whole, or else in part of it.

ARIST. It must.

PAR. Well, suppose it manifests itself in the whole, must it not either be co-extensive with the One throughout the whole range of the latter, or else contain it?

ARIST. Evidently.

PAR. Then if smallness is co-extensive with the One, it will be equal thereto; if it contains it, it will be greater.

ARIST. That is so.

PAR. Now can relative smallness be equal to, or greater than, anything, thereby performing the function of relative greatness or of equality instead of its own?

ARIST. No, it cannot.

PAR. Smallness, therefore, cannot reside in the One as a whole, but only in a part thereof—if at all.

ARIST. Yes.

PAR. Nor again in the whole of the part; otherwise it will act in the same way as it would do in relation to the whole; i.e. it will be equal to, or greater than, any part whatsoever in which it resides.

Arist. Inevitably.

Par. The result is that smallness will never be present in anything; it never manifests itself either in a part or in the whole, so there will be nothing small but only smallness itself.

Arist. It seems not.

Par. Consequently greatness will not be present either. Otherwise something other than greatness itself would be 'greater than', viz. that in which this greatness resided, despite the non-existence of a corresponding small, which it must necessarily exceed if it is to be great; but no such small can possibly exist, because there is no smallness present anywhere.

Arist. True.

Par. Further, there is nothing than which greatness itself is greater, except smallness itself; and vice versa.

Arist. No, nothing.

Par. Therefore, things other than the One are neither greater nor less than it, since they have neither greatness nor smallness; it is in the nature of these two to exceed and be exceeded, *not* in relation to the One, but as between themselves. Nor, again, can the One, having neither greatness nor smallness, be greater or less than they, or than other things.

Arist. Clearly not.

Par. Very well then, if the One is neither greater nor less than other things, it can neither exceed nor be exceeded by them.

Arist. That is unquestionable.

Par. Now that which neither exceeds nor is exceeded must of absolute necessity be in an equality, and therefore equal.

Arist. What else can it be?

Par. Moreover, the One will stand in this very relation to itself. Since it has neither greatness nor smallness, it can neither exceed nor be exceeded by itself; it must be in an equality with, and hence equal to, itself.

Arist. Of course it must.

Par. Therefore the One is found to be equal to itself and to other things.

Arist. Apparently.

Par. Yet again, since it is within itself, it must also be round about outside itself; as container it will be greater, and as contained less, than itself. [151] In other words the One will be both greater and less than itself.

ARIST. It will.

PAR. Is it not also necessarily true that there is nothing besides the One and things other than the One?

ARIST. Of course.

PAR. Furthermore, whatever is must always be somewhere.

ARIST. Yes.

PAR. And will not that which is in something be in it as a less in a greater? Only so can one thing be in another.

ARIST. I agree.

PAR. But since there is nothing else, besides the One and the Many, and they must be in something, does it not follow straightway that they are in one another—the One in the Many and vice versa—or nowhere at all?

ARIST. Evidently.

PAR. Therefore since the One is in the Many, the latter must be greater than the One and contain it, and the One less than the Many and be contained by them. But because the Many are in the One, the One must, by the same reasoning, be greater than the Many, and the Many less than the one.

ARIST. So it seems.

PAR. Therefore, the One is both equal to, greater than, and less than, itself and everything else.

ARIST. Clearly.

PAR. Again, being greater and less and equal, it must be of equal, more and fewer measures with itself and with everything else, and if of measures, then of parts also.

ARIST. Indeed it must.

PAR. Well, being thus of equal, more and fewer measures, it must likewise be less than, greater than, and equal to, itself and everything else in number also.

ARIST. How do you mean?

PAR. If it is greater than anything, it must also, presumably, be of more measures than that thing, and of parts corresponding in number to those measures. And the same principle will apply if it is less than, or equal to, anything.

ARIST. Quite so.

PAR. Being, then, (a) greater than, (b) less than, and (c) equal to itself, must it not be of (*a*) more, (*b*) fewer, and (*c*) equal measures with itself; and if of measures, then of parts too?

ARIST. Naturally.

PAR. Consequently, being of (*a*) an equal number of parts, (*b*) more parts and (*c*) fewer parts, it must be numerically (*a*) equal to, (*b*) greater than and (*c*) less than itself.

ARIST. I follow you.

PAR. And the same will be true, will it not, of the One's relations with everything else? Since it is clearly (*a*) greater than they, (*b*) less than they and (*c*) equal to them in magnitude, it must also be numerically (*a*) superior, (*b*) inferior and (*c*) equal to them.

ARIST. It must.

PAR. Once again then, it seems that the One will be numerically (*a*) equal to, (*b*) more than and (*c*) fewer than itself *and* everything else.

ARIST. It will.

PAR. Next we may ask whether the One has also duration; as having duration can it (*a*) both be and become and (*b*) neither be nor become, younger and older than itself and other things?

ARIST. What is your opinion?

PAR. In the first place, since it *is* one, it must of course *be*.

ARIST. Yes.

PAR. In the second place, to *be* is surely the possession of being with present duration, just as [152] *was* and *will be* are respectively participation therein with past and future duration.

ARIST. It is.

PAR. Consequently, since the One has being, it has duration.

ARIST. Certainly.

PAR. And progressive duration?

ARIST. Yes.

PAR. Therefore, since it progresses in duration, it must always be becoming older than itself.

ARIST. It must be.

PAR. Bear in mind, however, that that which is becoming older becomes older than something which is all the time becoming younger.

ARIST. Exactly.

PAR. So because the One is becoming older than itself it must become older than a self which is becoming younger than itself.

ARIST. Inevitably.

PAR. Consequently it is becoming both younger and older than itself.

ARIST. Yes.

PAR. But exactly when, I ask, *is* it older? Surely when the process of becoming is in the *here and now* which links the past and the future. On the road from Has-been to Hereafter we can scarcely by-pass the present.

ARIST. Indeed no.

PAR. So when it comes to the present it ceases to become older; i.e. it is no longer in process of becoming, but actually *is* older; so long as it advances it will never be overtaken by the present. That which is advancing is in a state of contact both with the present and with the future, leaving the present behind and entering upon the future, and thereby standing between the two.

ARIST. That is correct.

PAR. But if it is impossible for anything in process of becoming to by-pass the present, it must be true to say that whenever such a thing reaches the present, it ceases from becoming and *is* then whatever it is in process of becoming.

ARIST. Undoubtedly.

PAR. The One therefore, when in process of becoming older it reaches the present, ceases to *become* older; it *is* then older.

ARIST. Most definitely.

PAR. Older, I mean, than that than which it was becoming older, i.e. than itself.

ARIST. Yes.

PAR. And the older is older than a younger.

ARIST. It is.

PAR. Consequently the One *is* also younger than itself when, in the process of becoming older, it reaches the present.

ARIST. Inevitably.

PAR. Furthermore the present is always with the One throughout its existence; for at any given moment when it is, it is *now*.

ARIST. Beyond a doubt.

PAR. Therefore the One at *every* moment is and is becoming both older and younger than itself.

ARIST. So it appears.

PAR. And is this being or becoming of longer duration than this process itself, or is it of equal duration therewith?

ARIST. Of equal duration.

PAR. But surely things which are or become for an equal length of time are of the same age.

ARIST. Undoubtedly.

PAR. And that which is of the same age is neither older nor younger.

ARIST. Certainly not.

PAR. Therefore the One, since it both is and becomes for a time equal with itself, neither is nor becomes younger nor older than itself.

ARIST. I agree.

PAR. Or than other things.

ARIST. [153] I really can't say.

PAR. But this much you can say: If things other than the One are in fact others and not *an* other, they are more than one. If they were *an* other, they would be one; but being others they are more than one, i.e. they must have plurality.

ARIST. Yes, they must.

PAR. And being a plurality their number must be greater than that of the One.

ARIST. Beyond a doubt.

PAR. I ask you then: which terms of a number-series shall we say are prior in generation and existence, the greater or the less?

ARIST. The less.

PAR. The first term therefore is the least, i.e. the One: do you agree?

ARIST. Yes.

PAR. Consequently the One came into being first of all things which have number; and all things else have number if they are in fact others and not *an* other.

ARIST. They have.

PAR. And if the One came into being first, it presumably did so *before* the Many, and they *after* it; but things which have come into being afterwards are younger than what came into being before them. The result is that the Many must be younger than it, and the One older than they.

ARIST. Assuredly.

PAR. Wait, though. Can the One possibly have come into being contrary to its own nature?

ARIST. Impossible.

PAR. But the One, we saw, has parts, and therefore a beginning, an end and a middle.

ARIST. Yes.

PAR. Now you will surely agree that, in the case both of the One and of the Many, the beginning comes into being first, and then all the rest until the end is reached.

ARIST. Naturally.

PAR. Moreover we shall have to admit that 'all the rest' are parts of the whole or one; the latter has only come into being as such when the end is reached.

ARIST. We shall have to admit that.

PAR. Now, as I see it, the end comes into being last of all, and it is the nature of the One to do so along with it. Therefore since the One cannot come into being otherwise than in accordance with its nature, and since it comes into being along with the end, it must of its very nature come into being last of all.

ARIST. Apparently.

PAR. Therefore the One is younger than the Many which are in turn older than the One.

ARIST. I see your point now.

PAR. You do? Then how about this further point? Take the beginning (or any other part) of the One or anything else, and recognize it as *a* part, not several parts: must it not be one, since it is *a* part?

ARIST. It must.

PAR. Consequently the One must come into being along with the first thing to do so, and also with the second, nor can it be absent from the generation of any other term, throughout the process of addition to any series, until, the final term being reached, the complete unity emerges; it is, I say, inevitably present in the generation of middle, end, beginning and any other term you like to name.

ARIST. True.

PAR. Therefore the One is of the same age with the Many; so unless there is an inherent contradiction in its very nature, it must come into being not before or after, but simultaneously with the Many. [154] This leads us to the conclusion that the One can be neither older nor younger than the Many, nor they than it; and yet our previous argument demonstrated that it is both older and younger than they, and vice versa.

ARIST. Exactly.

PAR. Enough then of what *is* and *has become*. Now what about this thesis, that the One (*a*) is and (*b*) is not *in process of becoming* both older and younger than the Many, and vice versa? Do the same principles apply in the case of becoming as in that of being, or do they not?

ARIST. I really don't know.

PAR. Well, I can tell you this much at any rate: if one thing *is* older or younger than another it can never *become* older or younger still by more than the initial difference in their original dates; for if you add equals to unequals you will always get a difference (in time or any other measure) equal to the original difference.

ARIST. Certainly.

PAR. Therefore no existent can ever be in process of becoming older or younger than another, owing to a permanent equal difference in date; one existent *is* and *has become* older, another younger, but neither is *in process* of becoming so.

ARIST. True.

PAR. Therefore the existent One is never *in process of becoming* older or younger than the existent Many.

ARIST. No.

PAR. I wonder, on the other hand, whether there is not a standpoint from which we may look upon them as in process of becoming older and younger.

ARIST. What standpoint?

PAR. That from which we saw the One to be older than the Many and vice versa.

ARIST. Yes?

PAR. If the One is older than the Many it has presumably been in existence for longer than they have.

ARIST. Yes.

PAR. Think now: if to a greater period of time and to a lesser we add an equal, will the greater d:ffer from the lesser by an equal or by a smaller fraction?

ARIST. By a smaller.

PAR. We cannot, therefore, say that the original difference in age between the One and the Many will continue into the future; as the ages of both are increased by an equal period of time, the difference between them will be steadily diminishing —or will it not?

ARIST. Certainly it will.

PAR. Now surely that which differs less in age from something than it formerly did must be becoming younger than it was in relation to those things with respect to which it was formerly older.

ARIST. Agreed.

PAR. And if the One is becoming younger the Many must in turn be becoming older than they were with respect to the One.

ARIST. Certainly.

PAR. So what has come into being later in point of time is in process of becoming older in relation to what has come into being earlier and is older than it. It never *is* older than the other, but is always in process of *becoming* so, because the other is constantly gaining in recency and itself in antiquity. [155] On the other hand, that which is older than something younger is likewise in process of becoming younger than it. As they advance in opposite directions the senses in which they become are opposite to one another; the younger is *in process of* becoming older than the elder and the elder younger than the younger, though it is impossible that they should ever have become so. If this latter eventuality were possible, they would no longer be in process of becoming, but would actually *be*. In point of fact, however, they are in process of becoming respectively older and younger than one another. The One is in process of becoming younger than the Many, for we have seen that it is older and came into being before them; and the Many are in process of becoming older than the One, since they came into being after it. And the same reasoning applies to the relation of the Many to the One, thanks to our proof that they are older by virtue of their having come into being earlier.

ARIST. That appears to be true.

PAR. Very well, then, in so far as nothing is ever in process of becoming older or younger than anything else, because the difference between their ages is constant and equal, the One can be in process of becoming neither older nor younger than the Many, nor the Many than the One. But in so far as there is inevitably constant variation of the fraction whereby the age of that which comes into being earlier differs from that which does so later, the Many must be becoming both older and younger than the One, and vice versa.

ARIST. Quite right.

PAR. Here then is the net result of all our arguments: (a) The One *is* and is *in process of becoming* older and younger than itself and than the Many; and also (b) neither *is* (*are*) nor is (*are*) *in process of becoming* either older or younger than itself or than the other(s).

ARIST. Absolutely true.

PAR. Now, seeing that the One has duration and the property of becoming older and younger, does not its having duration mean that it has past, present and future?

ARIST. Certainly it does.

PAR. The One, therefore, was, is and will be; it was becoming, is becoming and will become.

ARIST. Of course.

PAR. It may accordingly stand in this or that relation: did so, does so and will so stand.

ARIST. Yes indeed.

PAR. Thus it can be known, judged and perceived; in fact we are here and now subjecting it to all these operations.

ARIST. Correct.

PAR. There is in fact a name and a formula for it; i.e. it is named and discussed, and whatever characters belong to the Many belong also to the One.

ARIST. That is all perfectly true.

PAR. Let us take up the point yet a third time. Supposing the One to be such as we have described, in other words both one and not one, many and not many, and having duration: must it not follow (a) that because it exists, it at some time has being, and (b) on the other hand, because it does not exist, it at some time has not being?

ARIST. Undoubtedly.

PAR. Now can it possibly not have being at the very time when it has or vice versa?

ARIST. It cannot.

PAR. At one time, therefore, it has being, and at another has not; that is the only way in which it can both have and not have the same thing.

ARIST. [156] Quite right.

PAR. Consequently there must also be a time when it is acquiring being, and another when it is losing it. How can it possibly now have and then not have the same thing unless there is a time when it acquires and a time when it loses that thing?

ARIST. That would be altogether impossible.

PAR. And would you call the process of acquiring existence 'coming into being'?

ARIST. I would.

PAR. And the process of losing being, 'perishing'?

ARIST. Certainly.

PAR. Seeing, therefore, that the One acquires and loses existence, we may say that it comes into being and perishes.

ARIST. It must do.

PAR. Considering now that it is both one and many, and comes into being and perishes, its plurality must surely perish when it becomes one and its unity when it becomes many.

ARIST. Indeed yes.

PAR. Moreover, since it becomes one and many, is it not thereby subject to disgregation and aggregation?

ARIST. Too true.

PAR. Also, when it becomes like and unlike, to assimilation and dissimilation. Is that not so?

ARIST. Yes.

PAR. And when it becomes greater, or less, or equal, to increase, decrease or equalization?

ARIST. Exactly.

PAR. Again, when it is halted in motion, or is changed from rest to motion, it cannot of course exist in time at all.

ARIST. How do you make that out?

PAR. Well, assume it is first at rest and then in motion, or first in motion and afterwards at rest: it cannot be subject to those conditions without changing.

ARIST. No, it cannot.

PAR. Exactly when, then, does the change occur? It cannot do so
    when the subject is at rest, nor when it is in motion, nor
    within any period of time.

ARIST. Clearly not.

PAR. Very good; there must really be that paradoxical some-
    thing-or-other in which the subject must be at the actual
    moment of change.

ARIST. What 'something-or-other'?

PAR. Why, the *instant*. The word 'instant' would appear to
    signify that from which change takes place in either direction,
    or something of the sort. Change from the state of rest does
    not occur while the subject remains stationary, nor change
    from that of motion while the subject continues to move. No,
    between motion and rest there stands this paradoxical entity,
    the instant, which marks no period of time whatsoever. Into
    it and from it the moving or stationary subject changes
    respectively towards rest or motion.

ARIST. That seems the inevitable conclusion.

PAR. The One likewise, since it both moves and is at rest, must
    change from either state to the other; only so can it do both.
    Since it changes, it changes instantaneously, and in doing so
    can be in no time at all; it can then be neither moving nor at
    rest.

ARIST. No.

PAR. Right; now is the same true of its other changes—from
    being to perishing, [157] from not-being to coming into being?
    Is it at such times between certain kinds of motion and rest,
    so that one may then describe it as neither existent nor non-
    existent, neither coming into being nor perishing?

ARIST. Apparently so.

PAR. By the same reasoning of course, when it is changing from
    unity to plurality or vice versa, it is neither one nor many,
    neither in process of disgregation nor of aggregation. So too
    when it is in transit from likeness to unlikeness or vice versa,
    it is neither like nor unlike, neither in process of assimilation
    nor of dissimilation. Again, as it passes from small to great or
    equal or vice versa, it can be neither small nor great nor
    equal; it cannot be in process either of increase, decrease or
    equalization.

ARIST. Evidently not.

PAR. The One then must exhibit all the foregoing characters, if it exists.

ARIST. It cannot do otherwise.

[*The Third Antinomy* [1]]

PAR. We must now, I think, ask ourselves this question: If the One is, what character belongs to the Many?

ARIST. Yes, we must consider that.

PAR. Let me put it in this way: If the One is, what must we predicate of the Many, which are other than the One?

ARIST. Fair enough.

PAR. Well, since the Many are other than the One, the One is not the Many; if it were, they could not be other than the One.

ARIST. Agreed.

PAR. Wait though: the Many are not *entirely* without unity but have it in some way.

ARIST. In what way?

PAR. The Many, being other than the One, must have parts; if they had no parts they would be absolutely one.

ARIST. True.

PAR. But we said that parts are parts of something which is a whole.

ARIST. We did.

PAR. Now the whole must be a unity consisting of a plurality, and the parts will be parts of that unity; each of the parts must be part not of a plurality, but of a whole.

ARIST. How so?

PAR. If something were part of a plurality which included that thing, the latter would of course be part of itself (which is impossible), and also of every single member of the plurality, since it is assumed to be part of them all. If there is one of them of which it is not a part, it will be a part of them all, with the exception of that one; so it will not be a part of each and every member, and, not being a part of each, it will be no part of *any* member of the plurality. But if something is related— whether as a part, or in any other respect—to *no* member of a plurality, it cannot possibly stand to *all* in the relation which it bears to *none*.

[1] If the One is, i.e. if there is unity which is something real, all kinds of predicates can be both affirmed and denied of the Many.

ARIST. I follow.

PAR. Consequently a part is not part of a plurality, nor of all, but of a single pattern, of a single something-or-other formed of all its components into one complete entity which we call a 'whole'. This it is of which the part is a part.

ARIST. Exactly.

PAR. Therefore if the Many have parts, they must also have wholeness or unity.

ARIST. Sure.

PAR. Very well then, the Many must be a single complete whole having parts.

ARIST. They must.

PAR. Yes, and the same reasoning applies also to each part; each must have unity. For if each of them is a part, [158] the very use of the word 'each' indicates that it is *one* part, distinct from the others, existing on its own; otherwise the word 'each' is inapplicable.

ARIST. Correct.

PAR. Now it is perfectly clear that while such a part *has* unity it is something other than unity; else it would not *have* unity but would itself *be* unity. In point of fact, however, we know for certain that nothing except the One itself can possibly *be* unity.

ARIST. Naturally not.

PAR. But both the whole and the part must *have* unity. The former will be a single whole of which the parts are parts; the latter (whatever is part of a whole) will be an individual part of the whole.

ARIST. Quite so.

PAR. And will not these things which *have* unity be, that fact notwithstanding, other than the One?

ARIST. Of course.

PAR. And the Many will presumably be a plurality; for if they were neither one nor more than one, they would be nothing at all.

ARIST. Of course not.

PAR. Now since things which have the unity of a part and those which have the unity of a whole are more than one, does it not immediately follow that the actual recipients of this unity are indefinitely numerous?

ARIST. Why so?

PAR. Look at it this way. At the precise instant when they are acquiring unity, it is clear that they neither *are* a unity nor *have* unity.

ARIST. That is quite plain.

PAR. Therefore they are manifolds in which there is no unity.

ARIST. True.

PAR. Then if we choose mentally to subtract the smallest conceivable portion from such a manifold, must not the portion itself, having no unity, itself be a manifold and not a unit?

ARIST. It must.

PAR. Thus if we consider either the whole or its part in abstraction from the process of being formed into a unity, and apply to it the same mental operation, we shall find that each successive part examined is indefinitely numerous.

ARIST. Certainly we shall.

PAR. But when each several part has become a part, they are at once limited relatively to each other and to the whole, and the whole is limited in relation to its parts.

ARIST. Undoubtedly.

PAR. Apparently, then, as a result of association between the One and the Many, there is born within the latter a new character which provides them with a reciprocal limit, whereas their own distinct character entails absence of limit.

ARIST. So it appears.

PAR. Consequently the Many, both as wholes and as parts, are unlimited and at the same time have limit.

ARIST. Assuredly.

PAR. Are they also like and unlike one another and themselves?

ARIST. Why should they be?

PAR. Well, in so far as they are all, of their intrinsic nature, limitless, they must have one and the same characteristic.

ARIST. Quite.

PAR. Again, in so far as they all have limit, they must likewise have one and the same characteristic.

ARIST. Granted.

PAR. But in so far as they have both characters, being limited and limitless, they are affected by contrary characteristics.

ARIST. [159] Yes.

PAR. And contraries are the extremes of unlikeness.

ARIST. They are.

PAR. So in the light of each character singly they are like themselves and like each other; but in the light of both together they represent extremes of contrariety and unlikeness.

ARIST. I cannot avoid your conclusion.

PAR. Thus the Many must be like and unlike themselves and one another.

ARIST. Exactly.

PAR. Well then, having found this to be true of them, we shall have no further difficulty in recognizing that the Many are simultaneously identical with and different from each other, in motion and at rest—in fact, that they have all sorts of contrary characters.

ARIST. You are perfectly right.

[*The Fourth Antinomy* [1]]

PAR. Suppose then we take these last points as proved, and go on to ask the following question: If the One is, must not all we have said be denied of the Many, as well as affirmed?

ARIST. Yes, let us do that.

PAR. Well, let us start again at the beginning with the question: If the One is, what character must belong to the Many?

ARIST. Fair enough.

PAR. Good. Then must not the One be separate from the Many and vice versa?

ARIST. Why so?

PAR. Because there is presumably nothing else besides these— nothing else, I mean, other than the One and at the same time other than the Many, so that when we have said 'the One and the Many', we have named everything.

ARIST. Yes, those two terms cover everything.

PAR. Therefore there is nothing else left in which both the One and the Many might reside.

ARIST. No, nothing.

PAR. Consequently the One and the Many are never identically located.

ARIST. Apparently not.

[1] If the One is, i.e. if all that exists is an undifferentiated unity, nothing can be either affirmed or denied of the Many.

PAR. Therefore they are separate.

ARIST. Yes.

PAR. Nor can we recognize the truly one as having parts.

ARIST. No.

PAR. Therefore, neither the One as a whole nor parts of it can be in the Many, since it is separate from the latter and has no parts.

ARIST. True.

PAR. So it is quite impossible for the Many to have any share in unity, seeing that they have it neither partially nor as a whole.

ARIST. Quite impossible.

PAR. In no way, therefore, can the Many be described as one; there is no unity in them.

ARIST. No.

PAR. And therefore the Many cannot even be many; otherwise each of them would be one part of the whole. So it amounts to this, that the Many are neither one nor many, neither whole nor parts, since they have no unity at all.

ARIST. True.

PAR. Therefore the Many are neither themselves two, nor is there a pair or triplet among them, for they are absolutely devoid of unity.

ARIST. That is so.

PAR. It follows likewise that the Many are neither like nor unlike the One, nor is there any similarity or dissimilarity among themselves, otherwise they would have two contrary forms within themselves.

ARIST. Obviously.

PAR. And we saw that things which have not even unity cannot possibly have duality of any kind.

ARIST. We did.

PAR. Consequently the Many are neither like nor unlike, nor both together. [160] If they were like, or unlike, they would have one of two contrary forms, and if they were both together they would have the two; but these have been proved impossibilities.

ARIST. They have.

PAR. Therefore they are neither the same nor different, neither in motion nor at rest, neither come into being nor perish, are neither greater, less, nor equal, nor indeed have any other character of this kind. For if any such character can be ascribed to the Many, it will mean also that they have unity, duality, triplicity, odd and even number—from the possession of which we have shown them to be barred by their total lack of unity.

ARIST. Perfectly true.

PAR. Well then, we can only conclude that if the One is, it is all things and is nothing, in relation both to itself and to the Many.

ARIST. Quite so.

[The Fifth Antinomy [1]]

PAR. Enough of that. Our next question, I think, must be this: If the One is not, what will be the consequences?

ARIST. Yes, we must consider that.

PAR. Then what is the significance of the postulate 'If the One is not'? Is there any difference in meaning between it and 'If the not-one is not'?

ARIST. Of course there is.

PAR. Is there only a *difference* of sense? Surely the statement 'if the not-one is not' is the *direct contrary* of 'if the One is not'.

ARIST. Certainly it is.

PAR. Suppose now we say: 'If greatness is not', and 'If smallness is not', and so on; we are obviously assuming the non-existence of something different in each case.

ARIST. Indeed we are.

PAR. Clearly then, in the present case, when it is pretended that 'the One is not', the assumed non-existent is something different from other things, and we know what it is.

ARIST. We do.

PAR. Therefore when a man speaks of 'one', he is referring (*a*) to something known and (*b*) to something different from other things. This holds good whether he asserts *or* denies its existence: his denial will in no way obscure our recognition of what is denied to exist or of its being different from other things. Do you agree?

ARIST. I cannot do otherwise.

PAR. Very well, we must begin inquiring: If the One is not, what will be the consequences? Now we must, in the first

---

[1] If the One is not, i.e. if all that exists is *not* an undifferentiated unity, it is susceptible of all kinds of affirmation and denial.

place, allow that it *can be known*; otherwise the meaning of the words 'if the One is not' would be unknown.

ARIST. True.

PAR. Secondly, we must allow that the Many are different from it; otherwise it could not be described as different from them.

ARIST. Granted.

PAR. Therefore it has differentiality as well as knowability. When somebody says 'the One is different from the Many', he is referring to *its* differentiality, not to that of the Many.

ARIST. Evidently.

PAR. Moreover the non-existent One is recognizable as a *that*, as a somewhat, as standing in various relation to *this so-and-so* and *these so-and-so*, and the like. If it had not the character of being a somewhat, etc., it would not have been possible to speak either of the One or of things different from the One, nor could anything be related to or predicated of it.

ARIST. True.

PAR. On the assumption that the One 'is not', it cannot of course exist; but there is nothing to prevent its having many characters [161]. It *must* in fact have them, if it is this One and not some other thing that is non-existent. If, however, it is neither the One nor *this* that is to be non-existent, and our reasoning is to be concerned with some other thing, we must not so much as utter a sound. If on the other hand our initial postulate is that *this One* (not some other thing) does not exist, the character of a *this* must belong to it and a number of other characters as well.

ARIST. Definitely.

PAR. Therefore it has unlikeness to the Many; for the Many, because they are other than the One, must be of other character.

ARIST. Yes.

PAR. And because they are of other character they must be diverse, what?

ARIST. Naturally.

PAR. And the diverse must be unlike?

ARIST. Yes, unlike.

PAR. Now since they are unlike the One, there must obviously be such a thing as unlikeness by virtue of which they are unlike.

ARIST. There must be.

PAR. Therefore the One also will possess unlikeness, in relation to which the Many are unlike it.

ARIST. Apparently.

PAR. And if it has unlikeness to the Many, must it not have likeness to itself?

ARIST. Exactly why?

PAR. If the One has unlikeness to the One, we are of course no longer discussing any such thing as the One; our hypothesis will no longer have reference to the One, but to something else.

ARIST. It will.

PAR. But it *has* reference to *nothing* else.

ARIST. No.

PAR. In that case the One must have likeness to itself.

ARIST. It must.

PAR. Furthermore, the One is not equal to the Many. If it were it would at once *be* and be *like* them in virtue of its equality. Both eventualities, however, are impossible, since the One is non-existent.

ARIST. Quite impossible.

PAR. Then since it is not equal to the others they can surely not be equal to it.

ARIST. No, they cannot.

PAR. Do you agree that things which are not equal are unequal?

ARIST. Yes.

PAR. And that things are unequal by virtue of inequality?

ARIST. Sure.

PAR. The One, therefore, has inequality, relatively to which the others are unequal to it.

ARIST, It has.

PAR. But 'inequality' implies 'great and small'.

ARIST. It does.

PAR. Therefore great and small are properties of a One such as we have in mind.

ARIST. Indubitably.

PAR. Now great and small are invariably disjointed.

ARIST. Yes.

PAR. Hence there is always something intermediate between them.

ARIST. There is.

PAR. Well, can you name such an intermediate other than equality?

ARIST. No, I cannot.

PAR. Therefore anything which has greatness and smallness must also have equality, which is intermediate between them.

ARIST. That is clear.

PAR. Apparently, then, the non-existent One must have equality, greatness and smallness.

ARIST. Seemingly it must.

PAR. Yes, and it must also in some sense have being.

ARIST. But *how*?

PAR. It must be as we describe it; otherwise we are not speaking the truth when we say that the One is non-existent. If what we say is true you will surely admit that it represents actual fact.

ARIST. Yes, I grant you that.

PAR. And since we maintain the truth of what we say, we are obliged on that account to maintain that our words are a statement of fact.

ARIST. [162] We are.

PAR. Evidently then the One *is* existent. If it is *not* non-existent, if it moves in the slightest degree from being to not-being, it will forthwith *be existent*.

ARIST. No question about that.

PAR. Accordingly, if it is not to exist, it must have 'being-non-existent' in order to tie it down to non-existence, just as the existent must have 'not-being-non-existent' in order that it may completely exist. The only possible way for the existent to be and the non-existent not to be is as follows: the existent, if it is to exist completely, must have (*a*) being (i.e. being-existent) and (*b*) not being (i.e. not-being-non-existent); whereas the non-existent, if it is to be absolutely non-existent, must have (*a*) not-being (i.e. not-being-existent) and (*b*) being (i.e. being-non-existent).

ARIST. How right you are!

PAR. Very well. Since the existent has not-being and the non-existent has being, it follows that the One also, since it does not exist, must have *being* in order that it may *not be*.

ARIST. True.

PAR. There you are then: the One has being, because it does not exist!

ARIST. Exactly.

PAR. And not-being too, for the same reason.

ARIST. Of course.

PAR. Now is it possible for a thing which somehow *is* to *be not* so, unless it changes from the former state?

ARIST. No, it is not.

PAR. In other words, every such statement 'it is thus and it is not thus' implies change.

ARIST. Inevitably.

PAR. And change, we must surely allow, is motion.

ARIST. It is.

PAR. Now we have agreed that the One both is and is not.

ARIST. Yes.

PAR. Then it is evidently thus and also not thus.

ARIST. Evidently.

PAR. The non-existent One therefore is clearly in motion, since we have found it to change from being to not-being.

ARIST. Yes, that seems to follow.

PAR. Again, if it is nowhere at all—an inevitable corollary of its non-existence—it is manifestly incapable of moving from here to there.

ARIST. Of course it is.

PAR. Its motion, therefore, cannot be transference.

ARIST. No.

PAR. Nor can it be rotation in the selfsame place, for it has no contact whatever with the selfsame. The selfsame is existent, and the non-existent cannot possibly be within any existent.

ARIST. No, it certainly cannot.

PAR. Consequently the non-existent One cannot rotate in something in which it is not.

ARIST. Indeed no.

PAR. Nor can the One, whether existent or non-existent, vary from itself in respect of quality; otherwise our discussion would no longer be concerned with the One but with something else.

ARIST. Correct.

PAR. Then if it neither varies in quality nor rotates in the selfsame place, nor is transferred from here to there, how else can it possibly move?

ARIST. Exactly. How?

PAR. Now the motionless must be at rest, and that which is at
rest must be stationary.

ARIST. Of course.

PAR. Apparently then the non-existent One is both stationary
and in motion.

ARIST. So it seems.

PAR. But again, if it moves it must of absolute necessity change
in quality; for in so far as a thing has been moved, [163] it is
no longer in its original state, but in another.

ARIST. Agreed.

PAR. And therefore since the One moves it also changes.

ARIST. Yes.

PAR. And if it never moves at all it can never change.

ARIST. No.

PAR. Therefore the non-existent One, in so far as it moves,
changes; but in so far as it does not move, it does not change.

ARIST. So it seems.

PAR. Now a changing thing inevitably comes to be other than it
was, and perishes out of its former state, while that which is
not changing can neither be coming to be, nor perishing.

ARIST. Perfectly true.

PAR. So too, therefore, with the One: though non-existent, it is
both coming to be and perishing because it *is* changing; but
because it is also *not* changing, it is neither coming to be nor
perishing.

ARIST. Quite so.

[*The Sixth Antinomy* [1]]

PAR. Now let us go back again to the beginning and see whether
or not we shall arrive once more at the same conclusion.

ARIST. By all means.

PAR. Very well then: If the One is not, what consequences will
follow? That is the question.

ARIST. Yes.

PAR. When we use the phrase 'is not', it signifies merely the
absence of being from that of which we are saying that it is not.

ARIST. Just that and nothing else.

---

[1] If the One is not, i.e. if there is no unity whatever in things, nothing can
be either affirmed or denied of it.

PAR. Then when we say that such and such a thing 'is not', do we mean that in one sense it is not and in another sense is? Or are we using the phrase 'is not' without qualification, to signify that the thing which is not is not (i.e. has not being) in any sense whatever?

ARIST. We use it absolutely, without qualification.

PAR. Therefore, that which is not cannot 'be' or 'have being' in any sense whatever.

ARIST. No, it cannot.

PAR. And what is 'to come into being', or 'to perish'? Is the former anything else than to acquire being, and the latter anything else than to lose it?

ARIST. Nothing else than just that.

PAR. And that which has no part in being can neither acquire it nor lose it.

ARIST. Of course not.

PAR. Then assuming that the One is wholly and entirely non-existent, there is no sense whatever in which it can have, or lose, or acquire being.

ARIST. Quite so.

PAR. Consequently the non-existent One is neither perishing nor coming to be, for it has absolutely no part in being.

ARIST. Obviously not.

PAR. Nor, therefore, does it change in any way at all; if it suffered change we should at once have to conclude that it comes to be and perishes.

ARIST. True.

PAR. And if it does not change, it cannot possibly move.

ARIST. No.

PAR. But we shall not describe as stationary that which is no-where, for the stationary must be perpetually in one and the same something.

ARIST. It must.

PAR. Once again then we may never speak of the non-existent One as in motion or at rest.

ARIST. Certainly not.

PAR. Moreover it can have no active character; if it had it would thereby have being.

ARIST. Clearly.

PAR. [164] Hence it has neither greatness, smallness nor equality.

ARIST. No.

PAR. Nor again likeness to, or difference from, itself or the others.

ARIST. Evidently not.

PAR. Very well then, if it can have no character at all, can the Many possibly be anything to it?

ARIST. They cannot.

PAR. Therefore the Many are neither like it nor unlike, neither the same as nor different from it.

ARIST. No.

PAR. Right, then, can anything stand in any relation to it? Can it be qualified as 'something', or as 'this', or as related to a 'this' or an 'other', or as past, future or present? Can it be the object of knowledge, judgment, perception or discussion? Can it have any name? In a word, can the non-existent be qualified by anything actual?

ARIST. Certainly not.

PAR. Thus, the non-existent One had no character whatsoever.

ARIST. That certainly appears to be the case.

[*The Seventh Antinomy* [1]]

PAR. Here now is our next question: If the One is not, what is the position of the Many, which are other than the One?

ARIST. Yes, what is it?

PAR. Other, of course, they must be; if they were not even that we should not refer to them as such.

ARIST. Quite so.

PAR. But since we *are* so referring to them the Many must also be diverse from the One. 'Other' and 'diverse' are epithets which you presumably apply to the same thing.

ARIST. I do.

PAR. Now we speak of the diverse as diverse from something which is in turn diverse from it, and of the other as other than that which is other than it.

ARIST. Yes.

PAR. Therefore, if the Many are to be other, they must surely have something than which they are other.

[1] If the One is not, i.e. if all that exists is *not* an undifferentiated unity, we can make many assertions about the apparent character of the Many.

ARIST. They must.

PAR. What then can this be? They cannot be other than the One, for *ex hypothesi* there is no One.

ARIST. No.

PAR. Consequently they are other than one another; that is the sole remaining possibility, unless they are to be other than nothing.

ARIST. Correct.

PAR. Therefore they are other than one another as aggregates; they cannot be so as units, because there *is* no unit. Each group of them, it seems, is indefinitely numerous. If a man takes what appears to him the smallest of them all he will fare as does a sleeper in his dream: what he thought was one will be suddenly revealed as many, and what he took to be very small he will find enormous by comparison with its small components.

ARIST. Perfectly true.

PAR. The Many, accordingly, will be other than each other as such aggregates, since they are other without there being any unit.

ARIST. Undoubtedly.

PAR. Therefore there will be many aggregates, each of them seeming to be one but not *really* being so, because there is *ex hypothesi* no One.

ARIST. Quite.

PAR. And these many will seem to have a number because each appears to be a unit.

ARIST. Of course.

PAR. And some of them will appear to be even and others odd; but the appearance will be deceptive because it is assumed there is no One.

ARIST. It will.

PAR. Again I think there will appear to be among them a least; but this will also appear many and great when compared with each of its small components.

ARIST. [165] Inevitably.

PAR. Moreover each aggregate will seem to be equal to its numerous small constituents; it could not pass from seeming to be greater to seeming to be less, without appearing to reach the intermediate state, viz—apparent equality.

ARIST. I suppose not.

PAR. Surely too one aggregate will seem to be limited relatively to another, but to have neither beginning nor limit nor middle relatively to itself.

ARIST. Why not?

PAR. Because whenever the mind recognizes any part of them as one of the three, there will always appear to be a beginning before the beginning first recognized, another end ahead of the end first recognized, another and more central middle (though of less extent) within the middle first recognized. The reason of this is, that we are unable to grasp any of them as a unit, precisely because there is no One.

ARIST. Yes, I follow.

PAR. It seems to me, in fact, that every existent which the mind can apprehend must be split up into fractions like money into small change; what is thus apprehended will turn out to be an aggregate without a unit.

ARIST. True.

PAR. Now to a man beholding such a thing from afar off and obscurely, it must inevitably *seem* one thing; but as he draws nearer and observes more keenly, each of them must appear infinitely numerous because devoid of unity, which is non-existent.

ARIST. That of course must be so.

PAR. Accordingly, if there is no One, but only things other than the One, each of the latter must seem to be at once infinite and finite, One and Many.

ARIST. Exactly.

PAR. Will they not then appear to be both like and unlike?

ARIST. How do you account for that?

PAR. Well, they will resemble so many designs in perspective; seen from a distance all will appear to have one and the same character, and to be alike.

ARIST. True.

PAR. But as your observer draws near they will seem to be many and different, and owing to this semblance of difference they will appear diverse and unlike one another.

ARIST. They will.

PAR. Consequently these aggregates will of necessity appear to be simultaneously like and unlike themselves and each other.

ARIST. Certainly.

PAR. And therefore to be also identical with and different from one another, in contact and disjoint, moving with every kind of motion and absolutely stationary, coming into being and perishing, and also doing neither. Nor indeed shall we find any difficulty in running through a long list of similar conclusions, if the Many are but the One is not.

ARIST. I entirely agree.

[*The Eighth Antinomy* [1]]

PAR. Shall we go back to the beginning just once more and ask what will be the consequences if the One is not?

ARIST. By all means.

PAR. The Many of course will not be one.

ARIST. Naturally not.

PAR. Nor indeed a plurality of ones, otherwise there would actually be a unit among them. For if none of them is one, together they will be nothing, and therefore cannot even be a plurality of ones.

ARIST. True.

PAR. Well, since there is no unit among them, Many *are* neither one nor a plurality of ones.

ARIST. No.

PAR. [166] Nor do they even *appear* to be one or a plurality of ones.

ARIST. Why not?

PAR. Because the Many can have no possible connection whatever with a non-existent, and there is no non-existent in any of the Many, because a non-existent has no parts.

ARIST. That is a fact.

PAR. Consequently there is no semblance or appearance of the non-existent among the Many; it is downright impossible for the non-existent to be so much as thought of in relation to the Many.

ARIST. True.

PAR. Therefore if the One is not, none of the Many can be

[1] If the One is not, i.e. if there is no unity whatever in things, the Many cannot appear to be one, nor even a plurality of ones, and we can assert nothing at all about them.

thought of as one; nor again as a plurality of ones, for without the thought of 'one' there can be no thought of 'plurality'.

ARIST. There cannot.

PAR. Hence, if the One is not, the Many neither are, nor are thought to be, either one or a plurality of ones.

ARIST. Quite so.

PAR. Nor like or unlike.

ARIST. No.

PAR. Nor identical or different, nor in contact or disjoint. So too with the other apparent characters we mentioned earlier on; if the One is not, the Many neither have nor appear to have any of them.

ARIST. True.

PAR. Putting it in a nutshell then, it would be correct to say that if the One is not, there is nothing at all.

ARIST. Perfectly correct.

PAR. Good. And we may presumably go on to say this: Whether the One is or is not, both the One and the Many are and also are not, appear and do not appear to be, all manner of things, in relation both to themselves and to one another.

ARIST. You are perfectly right.

THEAITETOS

PERSONS OF THE DIALOGUE

Eucleides.
Terpsion.
Socrates.

Theodoros.
Theaitetos.

EUCLEIDES. [142] Hallo, Terpsion, just up from the country?

TERPSION. No, I've been here some time. Actually I was looking for you in the Agora and was surprised that I couldn't find you.

EUCL. As a matter of fact I was out of town.

TERP. Whereabouts?

EUCL. On my way down to the harbour I met Theaitetos being carried to Athens from the camp at Corinth.

TERP. Alive or dead?

EUCL. Alive, but only just. He's been badly wounded, and to make matters worse he's caught that epidemic which has broken out in the army.

TERP. Dysentery, you mean?

EUCL. Yes.

TERP. How unfortunate that such a man should be at death's door.

EUCL. A very gallant gentleman, Terpsion; only a few minutes ago I was listening to some people praising his conduct in battle.

TERP. No wonder; it would have been surprising if he had borne himself otherwise. But why did he not remain here at Megara?

EUCL. All he wanted was to get home. I begged him to stay, but he would have none of my advice. I accompanied him for some distance, and on my way back I recalled what Socrates had said about him and was amazed at this example of his prophetic insight. So far as I remember, Socrates met him shortly before his own death, when Theaitetos was a mere lad. They spent some time together in conversation and Socrates

67

was deeply impressed with his qualities. When I visited Athens he told me of what had passed between them and it was well worth hearing; he added that there was no doubt Theaitetos had a great future before him if he lived.

TERP. And he spoke the truth apparently. But what was that conversation? Could you repeat it?

EUCL. Good heavens no, not offhand at any rate. [143] But I made some notes at the time, as soon as I got home, and afterwards employed my leisure hours in writing down what I could remember. Whenever I visited Athens I used to question Socrates about such points as I could not recall and correct the manuscript on my return. So you see I have practically the whole conversation in black and white.

TERP. That's right; I have heard you mention it before. I have always been meaning to ask you to let me have a look at it. Why not run through it now? In any case I need a rest after trudging into town.

EUCL. So do I; having walked with Theaitetos all the way to Erineion I could do with a rest myself. Come along then; let us go along to my place, and while we are resting the boy shall read to us.

TERP. Splendid.

EUCL. Here now is the book, Terpsion. Notice the shape in which I have cast the dialogue. Instead of the narrative form used by Socrates when he told me about it, I have preferred direct speech as between him and his two interlocutors— Theodoros the geometer, and Theaitetos. I was anxious that my written account should not be cluttered up with bits of narrative breaking in on the conversation. You know, things like 'and I said' or 'and I remarked' whenever Socrates referred to his own words, and 'he agreed' or 'he would not agree' when it came to the reply. I therefore left out all such matter and represented Socrates as talking with them in person.

TERP. A very good idea too, Eucleides.

EUCL. Well, boy, take the book and read.

SOCR. If I were more interested, Theodoros, in Cyrene and its affairs I should ask you for the local news. I should want to

know whether any of the lads at Cyrene devote themselves to
geometry or to any other of the liberal sciences. As it is, I care
less for them than for my own fellow citizens, and am therefore anxious to learn which of our young men are likely to
make a name for themselves. I'm always doing my best to
obtain that kind of information, for which purpose I question
those with whom I find youth ready to associate. Now you
have a large following, as might be expected considering
above all your skill as a geometer. So, if you have come across
anyone worthy of note, I should like to hear about him.

THEOD. As a matter of fact, Socrates, I *have* met a fine young
Athenian, and it will pay you to listen while I describe him. If
he were good looking I should hesitate to say very much for
fear you might suspect me of being in love with him. Actually,
so far from being handsome—forgive my saying so—he is
rather like you, what with his snub nose and protruding eyes,
though these features are less noticeable in him. [144] So I
can speak without fear. I assure you that among all the young
men whom I have met—and I have come across a great many
—I have never found one of such extraordinary promise.
Never before have I seen or thought possible this combina-
ton of abnormal intelligence, uncommon gentleness and ex-
ceptional virility. As a rule, those who have such keen and
ready wits and such good memories as he are passionate and
quick tempered. They swing off course, like ships without
ballast, and are temperamental rather than strong willed;
whereas your steady sort, when called upon to study, are apt
to be dull and forget everything. But this young man's
approach to learning and inquiry, with the untroubled quiet-
ness of its smooth and sure advance, is like the silent flow of a
stream of oil. It is wonderful how he manages to achieve so
much at his age.

SOCR. That is good news; who is his father?

THEOD. I have heard the name but do not remember it. But here
is the lad himself, the middle one of those three coming
towards us. He and these friends of his have been rubbing
themselves down with oil in the portico outside, and now,
having done, they appear to be coming our way. See if you
recognize him.

SOCR. Yes, I do. His father was Euphronios of Sounion, just the

sort of man you describe his son to be. He was highly re-
spected—left a lot of money too. But I don't know the
youngster's name.

THEOD. Theaitetos is his name, Socrates; but I believe the
property has been squandered by trustees. All the same,
open-handedness is another of his admirable qualities.

SOCR. You give him a splendid character. Do ask him to come
and sit down with us.

THEOD. Certainly. Theaitetos! come here and sit by Socrates.

SOCR. Yes, do, Theaitetos; I want to have a look at myself and
see what my face is like. Theodoros tells me it resembles
yours. If each of us had a lyre, and he said they were both
tuned to the same pitch, would we just take his word for it or
would we first try to find out whether he spoke as a musician?

THEAIT. We should want to know that.

SOCR. And believe him if he turned out to be a musician, but
not otherwise?

THEAIT. Exactly.

SOCR. And now, if we are all interested in the so-called [145]
resemblance of our faces, we must presumably ask whether or
not the allegation is made by a skilled draughtsman.

THEAIT. I agree.

SOCR. Well, is Theodoros a portrait painter?

THEAIT. Not so far as I am aware.

SOCR. Nor a geometer?

THEAIT. Oh yes, he is, Socrates, very much so.

SOCR. And an astronomer, an arithmetician, a musician and in
general an educated man?

THEAIT. I think so.

SOCR. Then if, whether by way of a compliment or of disapproval, he says we have some physical likeness to one
another there is no particular reason why we should take any
notice.

THEAIT. Perhaps not.

SOCR. But suppose he praises the mind of one of us for virtue
and intelligence: surely there would be good reason why the
one who heard the other so commended should be anxious to
examine him, and why the latter should be keen to show his
gifts.

THEAIT. Certainly, Socrates.

SOCR. Now is the time then, my dear Theaitetos, for you to show *your* gifts, and for me to examine them. For I assure you that, often as Theodoros has spoken to me in praise of citizen or stranger, he has never praised anyone so highly as he was praising you a few minutes ago.

THEAIT. I am pleased to hear it, Socrates; but perhaps he was only joking.

SOCR. That would be quite unlike Theodoros. Come now, do not try to escape from your bargain on the pretext that his words were insincere. We don't want him to have to testify on oath. In any case, no one is going to accuse him of perjury; so don't be afraid to stand by your undertaking.

THEAIT. I suppose I must, if you say so.

SOCR. Tell me, then: you are studying geometry under Theodoros, I believe?

THEAIT. I am.

SOCR. Together with astronomy, harmonics and arithmetic?

THEAIT. I try hard to do so.

SOCR. So do I, my boy, from him and from anyone else who appears to understand these things. Although, generally speaking, I make fairly good progress, there is one small matter which puzzles me and which I should like to discuss with you and your friends. Tell me: isn't it true that learning about something means becoming wiser in that subject?

THEAIT. Of course.

SOCR. And what makes people wise is wisdom, I suppose.

THEAIT. Yes.

SOCR. And does this differ in any way from knowledge?

THEAIT. Does what differ?

SOCR. Wisdom. I take it that men are wise in those things whereof they have knowledge?

THEAIT. Of course.

SOCR. So knowledge and wisdom are identical?

THEAIT. Yes.

SOCR. Well, that is just what puzzles me; I cannot satisfy myself as to what exactly knowledge is. [146] Can we answer that question? What do you all say? Which of us is going to speak first? Everyone who misses shall 'sit down and be donkey', as children say when they play ball; anyone who gets through without missing shall be our king and shall be entitled to make us answer any question he likes to ask. Why the silence? I hope, Theodoros, that my love of argument is not making me rude; I only want to start a conversation so that we shall all feel at home with one another like friends.

THEOD. Nothing rude in that, Socrates. However, tell one of the lads to answer your questions; I'm not used to abstract discussion of this kind, nor am I ever likely to become so at my age. But it is quite in their line, and they stand a far better chance of improvement; youth, in fact, is capable of improvement in any and every direction. Stick to Theaitetos on whom you began: let him do the answering.

SOCR. Come, Theaitetos, you hear what Theodoros says. I don't imagine you will want to disobey him; it would in fact be quite wrong for you to turn down such a request from an older and wiser man. So do not begrudge me an answer: what do you think knowledge is?

THEAIT. Well, Socrates, I cannot refuse, since you and Theodoros ask me. Anyway, if I go wrong, the two of you are sure to put me right.

SOCR. Certainly, if we can.

THEAIT. In that case I think the things one can learn from Theodoros are knowledge—geometry and the other sciences you mentioned just now. Then there are cobblery and the crafts of other skilled workmen. Each and all of these are nothing else than knowledge.

SOCR. My word, you are generous, Theaitetos; so open-handed that, when asked for a single thing, you produce instead a whole variety.

THEAIT. What do you mean, Socrates?

SOCR. Maybe I'm talking nonsense, but I will tell you what I have in mind. When you speak of cobblery I take it that you mean precisely the knowledge of how to make shoes.

THEAIT. Exactly.

SOCR. And what about joinery? Are you not referring simply to the knowledge of how to make wooden furniture?

THEAIT. Quite so.

SOCR. In both cases therefore you are defining what the craft is knowledge of?

THEAIT. Yes.

SOCR. But my question, Theaitetos, was not 'What are the

objects of knowledge?' nor 'How many kinds of knowledge are there?' We were not trying to count them, but to find out what knowledge (the thing itself) really is. Is there nothing in that?

THEAIT. No, you are perfectly right.

SOCR. [147] Take another example. Suppose we were asked about some common or garden thing: for instance, what clay is. It would surely be ridiculous to answer 'potter's clay, oven-maker's clay and brick-maker's clay'.

THEAIT. Perhaps.

SOCR. To begin with, it is absurd to imagine that the questioner gathers any meaning from our answer when we use the word 'clay', no matter whose clay we call it—the doll-maker's or any other craftsman's. Surely you are not going to suggest that a man can understand a thing's name when he does not know what the thing is.

THEAIT. Of course not.

SOCR. Then 'knowledge of shoes' conveys absolutely nothing to him if he doesn't know what knowledge is.

THEAIT. No.

SOCR. A man, therefore, who has no conception of knowledge can derive no meaning from 'cobblery' or from the name of any other art.

THEAIT. That is true.

SOCR. So it is ridiculous to answer the question 'What is knowledge?' by naming one of the arts, and thereby saying 'knowledge of so-and-so'—which was not what the question called for.

THEAIT. I see your point.

SOCR. In the second place we are going an interminable way round when we might give a short and simple answer. For example, to the question about clay, the straightforward and obvious reply is 'earth mixed with moisture', regardless of *whose* clay it may be.

THEAIT. It appears easy now, Socrates, when put like that. Your question seems to involve a problem like one that came up not long ago when your namesake here, Socrates, and I were talking.

SOCR. What was that, Theaitetos?

THEAIT. Our friend Theodoros was proving to us something

about square roots, namely that the sides (or roots) of squares representing 3 square feet and 5 square feet are not commensurable in length with the line representing 1 foot; and he continued thus, taking each case in turn up to the root of 17 square feet. There, for some reason, he stopped. Now it occurred to us, since these square roots were apparently infinite in number, to look for a single collective term by which we should be able to designate all of them.

SOCR. And did you find one?

THEAIT. I believe we did. But let us have your opinion.

SOCR. Go on.

THEAIT. We divided number as a whole into two classes. Any number which is the product of a number multiplied by itself we likened to the square figures, and called it a 'square' or 'equilateral' number.

SOCR. Splendid!

THEAIT. Any intermediate number—[148] e.g. 3 or 5 or any other number that is not the product of a number by itself, but has one factor either greater or less than the other, so that the sides containing the corresponding figure are always unequal —we likened to the oblong figure, and called it an 'oblong' number.

SOCR. Fine; and then what?

THEAIT. All the lines which form the four equal sides of the plane figure representing the 'equilateral' number we defined as 'length', while those which form the sides of squares equal in area to the oblongs we called 'roots' (surds), as not being commensurable with the others in length, but only in the plane areas to which their squares are equal. And there is another distinction of the same sort in the case of solids.

SOCR. Brilliant, my young friends! I can't see Theodoros being prosecuted for giving false evidence.

THEAIT. But honestly, Socrates, I cannot answer your question about knowledge as we tackled that one about the length and the root. And yet you seem to want something of the kind; so it does appear after all that Theodoros was mistaken.

SOCR. Surely not. Why, suppose he had sung your praises as a runner, declaring that he had never met any young man capable of such speed and endurance on the course; and suppose you had then been beaten in a race by the champion at his best; do you think his praise would have been any the less justified?

THEAIT. No, I don't.

SOCR. Very well then, as I said just now, do you consider it a small matter to discover what knowledge is? Surely it is a very difficult question.

THEAIT. I should think it is; one of the most difficult of all.

SOCR. Then you must have confidence in yourself, and believe what Theodoros said. Be tireless in your quest for *any* definition, but above all for that of knowledge.

THEAIT. If it depends upon me doing my best, Socrates, the truth will emerge.

SOCR. Follow the road then that you have just mapped out so well. Take as a model your answer about the roots; just as you included the whole lot of them within a single character, so now try to designate the several kinds of knowledge by a single formula.

THEAIT. But I assure you, Socrates, I have often set myself to study that problem when I heard reports of the questions you ask. But I cannot convince myself that I have reached a solution, or that I have ever heard anyone else put forward the kind of answer you require. On the other hand I cannot put the subject from my mind.

SOCR. My dear Theaitetos, that is because your mind is not a vacuum. You are pregnant and in the throes of travail.

THEAIT. I don't know about that, Socrates. I merely tell you how I feel.

SOCR. [149] Good heavens, boy! have you never heard that I am the son of a fine buxom midwife called Phainarete?

THEAIT. Yes, I have heard as much.

SOCR. And have you also heard that I practise the same art?

THEAIT. No, never.

SOCR. Well I do; but be sure not to tell the others. It is not known that I possess this skill; so the ignorant describe me in other terms as an eccentric who drives men to distraction. Have you heard that too?

THEAIT. I have indeed.

SOCR. Shall I tell you the reason?

THEAIT. Please do.

SOCR. Consider the general practice of midwives and you will understand more clearly what I mean. You are doubtless aware that none of them ever attends other women in childbirth so long as she herself is capable of conceiving and bearing children, but only when she is too old to do so.

THEAIT. Of course.

SOCR. They say that is because Artemis, the patroness of childbirth, is herself childless. She would not allow barren women to act as midwives, because it is beyond the power of human nature to acquire skill without experience; and she therefore assigned the duty to women who were past child-bearing, as a mark of respect for their resemblance to herself.

THEAIT. Very likely.

SOCR. And is it not more than likely that no one is better qualified than a midwife to tell whether or not women are pregnant?

THEAIT. Certainly.

SOCR. Furthermore, by the administration of drugs and incantations, midwives can bring on or allay the pangs of travail as they wish, render a difficult birth easy and cause a miscarriage, if desirable, in the early stages of pregnancy.

THEAIT. That is so.

SOCR. You may also, perhaps, have noticed that they are expert matchmakers, knowing just exactly what union of man and woman will produce the best children.

THEAIT. Really?

SOCR. Oh yes; they pride themselves more on that than on cutting the umbilical cord. Consider the knowledge of the kind of plant or seed that should be set or sown in any given soil: does it go along with tending and harvesting the crops, or are they two different arts?

THEAIT. No, the same.

SOCR. In the case of a woman then, my friend, is skill in sowing separate from skill in harvesting?

THEAIT. I shouldn't think so.

SOCR. [150] No; only because of that wrong and unscientific method of bringing man and woman together, which is known as pandering, midwives are led by their own self-respect to avoid matchmaking, for fear of being charged with pandering. Yet your genuine midwife is the only efficient matchmaker.

THEAIT. Evidently.

SOCR. So much then for the midwife and her functions; but her achievement is less than mine. Women are not in the habit of sometimes bringing forth real children, and sometimes mere phantoms which can hardly be distinguished from the others. If they were, surely the midwife's highest and noblest task would lie in telling the unreal from the real.

THEAIT. I quite agree.

SOCR. Generally speaking, the art of midwifery as I practise it is very much like hers. But there are differences. First, my patients are men, not women; and secondly I am concerned not with bodies but with souls in labour. The supreme point, however, of my skill is its power to determine by every test whether a young man's mind gives birth to an empty phantom or to a living reality. I have this in common with a midwife, that I cannot give birth to wisdom; and there is some truth in the oft-repeated accusation that, though I question others I can never produce an answer, because there is no wisdom in me. Here is the reason: God compels me to serve as a midwife, but has prevented me from giving birth. I myself, therefore, am wholly devoid of wisdom, nor has any sage discovery been born to me as the offspring of my soul. Some of my associates at first appear abysmally ignorant. But as our acquaintance grows, all whom God favours make progress to an extent that seems amazing to others as well as to themselves, although it is evident that they have never learned anything from me; the many grand truths which they bring into the world have been discovered by themselves and from within. But the delivery is God's work and mine. The proof is as follows. Many who have been unconscious of the part I played and have despised me, attributing their success to their own efforts, have left me sooner than they should, either of their own accord or at another's instigation. Afterwards they have suffered miscarriage of their thoughts in consequence of evil company; and they have lost the children of whom I helped to deliver them by bringing them up badly, caring more for unreal phantoms than for the truth, until at length their ignorance has become manifest to themselves as well as to everyone else. [151] Such a one was Aristeides, son of Lysimachos, and there have been many others. When they come back, with melodramatic appeals for the renewal of our association, sometimes the divine spirit forbids it; but with others it is allowed, and these begin once more to make progress.

There is another way also in which my associates can be likened to women with child: night and day they are in travail and distress, far more so indeed than are women; and my art can bring on or still these labour pains. So much for them; but there are others, Theaitetos, whose minds appear to me never to have conceived at all. I realize that they have no need of me, and with all the goodwill in the world I serve them as a matchmaker. Thanks be to God, I am a pretty good judge of whose society will profit them: I have 'married' many of them off to Prodicos, and to other inspired sages.

Now for the point of all this long discourse, my friend. I suspect that, as you yourself believe, your mind is in labour with some thought it has conceived. Apply then to me as to a midwife's son who practises his mother's art, and do your best to answer the questions I shall put to you. It may be that when I examine your statements I shall judge one or other of them to be a mere phantom, devoid of reality; in which case I shall take it from you and throw it away. If that should happen, don't round on me like some wild beast as women do when robbed of their first-born. Dear boy, people have so often felt like that towards me, and have actually been prepared to bite me, for depriving them of some foolish notion. They do not see that I am doing them a kindness. They might as well imagine that I act thus from unkindness as believe God capable of ill will towards man; it is only that the moral law forbids me to acquiesce in a lie or to suppress the truth.

Come now, Theaitetos, start again and try to tell us what knowledge is. Never say 'I cannot'; for, under God, your own determination will enable you to do so.

THEAIT. Well, Socrates, with such encouragement from you of all people, it would be a shame not to do everything in one's power to give some kind of answer. It seems to me that one who knows anything is *perceiving* the thing he knows, and, so far as I can see at present, knowledge is nothing but perception.

SOCR. Good lad! Splendid! That's the way to express an opinion. Now let us examine your offspring together and see whether it is a living creature or a mere wind-egg. Perception, you say, is knowledge.

THEAIT. Yes.

SOCR. Well, the account you give of knowledge is, to say the least, respectable. [152] It is the one Protagoras used to give, except that he put it in a rather different way. He says, you will remember, that 'man is the measure of all things'—of the being of things that are and of the not-being of things that are not. You have doubtless read the passage.

THEAIT. Oh, frequently.

SOCR. He expresses himself, I think, in this sort of way: 'Any given thing is to me such as it appears to me, and is to you such as it appears to you'—you and I being men.

THEAIT. Yes, that is what he says.

SOCR. Well, a wise man is not likely to be talking nonsense; so let us follow up his statement. Is it not true that sometimes, when a particular wind is blowing, one of us feels cold and the other does not; or one feels just chilly and the other bitterly cold?

THEAIT. Certainly.

SOCR. In that case, then, are we to say that the wind in itself is cold or not cold? Or shall we agree with Protagoras that it is cold to the one who feels cold and not to the other?

THEAIT. I suppose we should agree with him.

SOCR. And further that it 'appears' so to each of us?

THEAIT. Yes.

SOCR. And 'appears' means that he 'perceives' it as such?

THEAT. It does.

SOCR. Then 'appearing' and 'perceiving' are the same thing in the case of what is hot, and so on. As each man *perceives* them, so they *are* to him.

THEAIT. Presumably.

SOCR. Perception, therefore, is always of something which *is*, and, since it is knowledge, it can never lie.

THEAIT. Evidently.

SOCR. Wait though: may it be that Protagoras was a very clever man who gave out this dark saying for the common herd like ourselves, and revealed the truth in secret to his disciples?

THEAIT. What do you mean by that, Socrates?

SOCR. I will tell you; and the doctrine is certainly one that deserves our attention. It means that nothing is one thing just by itself, and that you cannot rightly call it by a definite name or even ascribe to it any definite quality. No, if you call it large, it will be found also to be small, light if you describe it as heavy; and so throughout the whole gamut, because nothing is one thing or some thing or of any definite kind. All the things we commonly say 'are', actually are in process of becoming, as a result of motion, change and blending. It is wrong to say that they *are*, for none of them ever is; they are always becoming. In this matter you can take it that, with the exception of Parmenides, one philosopher after another is agreed—Protagoras, Heracleitos, Empedocles—as well as the leaders in both kinds of poetry, Epicharmos in comedy and Homer in tragedy. When the latter refers to 'Oceanos, origin of the gods, and mother Tethys', he implies that all things are the offspring of a flowing stream of change. Don't you take him to mean just that?

THEAIT. I do.

SOCR. [153] How, then, could anyone defy so great a host, with Homer at its head, and not make a fool of himself?

THEAIT. It would not be easy, Socrates.

SOCR. No, Theaitetos, it would not. There are adequate proofs for the doctrine that 'being' (or what we are pleased to call being) and 'becoming' result from motion, not-being and perishing from rest. The hot or fire, for example, which generates and controls everything else, is itself generated by movement and friction—both forms of change. That is how fire is produced, is it not?

THEAIT. Yes.

SOCR. Furthermore the animal kingdom is produced by these same processes?

THEAIT. So it is.

SOCR. Again, is not physical health destroyed by inactivity and idleness, but preserved largely by exercise and motion?

THEAIT. Yes.

SOCR. So too with the condition of the soul. The soul acquires information and is kept alive and improved by learning and practice—two forms of motion; whereas through inactivity, i.e. sloth and neglect of study, it learns nothing and forgets what it has learnt.

THEAIT. Exactly.

SOCR. Motion, therefore, is a good thing for both soul and body, and inactivity the opposite.

THEAIT. That seems to follow.

SOCR. I need hardly give you further examples, such as stagnant air and water, in which lack of movement causes corruption and decay, instead of keeping them fresh as motion does. Nor, surely, need I crown the argument by dragging in Homer's Golden Rope,[1] proving that he means by it nothing else but the sun, and thereby indicates that so long as the heavens and the sun go round, all things in heaven and earth are maintained in existence; whereas if they were slowed down to a standstill everything would be destroyed and the whole order of things be, as the saying is, 'turned upside down'.

THEAIT. I agree with your interpretation, Socrates.

SOCR. Go on, then, my friend, and apply the Protagorean thesis. First as regards sight: what you call 'white colour' must not be conceived as something distinct outside your eyes, nor yet inside them. You must not assign it any definite place; otherwise, of course, it would *be* in a fixed place and remain there, instead of arising in a process of becoming.

THEAIT. I don't follow you.

SOCR. Let us proceed on the lines of what we said just now, and assume there is no single thing that is in and by itself. We shall then realize that black or white or any other colour you care to name is the result of a meeting of our eyes with the appropriate motion. What we say *is* [154] such and such a colour will be neither that which encounters nor that which is encountered, but something which has arisen between the two and is peculiar to each percipient. Or would you maintain that every colour appears to a dog or any other brute beast just as it does to you?

THEAIT. Indeed I would not.

SOCR. Again, does anything appear the same to another *man* as it does to you? Are you sure of that? I will go so far as to suggest that you are very much more certain that it does not even appear the same to you, because you yourself never remain in the same condition.

THEAIT. I agree with what you suggest.

SOCR. So, if that against which we measure ourselves, or which

[1] *Iliad*, viii. 18 ff.

we touch, really were large or white or hot, it would never become different as soon as it encountered a different person, supposing that it does not itself change. Moreover if that which measures itself, or does the touching, really were large or white or hot, then, when a different thing encountered it or were modified in some way, it, on its side, if it were not affected in itself, would not become different. On the assumption now current, my friend, that things have permanent qualities, we are too easily led into making statements which Protagoras and anyone else who adopted his view would call strange and ridiculous.

THEAIT. What do you mean? What statements?

SOCR. Here is a simple illustration which will fully explain my meaning. If you compare six dice with four, we say that the six are more than the four or half as many again; but if you compare them with twelve we say they are fewer or only half as many. There is nothing else we can say—or is there?

THEAIT. Certainly not.

SOCR. Suppose then that someone like Protagoras asks you: 'Theaitetos, can anything become greater or more otherwise than by increase?' What will you reply?

THEAIT. Well, Socrates, if I were to express an opinion with reference to this last question I should answer No; but thinking back to your earlier question I should say Yes, for fear of contradicting myself.

SOCR. Well said, sir! But that 'Yes' of yours reminds me of Euripides: 'My tongue hath sworn, no oath is on my soul.'

THEAIT. There's something in that.

SOCR. Now if you and I were two clever fellows who had discovered all there is to know about the mind of man, we should most likely devote the remainder of our time to testing one another's strength in a sophistic battle of words. But being ordinary people we shall want in the first place to study the notions we have in our own minds and find out whether or not they are consistent one with another.

THEAIT. That is certainly what I should like to do.

SOCR. So should I. In that case, since we have plenty of time we will look at the question again, quietly and [155] patiently, making an honest examination of ourselves in an attempt to discover what exactly are these notions in our minds. With

regard to the first of them I imagine we shall assert that
nothing can ever become greater or less, either in size or in
number, so long as it remains equal to itself. Is it not so?

THEAIT. Yes.

SOCR. And, secondly, that anything to which nothing is added
and from which nothing is subtracted is neither increased nor
diminished, but that its amount always remains the same.

THEAIT. Undoubtedly.

SOCR. And must we not say, thirdly, that a thing which was not
at an earlier point of time cannot *be* at a later point without
becoming and being in process of becoming?

THEAIT. I agree.

SOCR. Those three assumptions, I fancy, war with one another
in our minds when we make such statements about the dice;
or when we say that I, being of the stature you now see,
without either increasing or diminishing in height, may within
a year be taller (as I now am) than a lad like you, and afterwards shorter, not because my bulk has grown less, but
because you have grown taller. For apparently I am later
what I was not earlier, and yet have not become so; for
without the process of becoming the result is impossible, and
I could not be in process of becoming shorter unless I dis-
carded some of my bulk. I could provide you with innumerable other examples, if we are to accept these. You doubtless
follow me, Theaitetos; at all events I do not imagine that such
puzzles are outside your experience.

THEAIT. On the contrary, Socrates, it is extraordinary how they
get me wondering whatever they can mean. Sometimes the
very contemplation of them makes me feel quite dizzy.

SOCR. I see. Theodoros did not estimate your nature so badly
after all. This sense of wonder is characteristic of a philosopher; wonder, in fact, is the very source of speculation, and he
who made Iris the daughter of Thaumas was a good genea-
logist. Now do you begin to understand the significance of all
this which follows from the doctrine we are attributing to
Protagoras? Or is it not yet clear?

THEAIT. No, not yet.

SOCR. Then doubtless you will be grateful if I help you to discover the truth hidden in the thought of a man—or rather, of
men—so distinguished.

THEAIT. I shall indeed be grateful, very grateful.

SOCR. Well, look around and see that none of the uninitiated overhears us. By the uninitiated I mean those who fancy that nothing is real except what they can grasp firmly with their hands, and who deny that actions or processes or anything invisible can share in reality.

THEAIT. What hard, repellent folk they sound!

SOCR. So they are too, quite without refinement. [156] Others, whose secrets I am going to reveal to you, are much more subtle. Their first principle, upon which all that we said just now depends, is an assumption that the universe is really motion and nothing else. And there are two kinds of motion: each is manifested in countless ways; but they differ in that one has the power of acting, and the other of being acted upon. From the intercourse and friction of these two arise offspring, numerically infinite, but in pairs of twins. One of these twins is a thing perceived, the other a perception, whose birth always occurs simultaneously with that of the thing perceived. Now we give the perceptions such names as 'seeing', 'hearing', 'smelling', 'feeling cold', 'feeling hot'; and again there are what we call pleasures, pains, desires, fears and so on. The nameless ones are legion, though names have been devised for a great many. The brood of things perceived is invariably born at the same moment with one or other of these: with instances of seeing there are born colours of corresponding variety; with instances of hearing a similar variety of sounds; and with all the other perceptions, the corresponding things perceived. Now, Theaitetos, what light do these facts cast on what has gone before? Do you see?

THEAIT. Not exactly, Socrates.

SOCR. Listen then, and I will try to explain. They suggest of course that all these things are, as we were saying, *in motion*; but their motion has a quickness or slowness. The slow kind has its motion without change of place and in relation to what comes within its orbit, and thereby generates offspring; but the offspring thus generated are more rapid, because they move from place to place and their motion is essentially locomotion. Whenever, therefore, an eye and some other appropriate object come within range of one another and give birth simultaneously to, say, whiteness and to the corresponding perception—things that could never have been produced if either of the two had approached any other object—then, as the vision from the eyes and the whiteness from the thing that co-operates in giving birth to the colour pass through the intervening space, the eye becomes filled with vision and so begins at that moment to see, becoming not *vision* but a *seeing eye*; while the colour's other parent is filled with whiteness and becomes, in turn, not whiteness but a white thing—stock, stone, or whatever it be that happens to be so coloured.

And all the rest (hard, hot, etc.) must be regarded in the same way: as we said earlier on, none of them has [157] any being just by itself, but all things of every kind arise from intercourse with one another, in consequence of their motion; for it is impossible to have any 'firm notion', as the phrase is, of either the active or the passive element in them, in any single case, as having any being. For there is no such thing as an agent until it encounters a patient nor vice versa.

The upshot of all this, as we said at the beginning, is that nothing *is* one thing just by itself, but is always *in process of becoming* for someone or other; 'being' must be cancelled out, although we have been led by the inadvertence of habit to use that word several times, even during the past few minutes. But according to these wise men, we should not employ such expressions as 'something', 'somebody's', 'mine', 'this', 'that' or any other word that implies bringing things to a halt. Rather, we should speak, in the light of fact, of what is 'becoming', 'being produced', 'perishing' and 'changing'. For anyone who makes a statement that implies that things are at a standstill is easily refuted. We ought to speak in this way both with reference to individual things and to such collective entities as 'man', 'stone' or any living creature or kind. Does all this satisfy you, Theaitetos? Does it suit your palate..

THEAIT. Well, Socrates, I really don't know. I can't even make up my mind about you, whether you are voicing your own beliefs, or simply testing me.

SOCR. You forget, my friend, that I personally know nothing about such matters, and lay no claim to produce offspring of my own. I am merely acting as midwife to you, and for that purpose uttering incantations and inviting you to taste the varied delicacies from Wisdom's table, until I succeed in helping forth *your* opinion to the light of day. That done, I shall see whether it is just a wind-egg or a living child. Meanwhile be brave and patient; answer my questions boldly and tell me just exactly what you think.

THEAIT. Ask away.

SOCR. Once again then, do you approve the theory that nothing *is*, but is always *becoming*, good, beautiful and so on?

THEAIT. Well, when I hear you explain it as you did, it seems to me altogether satisfactory and quite acceptable as you have stated it.

SOCR. Maybe, but that is not the end of the matter. What about dreams and diseases, especially madness and all the errors of sight, hearing, etc., which are said to proceed therefrom? You know of course that in all these cases the theory in question is supposed to be acknowledged as disproven. The argument is that [158] in madness, disease and so forth we undoubtedly have false perceptions, and so far from it being true that whatever *appears* to any individual actually *is*, on the contrary, no such appearance is ever real.

THEAIT. Quite true, Socrates.

SOCR. Upon what argument, then, can one fall back if one holds that perception is knowledge, and that whatever appears to any given man actually *is* so far as he is concerned?

THEAIT. Well, Socrates, I hesitate to say that I have no reply, because you pulled me up a little while ago for saying that. As a matter of fact, I cannot deny that madmen and dreamers believe what is false when the former imagine they are gods and the latter think they have wings and are flying in their sleep.

SOCR. Surely you have not overlooked another difficulty that arises in this connection, especially about sleeping and waking.

THEAIT. What difficulty is that?

SOCR. A question which I fancy you have frequently heard asked: to what evidence could we point if someone asked us here and now whether we are asleep or awake, dreaming all our passing thoughts or talking with one another in the waking state?

THEAIT. No, Socrates, I don't see how it can be proved one way or the other; for between the two conditions there is in all particulars as exact a correspondence as between strophe and antistrophe in a choral hymn. Take our conversation up to this point: there is no proof that it is not one we merely think in sleep that we are carrying on; and when we dream that we are narrating other dreams the two states are remarkably alike.

SOCR. You realize then that the door is wide open to doubt, when we cannot even be certain whether we are awake or asleep. In fact, since our time is equally divided between sleeping and waking, in each condition our mind stoutly maintains that its convictions at any given moment are certainly true; so that for equal periods we affirm the reality of the dream world and of the waking world, and are just as confident of being right in either case.

THEAIT. Exactly.

SOCR. And the same is true of disease and madness, except that the periods of time are unequal.

THEAIT. Yes.

SOCR. Well, is truth to be determined by length or shortness of time?

THEAIT. No, that would be unreasonable from many points of view.

SOCR. Do you know any other sure means of demonstrating which set of beliefs is true?

THEAIT. I don't think I do.

SOCR. Then listen while I tell you how these cases would be explained by those who hold that whatever at any time *seems* to anyone *is true* for him. They would begin, I imagine, by asking this question: 'Theaitetos, if one thing is entirely different from another, can it possibly be in any respect capable of functioning (actively or passively) in the same way as that other? Remember, we are not assuming the thing in question to be partially the same and partially different, but wholly and entirely different.'

THEAIT. It is impossible, on that assumption, for it to have any-thing at all in common, either in its [159] capabilities of function or in any other respect.

SOCR. Have we not then also to admit that such a thing is unlike the other?

THEAIT. I agree.

SOCR. So if perchance something comes to be like or unlike

either itself or something else, we shall say that when it has become like it becomes 'the same', and when unlike, 'different'.

THEAIT. We shall have to.

SOCR. Now we said earlier, did we not, that the number of things that function actively or of those that function passively is unlimited?

THEAIT. Yes.

SOCR. And further, that when any of these is 'married' to one different 'spouse' after another, the offspring resulting will be not the same but different.

THEAT. Of course.

SOCR. Good. Then let us take me or you or anything else to which the principle applies—Socrates in health and Socrates ailing: are we to say that one of these is 'like' the other, or 'unlike'?

THEAIT. Are you in fact asking whether 'Socrates ailing' considered as a whole is like 'Socrates in health' as a whole?

SOCR. You grasp my meaning perfectly; I am asking exactly that.

THEAIT. Well, I should say 'unlike'.

SOCR. And therefore, because unlike, a different thing?

THEAIT. Necessarily.

SOCR. And you would say the same of 'Socrates asleep' or in any other of the states we mentioned?

THEAIT. Yes.

SOCR. Then any one of the objects whose nature it is to act upon something else will treat me as a different thing, according as it finds Socrates in health or ailing?

THEAIT. Inevitably.

SOCR. And therefore a union of myself as acted upon and the thing that acts upon me will produce different offspring in the two cases?

THEAIT. Of course.

SOCR. Now when I am in good health and drink wine, it seems to me pleasant and sweet.

THEAIT. It does.

SOCR. The reason is that, according to the explanation we accepted just now, agent and patient give birth to sweetness and a perception or sensation, two simultaneous movements through space. The sensation on the side of the patient makes the tongue percipient; while as regards the wine, the sweetness, spreading itself over the wine, causes it to be and to appear sweet to the healthy tongue.

THEAIT. That was certainly the explanation we accepted.

SOCR. But when it finds me ailing, in the first place it does not really find the same person; for it now encounters someone unlike the other.

THEAIT. True.

SOCR. Consequently this pair—Socrates ailing and the drinking of the wine—give birth to different offspring, viz. a sensation of bitterness in the locality of the tongue, and in that of the wine a bitterness which is engendered as a movement there. The wine becomes, not bitterness, but bitter; and I become, not a sensation, but sentient.

THEAIT. Perfectly correct.

SOCR. Certain conclusions follow. (a) I for my part shall never become percipient of anything else in exactly this way; for of a different object there is a different perception, and in acting upon its percipient [160] it acts upon someone who is in a different state and therefore a different someone. (b) As for the thing that acts upon me, it can never, by encountering someone else, give birth to the same offspring or come to be of exactly this quality; for by producing another thing from another someone it will come to be of another quality.

THEAIT. Exactly.

SOCR. Again (c), I shall not come to have this sensation all on my own, nor will the object come to be such as it does all on its own.

THEAIT. No.

SOCR. On the contrary, when I become percipient, I must necessarily become percipient *of something*; for it is impossible to become percipient and perceive nothing; and likewise the object, when it becomes sweet or bitter or what not, must necessarily become so *to someone*; it cannot become sweet but sweet to no one.

THEAIT. Perfectly true.

SOCR. With the result, I suppose, that the object and I are or become—whichever term we adopt—*for one another*. Necessity links together our existence, but links neither of us to anything else, nor each of us to himself; so we are linked only to one another. Hence, if a man says that something 'is' or 'becomes', he must refer to it as being or becoming in some way *relative to something*; he must not speak or allow others to speak of a thing being or becoming anything just in and by itself. That is the upshot of our discussion.

THEAIT. I entirely agree, Socrates.

SOCR. Therefore, since what acts upon me is for me and for me alone, I, and I alone, perceive it.

THEAIT. Granted.

SOCR. In that case my perception is true for me. Why? Because its object is always real for me, and I am, as Protagoras says, judge of the exister ce of what is real for me, and of the non-existence of what is not so.

THEAIT. Apparently.

SOCR. If then I am infallible, and my mind never errs as to what is or becomes, can I possibly fail to have knowledge of the things of which I am percipient?

THEAIT. Of course you cannot.

SOCR. You were therefore quite right in saying that knowledge is nothing else than perception; and we find complete identity between the following theories: (*a*) the doctrine of Homer, Heracleitos, and all their followers, namely, that all things move like flowing rivers; (*b*) the teaching of the great philosopher Protagoras that 'Man is the measure of all things'; and (*c*) Theaitetos' view that, in the light of (*a*) and (*b*), perception is knowledge.

Is that right, Theaitetos? What about calling this your new-born child which I have brought to birth? What do you say?

THEAIT. It is the only thing to do, Socrates.

SOCR. Well, at any rate, we have at long last, and not without pain, managed to bring this creature into the world, whatever it turns out to be. After its birth of course it must be carried round the hearth; we must look at it from every point of view to be sure we are not deceived by a lifeless wind-egg not worth rearing. [161] On the other hand you may think that a child of yours must be reared at any cost and not exposed. Can you bear to see it examined and not be too angry if your first-born is taken from you?

THEOD. Theaitetos can stand that, Socrates; he is not at all bad tempered. But hurry up and tell us if the conclusion is wrong.

SOCR. You have an absolute craze for discussion, Theodoros. A fine thing to treat me like a kind of sack full of arguments, and imagine I can easily pull out a proof to invalidate our conclusion! You do not understand my method: the arguments never come from me, but always from the person with whom I am talking. I have only the slight advantage of being able to elicit some account of the matter from another's wisdom and to deal with it fairly. So now I shall put forward no explanation of my own, but try to extract it from our friend here.

THEOD. That is the better way, Socrates; go ahead.

SOCR. Well then, Theodoros, do you know what amazes me about your friend Protagoras?

THEOD. Tell me.

SOCR. The first sentence of his book. In general, I admire his statement that what *appears* to anyone actually *is*; but I am surprised that he did not begin his treatise *On Truth* by saying that a pig, a baboon or some sentient creature still more outlandish is the measure of all things. There would have been a certain grandeur in so contemptuous an introduction, pointing out that while we applauded him for wisdom almost divine, he was after all no more intelligent than a tadpole, let alone any other human being. What else is there to say, Theodoros? Assuming that what every man believes in consequence of perception is actually to be true for him; assuming that, just as no one is to be recognized as a better judge of another's experience, so no one has a better right to decide whether what his neighbour thinks is true or false, and (as we have several times observed) every man is to have his own beliefs for himself alone and they are all right and true: on these assumptions, I ask you, my friend, how comes it that Protagoras is so wise as to justify his setting up to teach others in return for large fees; and how comes it that we are so comparatively ignorant that we need him as our schoolmaster, when each of us is the measure of his own wisdom? Must we not conclude that Protagoras speaks in this fashion by way of 'playing to the gallery'? I say nothing of my own case or of the fatuity to which my art of midwifery is reduced, and surely too the whole business of philosophical discussion; for to undertake the scrutiny and testing of another's notions and beliefs when [162] those of every man are right, is a tiresome and outrageous piece of folly, if Protagoras' Dame Truth is really truthful and not simply amusing herself with delivering oracles from the awful sanctuary of his book.

THEOD. Well, Socrates, as you said a little while ago, Protagoras was my friend, so I would rather not have the good man refuted through any admissions on my part; but I should be equally disinclined to oppose you against my own convictions. So have another go at Theaitetos; he seemed to be following your line of argument very well just now.

SOCR. If you went to Sparta, Theodoros, and called in at a wrestling school, would you think it fair to watch the naked trainees, some of them in poor condition, and not strip so as to let them have a look at your own physique?

THEOD. Why not, provided they made no objection and allowed me to do so, just as I now believe I can persuade you to let me be a mere spectator? One is a bit stiff at my age; try a fall with someone younger and more agile without dragging me into the ring.

SOCR. Well, Theodoros, 'what likes you mislikes not me', as the saying goes. I must pick Theaitetos' brains once more. Tell me now, first, Theaitetos, in connection with that last criticism of mine: are *you* not surprised that your wisdom turns out all of a sudden to be on a level with that of any man, and even of any god? Do you think that Protagoras' aphorism about the measure applies any less to gods than to men?

THEAIT. Certainly not. And as for your other question, I am more than surprised. When we were discussing what is meant by the doctrine that what seems to a man really *is* to him who thinks it so, I was perfectly satisfied with the theory; but now, all at once, I have begun to take a very different view.

SOCR. That, my dear boy, is because you are young; you listen to plain rubbish and are taken in by it. Protagoras, or someone representing him, will have an answer ready. He will say: 'You good folk sitting together there, boys and old men, this is a lot of bounce. You drag in the gods, the question of whose existence or non-existence I deliberately exclude from my lectures and writings, and you make statements having a mere popular appeal such as this: "How odd that any human being is to be no better in point of wisdom than the lowest of brute beasts!" You rely upon what seems probable, without offering the slightest argument or proof. If Theodoros, or indeed any other mathematician, saw fit to base his geometry on likelihood he would not be worth a farthing. So you and Theodoros would be well advised to ask yourselves [163] whether you are going to allow such important questions to be decided by facile appeals to unsubstantiated probability.'

THEAIT. No, Socrates, you would not call that right any more than we should.

SOCR. Apparently, then, we must approach the question by another road. That is what you and Theodoros think.

THEAIT. We certainly do.

SOCR. Well then, let us look at it in this way—I mean, this question whether knowledge is or is not, after all, the same thing as perception. For that, you doubtless remember, was the pivot upon which the whole of our discussion turned; it was to answer that question that we stirred up all this swarm of eccentric theories, wasn't it?

THEAIT. Quite true.

SOCR. Right. Then shall we agree that whenever we perceive something by sight or hearing we thereby know it? For instance, in the case of a foreign language we have yet to learn, are we to say that we do not hear the sounds made by a foreigner when he speaks, or that we both hear and know what he is saying? Or again, suppose we don't know the letters of a foreign alphabet: are we to maintain that we don't see them when we look at them, or that by seeing them we know them?

THEAIT. Surely, Socrates, we shall say that we know just so much of them as we see or hear. In the case of the letters, we both see and know their shape and colours; in that of the spoken language we hear and at the same time know the rise and fall of the tonic accents; but we do not perceive by sight and hearing and we have not the information that a schoolmaster or an interpreter could give us about them.

SOCR. Good for you, Theaitetos! I don't think I'll raise objections to that, for fear of delaying your growth. But look at this next difficulty looming up. How are we going to cope with it?

THEAIT. What difficulty?

SOCR. I'll tell you. Suppose someone were to ask: 'Is it possible for a man who has once come to know something and still

retains a memory of it, not to *know* that very thing he remembers at the moment when he remembers it?' Perhaps I
am being rather long-winded. What I mean is: Can a man who
has become acquainted with something not know it when he
remembers it?

THEAIT. Of course not, Socrates; the suggestion is absurd.

SOCR. Well, I may be talking nonsense. But look here: am I not
right in saying that you call seeing 'perceiving', and sight
'perception'?

THEAIT. I do.

SOCR. Then, according to what we said just now, a man who
sees something enjoys from that moment knowledge of what
he sees?

THEAIT. Yes.

SOCR. Again, you admit there is such a thing as memory?

THEAIT. Yes.

SOCR. Memory of nothing, or of something?

THEAIT. Of something, obviously.

SOCR. Of what he has become acquainted with or, in other
words, perceived—that kind of things?

THEAIT. Of course.

SOCR. So a man sometimes remembers what he has seen, does
he?

THEAIT. Yes.

SOCR. Even when he shuts his eyes? Or does he forget when he
does that?

THEAIT. What a preposterous idea!

SOCR. [164] But we *must* say just that if we are to save our earlier
statement, which otherwise falls to the ground.

THEAIT. My word, I have an inkling you're right; but I don't
understand exactly how. Do please tell me.

SOCR. Let me explain. We laid it down that a man who sees
enjoys from that moment knowledge of what he sees, because
it is agreed that sight or perception and knowledge are all the
same.

THEAIT. Granted.

SOCR. But if this man who sees and acquires knowledge of what
he has seen shuts his eyes, may we take it that he remembers
the thing although he does not see it?

THEAIT. Yes.

SOCR. But 'does not see' is equivalent to 'does not know', if we assume that 'sees' and 'knows' means the same.

THEAIT. True.

SOCR. Consequently a man who has come to know a thing and still remembers it does not know it, because he does not see it; and we said that would be an outrageous proposition.

THEAIT. You are perfectly right.

SOCR. Evidently, then, if we hold that knowledge and perception are the same, we arrive at an impossible conclusion.

THEAIT. So it seems.

SOCR. Then we shall have to say they are different.

THEAIT. I suppose so.

SOCR. Then what can knowledge be? We must apparently start all over again. But half a minute, Theaitetos. What are we doing?

THEAIT. About what?

SOCR. It seems to me we are behaving in this matter like a third-rate gamecock, springing away from the argument and beginning to crow over it before we have disproved it.

THEAIT. How is that?

SOCR. It seems we are content with having reached an agreement based on mere verbal consistency and to have got the better of the theory by the methods of a professional disputant. We claim to be seeking wisdom, not contending for a prize, but we are unconsciously behaving just like those formidable controversialists.

THEAIT. I still don't see what you are driving at.

SOCR. Well, I will do my best to make the point clear. We were asking whether a man who had become acquainted with something and remembered it could fail to know it. Next we showed that a man who first sees something and then shuts his eyes remembers but does not see; from which we inferred that he simultaneously remembers the thing and does not know it. That, we said, is impossible. Hence, no one was left to 'tell Protagoras' tale', or yours for that matter, about the identity of knowledge and perception.

THEAIT. Evidently.

SOCR. That would not be so, I fancy, if Protagoras were still alive. He would have had a good deal to say in defence of his child. But he is dead, and here we are riding roughshod over the orphan. Even its appointed guardians, of whom Theodoros is one, will not come to its rescue. However, we will risk our own necks to make sure that it has fair play.

THEOD. Actually, Socrates, it is rather Callias, the son of Hipponicos, who is the guardian of Protagoras' offspring. [165] I myself turned at quite an early age from abstract speculation to geometry. Even so I shall be thankful for any assistance you can give him.

SOCR. Well said, Theodoros! You shall see what my help is worth. For a man might embrace still stranger conclusions than those in which we landed just now, if one were as careless in the use of words as we generally are in our assertions and denials. Shall I explain this to you or to Theaitetos?

THEOD. To all of us; but let the younger of us two answer your questions. He will be less humiliated if tripped up.

SOCR. Very good. Now I am going to ask the most tantalizing question of all, which I take to be this: Can an individual know something and at the same time not know that which he knows?

THEOD. Come on, Theaitetos, what's the answer to that?

THEAIT. I should say it is quite impossible.

SOCR. Not if you maintain that seeing is knowing. How are you going to tackle a question from which there is no escape, when you are caught like a wild beast in a trap and some brazen-faced fellow puts his hand over one of your eyes and asks if you can see his cloak with the eye that is covered?

THEAIT. I imagine I would say: 'Not with that eye, but I can with the other.'

SOCR. Then you both see and do not see the same thing at the same time?

THEAIT. In a kind of way, yes.

SOCR. And he will reply: 'That is no answer; I was not asking about the kind of way, but whether when you knew something, you also do *not* know it.' In the present instance you are manifestly seeing something which you do not see, and you have agreed that seeing is knowing, and that not seeing is not knowing. Now draw your own conclusion as to what follows.

THEAIT. I reckon that it contradicts my theory.

SOCR. Yes, dear boy, and you might have been driven into the same corner by a number of other questions: whether knowing can be acute or dim; whether it is possible to know at close quarters what cannot be known from a distance, or to know the same thing with varying intensity. Once you have declared knowledge and perception identical, a light-armed mercenary in the war of words might lie in ambush for you with a thousand questions of this sort. He would strike at hearing, smelling and other senses and put you to rout, pressing his attack until you surrendered through sheer admiration of his incomparable skill; and then, leading you away captive and bound, he would proceed to bargain with you for such ransom as might be agreed between you. And now perhaps you may be wondering what arguments Protagoras will bring up to reinforce his position. Shall we try putting the words into his own mouth?

THEAIT. By all means.

SOCR. He will, I imagine, make all the points we have already made in his defence, and then [166] he will close with the enemy, observing with disdain: 'Your worthy Socrates finds a mere lad who is terrified at being asked whether it is possible for one and the same person to remember and at the same time not know one and the same thing. When the boy is scared into saying No, because he cannot foresee the consequence, Socrates turns the conversation in such a way as to make a fool of my unhappy self. But you simplify the thing far too much, Socrates. The facts are these: when you question someone in order to dissect an opinion of mine and he comes to grief, I personally am not refuted unless his answers are the same as I myself would have made; otherwise it is he who is refuted, not I. For example, do you suppose you will get anyone to admit that a man's memory here and now of some bygone experience is an impression of the same kind as one received during the original experience, which is now a thing of the past? It is nothing of the kind. Or again, will anybody hesitate to agree that it is possible for an individual to know and not to know the same thing? Or, if he dare not admit that, will he ever allow that a person who is changed is the same as he was before; or rather, if we are to take genuine precautions against one another's attempts to catch at words, will he allow that he is one person at all, and not several, indeed an infinite succession of persons, if the process of change is perpetuated?

No, my dear fellow,' he will say, 'prove yourself more liberal minded by attacking what I really say; and establish, if you can, that each one of us has not his own private perceptions, or that, recognizing them as private, it does not follow that what appears to each becomes—or *is*, if we may be permitted the word—for him alone to whom it appears. With your talk of pigs and baboons, not only do you yourself behave like an ignorant creature, but you encourage your disciples to adopt the same attitude towards my writings, which is most unfair. I firmly maintain that the truth is as I have written: each one of us is a measure of what is and of what is not; but there is a world of difference between one man and the next by virtue of the fact that what is and appears to one differs from what is and appears to another. I am not saying for a moment that wisdom and the wise man do not exist. A wise man, as I see him, is precisely a man who can change any one of us, when what is bad appears *and is* to him, by making what is good appear *and be* to him. Don't lay too much stress on the *words* of this statement; let me explain just what I mean. Remember how it was put earlier in the discussion: to an ailing man his food appears bitter and is so; to one in good health it is and appears the opposite. Now neither of these two persons is to be represented as wiser—that is out of the question—nor is the ailing man to be [167] set down as unwise because he thinks as he does, or the healthy man as wise because he judges differently. What is needed is a change from the one state to the opposite, for the other condition is better.

'So too in education it is necessary to bring about a change from the worse condition to a better; but whereas the doctor affects a change by means of drugs, the sophist does it by discourse. Not that anyone ever makes another who previously thought what is false think what is true (for it is impossible either to think what is not, or to think anything except what one experiences, and all experiences are true); rather, I believe, when somebody has depraved thoughts because of a depraved mentality one improves his mentality and thereby causes him to think correspondingly good thoughts. Some ignorant folk describe these new thoughts as 'true'; I should call them *better* than the others, but certainly not *truer*. As for the wise, my dear Socrates, so far from dubbing them frogs, I call them "physicians" when they have to do with the human body and "husbandmen" when plants are their concern. For I maintain that husbandmen also, when plants are ailing and have depraved sensations, endow them instead with good and healthy sensations; and furthermore that wise and honest orators replace with sound opinions the community's distorted view of what is right. For it is my belief that whatever courses of action seem right and commendable to any given State *are* right and commendable for the State in question, so long as it holds by them. But when those courses are, in any particular instance, bad for the citizens, the wise man substitutes others that are and appear more expedient. On the same principle the sophist, who can likewise educate his disciples along the right lines, is wise and entitled to large fees from them when their training is complete. In this sense it is true that some men are wiser than others and that no one thinks falsely; and you must put up willy-nilly with being a measure, since upon these foundations my doctrine stands firm. Now if you can dispute this doctrine in principle, do so by argument setting out the case for the other side. Or ask questions, if you prefer that method; so far from having terrors for an intelligent man, he should welcome it with open arms. There is, however, one rule you must obey: never be unfair in your questioning. It is very unreasonable that a man who cries up his concern for virtue should be time and again found guilty of unfairness in argument. He is unfair in that he turns a blind eye to the distinction between debate and conversation. The former need not be taken seriously, and one may do all in one's power to trip up an opponent; but conversation must be carried on in earnest, one party setting the other right by pointing out to him only those fallacies which are the fault of himself or of his earlier teachers. [168] If you observe this rule, your acquaintances will blame themselves, not you, for their confusion and perplexity. They will like you and seek your company; fleeing in disgust from themselves, they will take refuge in philosophy, hoping thereby to escape from their former selves and become different men. But if, as so many do, you behave in the opposite way, you will achieve something altogether different: instead of turning your companions into philosophers you will make them detest the whole business when they get older. Therefore if you take my advice you will meet us in that spirit of candour to which I have referred, without ill will or pugnacity, and frankly consider what we mean when we declare that all things are in motion and that whatever seems also *is*, for any individual or community. As for the question whether or not knowledge is the same thing as perception, you will consider it as a consequence of these principles, not (as you did a while ago) arguing from the everyday use of words and phrases, which the common run of men wrest to mean anything they please and thereby confuse one another in all sorts of ways.'

That, Theodoros, is as much as I can contribute to your friend's defence; it is not much, but I have slender means. Were Protagoras himself alive, we should have had a much more impressive performance.

THEOD. You are joking, Socrates; that defence of yours was a real *tour de force*!

SOCR. Thank you, my friend. Now tell me, did you notice that Protagoras took a dim view of us for addressing ourselves to a mere boy and taking advantage of the lad's timidity to circumvent his own theory in what he described as nothing but a display of wit, and that he urged us to treat his doctrine seriously?

THEOD. Yes, Socrates, I certainly did.

SOCR. Well then, shall we do as he says?

THEOD. By all means.

SOCR. Fine! But look, with the exception of yourself I am confronted with a whole lot of boys. So if we are to follow his injunction, you and I between us must supply the questions and answers. Only thus shall we 'treat his doctrine seriously' and escape being condemned by him as frivolous for discussing it with 'mere boys'.

THEOD. Good heavens! Surely Theaitetos can follow up an investigation better than many a greybeard.

SOCR. But not better than you, Theodoros; so don't imagine you can sit by [169] and leave me single-handed to protect your late lamented friend. Do please come with us just a little of the way, at all events until we know whether, as regards mathematical demonstration, you can help being a measure, or whether everyone is just as competent as you in astronomy and other sciences in which you have the reputation of an expert.

THEOD. No one finds it easy to escape cross-examination in your company, Socrates. It was foolish of me to say you would let me off and not drag me into the ring like the Spartans; you have something of Sciron about you. The Spartans simply tell a man to clear off if he will not wrestle. Your attitude is more reminiscent of Antaios; you will not release anyone who comes near you until you have forced him to strip and try his strength against yours.

SOCR. An admirable picture of my weakness, Theodoros! But I have more endurance than either Sciron or Antaios. I have encountered many a man whose strength in debate could be compared with that of Theseus or Heracles, and have taken many a hard knock; but I have so great a passion for this sport that I cannot give it up. So now your turn has come don't refuse a bout with me; it will be good for both of us.

THEOD. I say no more; lead on where you will. I must evidently endure whatever toils you spin for me, and submit to interrogation. But I shall not be able to oblige you beyond the point you have named.

SOCR. Far enough, thank you. And please keep a keen look-out; we don't want to slip into 'frivolous' argument and be blamed again for that.

THEOD. I'll do my best.

SOCR. Let us then start by tackling the theory of Protagoras at the same point as before. In other words let us see whether or not our disapproval was justified when we criticized it as making every individual self-sufficient in wisdom. Its author conceded that some persons were superior as regards what is better and worse, and these, he said, were wise.

THEOD. Yes.

SOCR. If he himself were present to allow that much, instead of our conceding it for him in our defence, there would be no need to reopen the question and make sure of where we stand. But in the present circumstances it might be urged that we are not authorized to make the concession on his behalf, so we shall do better by trying to reach a more complete and clear agreement on this point; for it makes a good deal of difference, whether or not it is so.

THEOD. True.

SOCR. [170] Let us then, as briefly as possible, get him to agree not through a third party, but from his own mouth.

THEOD. How?

SOCR. In this way. He says, does he not, that 'what seems true to anyone is true for him to whom it appears so'?

THEOD. Yes, that is what he says.

SOCR. Well now, Protagoras, we are expressing what seems true to a man, or rather to all men, when we say there is absolutely no one who does not consider that in some respects he is wiser than his fellow beings while in others they are wiser than he. For example, in times of great danger and distress, in war, in sickness or at sea, anyone who can take charge of the situation is always looked upon as a god and expected to prove himself a saviour, whereas in point of fact he is superior in nothing except knowledge of how to deal with a given set of circumstances. The world, I venture to say, is full of people searching for others who can instruct and control men and beasts and govern their activities, and on the other hand of people who think themselves qualified both to teach and to direct. What else is there we can say in all these cases, except that men do believe that wisdom and ignorance are present in their midst?

THEOD. There is no alternative.

SOCR. And they maintain that wisdom consists in thinking truly, and ignorance in false belief?

THEOD. Exactly.

SOCR. In that case, Protagoras, how are we to understand your doctrine? Are we to say that what men think is invariably true, or that it is sometimes true and sometimes false? Whichever line we take we are forced to the conclusion that their thoughts are not always true, but both true and false. Just consider, Theodoros: would you, or any disciple of Protagoras, be prepared to affirm that no one looks upon anyone else as ignorant or as guilty of false judgments?

THEOD. That is incredible, Socrates.

SOCR. Nevertheless it is a conclusion which follows inevitably from the doctrine that man is the measure of all things.

THEOD. How so?

SOCR. Well, when you have formed a judgment on some matter in your own mind and express an opinion about it to me, let us

grant that, according to the Protagorean theory, the said
opinion is true for you. But may not the rest of us turn critics
of your judgment; and, as critics, shall we always declare your
opinion true? Surely, thousands of men will on every occasion
set their opinion against yours, holding that your judgment
and belief are false.

THEOD. How right you are, Socrates: 'thousands and tens of
thousands', to use Homer's phrase; and they give me no end
of trouble.

SOCR. What then? Do you want us to say that in such a case
your opinion is true for you, but false for these 'tens of
thousands'?

THEOD. That seems to be the inescapable deduction.

SOCR. And what of Protagoras himself? Suppose not even he
believed that man is the measure of all things and the world in
general did not believe so either (as it actually does not):
presumably his *Truth* would be true for no one. [171] If,
however, he did believe it, but the majority of men did not
agree with him, then you must recognize, in the first place,
that it is more false than true by just so much as the number of
unbelievers exceeds the number of believers.

THEOD. I must indeed, if its truth or falsity is to vary with each
individual opinion.

SOCR. Yes, and in the second place it involves the prettiest of
conclusions. Protagoras, admitting as he does that everyone's
opinion is true, must acknowledge as true the belief of his
opponents about his own belief, namely, that he is wrong.

THEOD. Certainly.

SOCR. In other words, by admitting that the belief of those who
consider him wrong is true, he would acknowledge his own
belief to be false?

THEOD. Necessarily.

SOCR. But the others, for their part, do not admit themselves in
error, do they?

THEOD. No.

SOCR. And Protagoras again, according to his own book, admits
that his opinion of theirs is no more false than any other.

THEOD. Evidently.

SOCR. On every side then, beginning with Protagoras, his
opinion will be challenged; or rather Protagoras will join in

the general agreement. Once he admits to an opponent the truth of his contrary opinion, from that moment Protagoras himself will be admitting that neither a dog nor the man in the street is a measure of anything at all that he does not understand. Am I right?

THEOD. Yes.

SOCR. Consequently, since the *Truth* of Protagoras is challenged by everyone, it will be true for nobody—neither for himself nor for anybody else.

THEOD. We are running the poor fellow too hard, Socrates.

SOCR. But, my dear man, I can't see that we are going beyond the facts. It is quite likely of course that being older he was wiser than we are; if he could at this very moment shove his head through the ground there as far as the neck, he would most probably accuse me of talking nonsense and you for agreeing, before he sank out of sight and fled. However, I suppose we ought to rely on our own intelligence, such as it is, and continue to say what we think. Surely, for example, everyone would agree at all events to the proposition that some men are wiser and some more ignorant than others.

THEOD. I grant you that.

SOCR. And have I your backing when I say first that the doctrine will stand most securely on the position we marked out in our defence of Protagoras: that most things—hot, dry, sweet and everything suchlike—*are* for each person as they appear to him; and secondly that if there are cases in which the theory would allow that one man excels another, it might be willing to admit that, as regards health or disease, not any and every woman or child (or beast for that matter) knows what is good for it and is able to cure itself, but that here, if anywhere, one individual excels another?

THEOD. Yes, that seems to me correct.

SOCR. [172] And likewise as regards social life, the theory will maintain that whatever good and bad customs, rights and wrongs, or religious practices a given State decides to enact as lawful for itself, those customs, etc., really *are* lawful for it, and that in this connection no citizen or State is wiser than another. On the other hand, where it is a question of laying down what is and what is not expedient for it, once again, there if anywhere the theory will recognize that in respect of truth one counsellor is superior to another, and the decision of one State an improvement on that of another; it will hardly go so far as to claim that whatever enactment a given State *believes to be* for its advantage *will be* so beyond any possibility of doubt. But in the sphere of right and wrong or of religious practices, to which I am now referring, people are ready to insist that none of these things possesses by nature an existence of its own, but rather that the public decision becomes true at the moment it is reached and remains true so long as it continues in force; and those whose argument varies somewhat from that of Protagoras speculate on more or less the same lines. But one theory after another is catching up with us, Theodoros, the next always more important than the previous one.

THEOD. Well, Socrates, we have time on our hands.

SOCR. True enough. And it occurs to me now, as often before, how natural it is that those who have devoted much of their time to philosophical studies make fools of themselves when they stand up to plead in a court of law.

THEOD. What do you mean?

SOCR. Well, compare those who have spent a large part of their lives from youth upwards in the courts and such places with others who have been brought up on philosophy and similar pursuits, and you will find that the former have been trained as slaves, the latter as free men.

THEOD. In what way?

SOCR. In the way you mentioned: free men always have time for quiet and leisurely conversation. They will pass from one argument to another, just as we are now doing—we've already reached the third; like us, they will abandon the first and so on if the next is more attractive; nor do they care how long or for how short a time the discussion lasts, provided only it hits upon the truth. But your court orator is always in a hurry, driven by the water-clock. He has no opportunity to dwell on subjects of his own choice; no, his opponent stands over him, prepared to read the so-called schedule of points to which he will be bound by law to confine himself. His words are those of a slave arguing about another slave before a master who sits there holding in his hand a definite plea. Nor does the contest ever follow an uncertain course; it is always directed to the point at issue, and the race is often for the defendant's very life. [173] As a result of all this he becomes overwrought and filled with low cunning; he knows how to wheedle his master with fair words and work his way into favour, but his mind is twisted and narrow. Slavery endured from early years has warped and stunted his growth, depriving him of his free spirit, forcing him into tortuous paths, burdening his tender soul with doubts and fears. Unable to support this load with honesty and truth, he turns forthwith to deceit and the requital of wrong with wrong. Thus, bent and dwarfed, he passes from youth to manhood with no soundness in him, and proves himself—or so he thinks—an intellect with which to reckon.

So much for the orator, Theodoros. Shall I go on to describe that happy band of which we are members, or would you prefer to leave the topic and return to our original theme? After all, we must be careful not to abuse that right we claimed just now to vary our discourse.

THEOD. No, Socrates; let us first hear your description. As you so rightly said, we philosophers are not servants of the argument, which, on the contrary, must wait in expectation of the moment when we choose to follow up this or that point to a conclusion. We are under no judge's eye, nor are we a chorus in the theatre with a critical audience watching our performance.

SOCR. Very well then, if you so desire, let us speak of the most distinguished philosophers; the lesser lights may safely be forgotten. To begin with, from youth upwards they have never learned the way to the Agora; they do not even know the very whereabouts of the law courts, the Council House and other places of assembly. They never hear the proclamation of a decree or set eyes on the text of a law; while it never occurs to them, even when dreaming, to interest themselves in the rivalries of political clubs, in associations, dinner parties and junketings with flute-girls. Whether a particular citizen is of high or low birth or has inherited some defect from his ancestors on either side, are matters as far beyond a philosopher's ken as the proverbial number of pints in the sea. He is not even conscious that he knows nothing of all these things; if he stands aloof it is not to enhance his reputation, but because his body alone really dwells within the city walls, while his mind, disdaining all such matters as of no account, soars upon wings, as Pindar says, 'above the sky, below the earth', conning the heavens and measuring the plains, seeking everywhere the true [174] nature of everything as a whole, never sinking to what is near at hand.

THEOD. What do you mean, Socrates?

SOCR. The same as is suggested by that story about a witty Thracian maidservant who jeered at Thales when he was looking up to watch the stars and tumbled into a well. She thought him a fool for being so eager to know what went on in the sky that he could not see what lay at his feet. All who devote their lives to philosophy are subject to derision of this kind. A philosopher is in fact unaware of what his neighbour is doing, and, indeed, scarcely knows whether the creature is a human being at all; he is absorbed in the problem of what man really is, and what powers and properties distinguish such a nature from any other. Do you see what I mean, Theodoros?

THEOD. Yes; and you are right.

SOCR. Once again, then, my friend, whether in private conversation or on some such public occasion as a trial, when he is obliged to talk about what lies at his feet or stands before his eyes, the philosopher becomes a laughing-stock, not only for servant girls but for the whole crowd of bystanders; inexperience lures him into every kind of pitfall. His appalling clumsiness makes him appear utterly stupid. In the matter of personal abuse he can provide nothing whatsoever, because he knows no evil of any man, never having meddled with such things; and so in his perplexity he merely looks an ass. When people cry up their own or other men's virtues, his mirth is so clearly unaffected that he is set down as frivolous. When a tyrant or king is eulogized he imagines he is listening to the congratulations offered to some shepherd or herdsman for a record yield of milk; only it strikes him that the animal tended and milked by monarchs is more surly and malicious than are sheep or cows, and that such a herdsman, shut up in his castle and without a moment's leisure, must inevitably grow as rough and uncouth as do shepherds in their mountain folds. When he hears that so-and-so is wonderfully rich, owning ten thousand acres or more of land, he is not impressed, being used to contemplate the whole wide world. When they hymn the glories of high birth, declaring that some notable can point to seven generations of wealthy forbears, our philosopher thinks such praises indicate defective vision on the part of men [175] whose lack of education prevents them from keeping their eyes upon the whole and reflecting that every human being has had countless millions of ancestors, including any number of rich and poor, kings and slaves, barbarians and Greeks. To flaunt a catalogue of twenty-five generations going back to Heracles, son of Amphitryon, strikes him as curiously short-sighted. He laughs at a man who cannot rid his stupid mind of vanity by calculating that Amphitryon himself had a twenty-fifth, yea and a seventy-fifth ancestor, whose fortune in each case was purely accidental. But in all these matters the philosopher is derided by the common herd, partly because he appears arrogant, and partly because he is hopelessly at sea in day-to-day affairs.

THEOD. Your description is accurate in every detail, Socrates.

SOCR. On the other hand, my friend, when the philosopher drags a man upwards until he is ready to abandon such questions as 'What wrong have I done to you or you to me?' and to consider justice and injustice in themselves, what each of them is, and wherein they differ from one another and from everything else; or to cease quoting lines about the 'happiness of kings' and 'men possessed of gold', and concentrate on the meaning of kingship and all the business of human happiness and misery, what is the nature of each, and how our race can achieve the one and avoid the other—then, I say, when that small, shrewd, pettifogging mind has to render its account, then indeed our philosopher comes into his own. This time it is the other who feels dizzy—dizzy from hanging at such an unwonted height and gazing downward from mid air. Dumbfounded, stammering, he becomes a laughing-stock, not of servant girls or other uneducated folk, who cannot appreciate the situation, but of all those whose training has been the opposite of a slave's.

Such are the two characters, Theodoros. The one has been reared on freedom and leisure, and you call him a philosopher. He may be excused for appearing stupid or futile when confronted with some menial duty like bed-making, preparing a tasty sauce, or sweetening a speech with flattery. The other is an adept at such tasks, but has never learned to wear his cloak like a gentleman, or acquired the style of conversation [176] which alone can rightly celebrate the life divine and that of truly blissful men.

THEOD. Ah, Socrates! if you could convince all men as you have convinced me, there would be more peace and fewer evils in the world.

SOCR. Evils, Theodoros, can never be abolished, for the good must always have its opposite. Nor is there room for them in the divine world, but they must needs haunt this world of our mortality. And therefore it behoves us with all haste to flee the earth for an immortal home, in other words to make ourselves like unto the divine so far as that may be; and that again means becoming righteous with the aid of wisdom. But it is not at all easy to convince one's fellow men that the reasons for avoiding wickedness and seeking goodness are not that one should appear innocent and good, as is suggested by the world at large. That, in my view, is a lot of old wives' chatter; let us state the truth in this form. The divine shows no trace of unrighteousness, only the plenitude of righteousness; and there is nothing more like unto the divine than a human being who becomes as righteous as possible. Herein stands revealed a man's true spirit or cowardly ineptitude. For the knowledge of this is wisdom and real virtue; ignorance thereof is manifest poverty of intellect and character. All other forms of apparent power and wisdom among civil rulers are as base and vulgar as mere skill in handicrafts. It is far better, therefore, for a man whose words and deeds are unrighteous and profane not to conceive that villainy makes him a great man, glorying in his shame as people of that kind do when they think others speak of them as no fools, no 'useless burdens upon earth', but such as men should be if they are to weather the storms of public life. In actual fact they are what they fancy they are not, and all the more so because they cannot see it; for they are ignorant of the penalty of injustice, which is exactly what they most need to know. That penalty is not, as they imagine, flogging or death, which do not always overtake the malefactor, but one which cannot be escaped.

THEOD. What penalty do you mean?

SOCR. My friend, there are in the abiding nature of things two patterns, one of divine bliss, the other of godless misery. But the people in question are unaware of this truth; downright stupidity blinds them to the fact that [177] by acting unjustly they become less like the first of those patterns and more like the second. The penalty they pay is the life they lead, in accordance with the pattern they resemble. And yet, if we assure them that, unless they throw off their superior cunning, death will not introduce them to that other region which is utterly devoid of evil, but here on earth, for ever and ever, they will lead some kind of life similar to their own and in association with men as evil as themselves; if we tell them that, I say, our words will sound mere folly to their determined and unscrupulous minds.

THEOD. Quite true, Socrates.

SOCR. Yes, my friend, I know. But there is one thing about them: when you catch them alone and challenge them to explain their objections to philosophy, then, if they have the courage to sustain a long course of questioning and not run away, it is curious how they end by becoming dissatisfied with their own arguments; their much vaunted rhetoric somehow withers up, and they have no more to say than a child.

All this, however, is beside the point, and we must drop the subject, otherwise it will overflow its banks and swamp our original argument. Do you mind then if we go back to where we were before?

THEOD. Well, Socrates, I really prefer listening to your digressions; they are easier for a man of my age to follow. Still, if you wish it, let us retrace our steps.

SOCR. Good. Now we had reached the point of saying that those who come down on the side of a constantly changing reality, and maintain that what seems to an individual at any given moment *is* for him, would insist on their principle as of general application, emphasizing particularly, in regard to what is right, that whatever laws or regulations a State may decide on are certainly right for that State so long as they remain in force. But in the matter of what is good, we said that no one would dare go so far as to contend that whatever a State believes and declares expedient for itself is in fact expedient for so long as it is declared so to be, unless he meant that the

name 'expedient' would continue to be so applied; but that
would be making a joke of our subject. Don't you agree?

THEOD. Certainly.

SOCR. We will presume then that he does not mean the name,
but is referring to the thing that bears it.

THEOD. Fair enough.

SOCR. No matter what name the State may give it, expediency is
surely the aim of its legislation; and all its laws, to the full
extent of its belief and ability, are enacted as being for its own
greatest advantage. Does it make laws with any other goal in
view?

THEOD. [178] None at all.

SOCR. Then does it invariably hit the mark? Does not every
State often shoot wide?

THEOD. In my view mistakes are not infrequent.

SOCR. There is still more likelihood of everyone admitting that,
if we start from a question covering the entire class of things
to which the advantageous belongs. Expediency, I think you
will agree, has to do with future time. When we make laws,
we do so with the idea that they will be advantageous hereafter, and we can safely call this whole class 'what is going
to be'.

THEOD. Certainly.

SOCR. Here then is a question for Protagoras or one of his
disciples: 'Is it correct to say, Protagoras, that according to
you and your school man is the measure of all things (white,
heavy, light and all such qualities), that he possesses within
himself the standard by which to judge them, and when he
believes them to be such as he experiences them he believes
what is true and real for him?'

THEOD. The answer will be yes.

SOCR. The next question we shall ask Protagoras is this: 'Does
man possess within himself the test of what is going to be? In
other words, is it true to say that whatever a man believes will
come to pass actually does so for him who believes it? Take,
for example, heat. If someone who is not a doctor believes he
is going to catch a fever, i.e. that such and such a form of heat
is going to exist, and another man—a doctor this time—
believes the contrary, are we to suppose that the event will
turn out in accordance with one or other of these opinions, or

in accordance with both, so that to the doctor our layman will not be hot or feverish, but will be both to himself?'

THEOD. Oh, that would be absurd!

SOCR. And as regards the question whether a wine is going to be sweet or dry, surely the vine-grower's opinion will carry most weight, not that of a flute-player.

THEOD. Naturally.

SOCR. Then too the question may arise whether or not a musical composition is going to be discordant. Here, presumably, a physical training instructor's opinion will not be more reliable than a musician's as to what the former himself will afterwards judge to be in tune.

THEOD. Of course not.

SOCR. Again, when a dinner is in preparation the opinion of an invited guest who is no gourmet will be less authoritative than that of the chef as to the pleasure to be derived from the food. We need not as yet deal with what here and now *is* or already *has been* pleasant to any individual; but as regards what will in the future seem and be to anyone, is every man the best judge for himself, or would you, Protagoras—and I am thinking of arguments that would convince any one of us in a court of law—express a better opinion beforehand than anyone with no special training?

THEOD. Certainly, Socrates, in that connection Protagoras used to declare emphatically that he was superior to everyone else.

SOCR. With a vengeance he did! Nobody would have paid high fees for talking with him [179] if he had not convinced his pupils that absolutely no one, not even a prophet, was a better judge than himself of what was going to be and appear in the future.

THEOD. Perfectly true.

SOCR. Both legislation and the question of expediency, therefore, are concerned with the future; and everyone would agree that a State, in making laws, must often fail to provide for its own greatest advantage.

THEOD. Assuredly.

SOCR. Then we may fairly call upon your master to agree that one man is wiser than another and that the wiser man is the measure, whereas an ignorant man like myself is under no necessity to be a measure, as our recent defence of Protagoras tried to make me, whether I liked it or not.

THEOD. There, Socrates, I think you have the strongest weapon against the theory; but it is likewise assailable on the ground that it recognizes the validity of opinions held by others who stoutly deny the truth of what my old friend used to assert.

SOCR. The Protagorean doctrine in this respect, Theodoros, has many other weak points, enabling us to show that not every opinion of every person is true. But it is more difficult to assail the truth of what an individual experiences at a given moment —the source of his sensations and his corresponding judgments. Perhaps I am wrong in saying 'more difficult'. Maybe they are absolutely impregnable; those who maintain that they are crystal clear and are forms of knowledge may be right, and Theaitetos hit the nail on the head when he said that perception and knowledge are identical. We must therefore go into the doctrine more closely, as our recent defence of Protagoras enjoined; we must subject this moving reality to a more thorough examination, tapping its metal to hear if it rings false or true. As you are doubtless aware, it has been widely and furiously disputed.

THEOD. 'Furiously' is no exaggeration. The debate has actually assumed fresh violence in Ionia, where the school of Heracleitos is loud in support of the theory.

SOCR. All the more reason, my dear Theodoros, to study it carefully and to follow them upstream to its source.

THEOD. Indeed yes. For it is impossible to discuss these principles of Heracleitos—or, as you say, of Homer and even earlier sages—with the Ephesians themselves, who claim to be well acquainted with them; one might as well talk to a madman. True to their own textbooks, they are literally in perpetual motion: their ability to remain quiet while you expound an argument or ask a question, let alone to spend a while in the peaceful interchange of question and answer, [180] amounts to less than nothing; a minus quantity, in fact, is too high an estimate when describing the extent to which these fellows lack the very slightest modicum of repose. If you ask one of them a question, he pulls out pithy sayings, like arrows from a quiver, and lets fly at you; and as soon as you try to obtain some explanation of what these aphorisms mean, you will find yourself transfixed by another, tipped with some newfangled metaphor. You will make no progress whatever with any of them; nor, for that matter, do they themselves with one another. But they take very good care to leave nothing settled either in discussion or in their own minds; I suppose they regard settlement as something stationary, that hated foe to be banished at all costs from the world.

SOCR. Maybe, Theodoros, you have observed these folk at war but have never met them in conditions of peace; they are certainly no friends of yours. Doubtless they reserve such matters for leisurely explanation to their pupils, whom they wish to model upon themselves.

THEOD. Pupils be damned! My dear sir, there is no such thing as a pupil or teacher among them; they spring up of their own accord. Each one gets his inspiration wherever he can, and each considers his neighbour hopelessly ignorant. So, as I was going to say, you will never succeed in calling these people to account, either with or without their consent. We must therefore take over the question ourselves and treat it like a problem to be solved.

SOCR. That is a good idea. As to the problem, have we not here a tradition handed down from the early cosmologists, who veiled their meaning from the common herd in poetical figures? They declare that Oceanos and Tethys, the source of all things, are flowing streams and nothing is at rest. The more sophisticated moderns tell us the same in perfectly straightforward language; their words are addressed even to such common people as shoemakers, who are thus invited to discard the ingenuous belief that some things stand still while others move, and bow the knee to those who teach them that everything is in motion.

Wait though, I had almost forgotten the school of Parmenides, Melissos and others, who proclaim the very opposite, that reality 'is One and immobile: "Being" is the name of the All', and so forth. As against the Heracleiteans, they maintain that all things are a One, stationary in itself, having no space in which to move. How, my friend, are we to cope with these two warring groups? For we have gradually and unwittingly advanced to a point half way between their opposing lines; [181] and unless we manage to fight them off and make good our escape, we shall pay the penalty of the vanquished in a tug-of-war and be dragged to one side or other of the line. It seems to me then we had better start by looking at the party whom we mentioned first, the advocates of Flux. If we find their arguments sound we will help them to pull us over to their side, in hopes of thereby eluding the others; but if we are more convinced by those who favour the immovable Whole, we will seek shelter with them from this rebel force which would violate established frontier-lines. On the other hand, if both sides prove altogether unreasonable, it will be foolish for us to think that we, mere nobodies, have anything to contribute after scorning the high peaks of ancient wisdom. Do you think it worth while to go forward and risk the peril, Theodoros?

THEOD. Why, of course I do, Socrates: I couldn't bear to call a halt before we have thoroughly investigated the respective doctrines of both schools.

SOCR. Well, if you feel like that about it we must go ahead. Now I think we should begin our study of change by asking this question: When all is said and done, what exactly do they mean when they assert that all things are in process of change? In other words, do they mean to say that there is one kind of change or two? I believe there are two. But don't leave me alone in that opinion; you must be a party to the risk, so that, whatever happens, we may share a common fate. Tell me: when something removes from one place to another, or revolves in the same place, do you call the process change?

THEOD. Yes.

SOCR. Let that be one kind, then. And now suppose a thing remains unmoving in the same place but grows old, or turns from white to black, or from soft to hard, or alters in some other way: am I not right in saying that here we have another kind of change?

THEOD. Yes, of course.

SOCR. Very good. So I recognize two kinds of change, alteration and local movement.

THEOD. And you are correct.

SOCR. Well, having made that distinction, let us begin our talk with these people who say that everything is in process of change. First we will ask them: 'Do you say that everything changes in both ways—local movement and alteration—or that part undergoes both kinds of change, and part only one of the two?'

THEOD. Heaven knows what the answer would be. I rather think they would say 'everything changes in both ways'.

SOCR. Yes, my friend; otherwise they will find things at rest as well as things in process of change, and it will be no more accurate to assert that everything is changing than that everything is at rest.

THEOD. Perfectly true.

SOCR. Very well then, since they must be in process of change, and stability must be impossible anywhere, it follows that all things [182] are at all times subject to every kind of change.

THEOD. It does.

SOCR. Now just consider this point in the Heracleitean theory. You remember how we formulated their account of the genesis of heat, whiteness, etc.? We made them describe each one of these things as something that moves in space, simultaneously with a perception, between agent and patient; and that the latter becomes percipient, not a perception, while the agent comes to *have*, rather than to *be*, a quality. Maybe this word 'quality' appears to you outlandish; you may not understand it as a general expression, so let me give you some particular instances. The agent becomes neither heat nor whiteness, but hot or white, and so on with other such things. You no doubt remember how we expressed it earlier on. We said that nothing has any being as just one thing by itself; no more has the agent or patient, but as a result of their encounter with one another, in giving rise to the perceptions and the things perceived, the agents become endowed with some quality while the patients become percipient.

THEOD. Oh yes, I remember.

SOCR. Well now, do not let us worry about what other parts of their theory may or may not mean; let us concentrate upon the central theme of our discussion, and ask them this: 'Is it true that you believe all things to be in a continual state of flux, or change.'

THEOD. The answer is Yes.

SOCR. What, with both the kinds of change we have distinguished—local movement and alteration?

THEOD. Naturally, if they are to be completely in process of change.

SOCR. I take it then that if they were subject only to local movement without qualitative alteration, we should be able to say what qualities they have while in this perpetual state of flux.

THEOD. Exactly.

SOCR. But even here there is nothing constant: the thing in flux does not flow white but changes, so that the very whiteness itself is in flux and changes into another colour—unless of course we are going to convict the thing of permanence in this respect. How then can it ever be possible to give it the name of any colour and be sure of describing it correctly?

THEOD. How indeed, Socrates? And how can anything else of the sort to which you refer be called by its right name, if, while we are speaking, it continually evades us in the stream of change?

SOCR. Again, what are we to say about a perception of any kind —that, for example, of seeing or hearing? Does it by any chance abide in its own nature as seeing or hearing?

THEOD. Certainly not, if all things are in process of change.

SOCR. Very well then, if everything is changing in every kind of way, it is no more entitled to be called 'seeing' than 'not-seeing'; nor, for the same reason, has any other perception a right to be called 'perception' rather than 'non-perception'.

THEOD. I quite agree.

SOCR. Moreover, perception is knowledge, according to Theaitetos and me.

THEOD. Yes, that is what you said.

SOCR. Consequently our reply to the question, 'What is knowledge?' did not mean knowledge any more than not-knowledge.

THEOD. [183] Apparently.

SOCR. There you are, that's the result of our so-called improvement upon the first answer ('knowledge is the same as perception'), notwithstanding our anxiety to demonstrate its accuracy by showing that everything is in process of change. It seems that what we have actually discovered is that, if all things are in process of change, any answer to any question whatever is equally right: one may say it is so and it is not so— or 'becomes', if you wish to avoid a term that might bring our opponents to a standstill.

THEOD. You are right.

SOCR. Except, Theodoros, that I used the words 'so' and 'not so'. This 'so' is inadmissible: a thing which is 'so' would no longer be changing, and the same applies to 'not so'. Some new jargon will have to be devised for those who teach the Heracleitean theory, for at present they have no terms in which to cast their fundamental proposition—unless perhaps 'not even no-how'! That might be sufficiently indefinite for their purpose.

THEOD. Quite an appropriate idiom.

SOCR. So, Theodoros, we are rid of your friend Protagoras; we are not yet prepared to acknowledge that every man is the measure of all things, if he is not a man of practical wisdom. Nor are we going to allow that knowledge is perception, not, at any rate, on the theory that all things are in process of change—unless Theaitetos here has some objection.

THEOD. I'm glad to hear you say that, Socrates; for it was agreed that once these questions had been settled, and our discussion of Protagoras' theory closed, I should no longer be obliged to answer your questions.

THEAIT. No, Theodoros, you must keep going until you and Socrates, as was proposed just now, have discussed that other school which maintains that the All is at rest.

THEOD. Really, Theaitetos, a young man like you encouraging his elders to commit breach of contract! No, you must prepare to carry on the remainder of this argument with Socrates.

THEAIT. Certainly, if he wishes; though I should have been far happier just listening while you discussed the Eleatics.

THEOD. To offer Socrates the chance of an argument is like inviting cavalry to fight on level ground. Ask him a question and see what happens.

SOCR. As a matter of fact, Theodoros, I am not inclined to do what Theaitetos asks.

THEOD. Why ever not?

SOCR. My respect for Melissus and others who describe the universe as a One and immobile prevents me from treating them with any degree of flippancy. But there is one being whom I venerate above all—Parmenides. To me he is, in Homer's words, 'a reverend and awful' figure. I met him in his old age, when I was little more than a boy, and I thought there was a sort of depth in him that was terribly impressive. [184] I am afraid we might not even understand his words, let alone grasp the thought that lies behind them. More important still, there is a danger that the original subject of our discussion—the nature of knowledge—may be lost to view if we keep staring at a jostling crowd of topics that are quite irrelevant. Remember too that the question we are now raising covers an enormous field; it cannot in fairness be treated as a side issue, and an adequate study would take so long that we should never get down to our inquiry about knowledge. Neither course is acceptable. Our duty is to see whether my skill as a midwife can deliver Theaitetos, who is heavy with ideas of knowledge.

THEOD. That's what we must do then, if you think it best.

SOCR. Here now, Theaitetos, is a further point for your consideration. You told us that knowledge is perception, didn't you?

THEAIT. Yes.

SOCR. Now suppose someone asked 'With what does a man see white or black things and hear high or low tones?' I presume you would say 'With his eyes and ears'?

THEAIT. I would.

SOCR. To use words and phrases in a casual sort of way without much regard to precision is not generally a mark of ill-breeding; indeed there is something ungentlemanly in being too pernickety. But there are times when strict accuracy is imperative, and in this case I feel bound to take you up on the form of your reply. Just think a moment: is it more correct to say that we see and hear *with* our eyes and ears, or *through* them?

THEAIT. I should say we perceive *through* rather than *with* our various organs.

SOCR. Exactly. It would surely be odd, my boy, if there were a whole lot of senses tucked away inside us, like armed men in the Wooden Horse, and not combining into a single nature—a mind or whatever it is to be called—*with* which we perceive the objects of perceptions *through* the instrumentality of these senses.

THEAIT. Yes, that is far more likely.

SOCR. I am being so fastidious because I want to know whether there is some part of ourselves, the same in all cases, *with* which we apprehend black or white *through* the eyes, and other objects of other senses *through* other organs, so that, if challenged, you can refer all such acts of apprehension to the body? On second thoughts, however, it may be better for you to speak for yourself in reply to questions than for me to do all the work for you. Tell me then: do you admit that the various organs through which you perceive what is warm, hard, light or sweet are parts of the body, and not of anything else?

THEAIT. I do.

SOCR. And will you also allow that [185] what you perceive through one faculty cannot be perceived through another—objects of hearing, for example, through sight, or vice versa?

THEAIT. Certainly, I grant you that.

SOCR. So, if you have some thought about both objects at the same time, you cannot be having a perception taking in both at once through either the one organ or the other.

THEAIT. No.

SOCR. Now as regards sound and colour, have you not, in the first place, a certain thought which takes in both together, namely that they both *exist*?

THEAIT. Yes, I have.

SOCR. And also that each is different from the other and identical with itself?

THEAIT. Of course.

SOCR. And further, that both together are two, and that each separately is one?

THEAIT. Yes.

SOCR. Can you not, moreover, ask yourself whether they are like or unlike one another?

THEAIT. Undoubtedly.

SOCR. Then through what organ do you think all this about the pair of them? A factor common to both cannot be apprehended either through hearing or through sight. Here too is further evidence for the point I am trying to establish. If there were any way of discovering whether or not sound and colour are brackish, you would of course be able to tell me what faculty you would employ; it would clearly not be sight or hearing, but some other.

THEAIT. Of course—the faculty that works through the tongue.

SOCR. Very good. But through what organ does that faculty

work which reveals to you what is common not only to sound and colour but to all things—what you mean by 'exists', 'does not exist' and the other terms used of them in the questions I put to you just now? What kind of organs will you recognize, corresponding to all these terms, through which the perceiving part of us perceives each one of them?

THEAIT. You mean existence and non-existence, likeness and unlikeness, sameness and difference, unity and plurality as applied to them; and your question evidently includes 'even' and 'odd' and every notion of that kind. You want me to tell you through what bodily organs our mind perceives these. Am I right?

SOCR. You follow me exactly, Theaitetos; that is just what I am asking.

THEAIT. Really, Socrates, I haven't an idea, except that there is no special organ for apprehending these things, as there is for apprehending colour, sound, etc. I am quite sure that the mind in itself is its own organ for viewing what is common to all things.

SOCR. Why, Theaitetos, you are handsome after all, not ugly as Theodoros described you; for in debate 'handsome is that handsome speaks'. That is a charming discovery; but you are also my benefactor in having saved me from a very long argument, if you are perfectly satisfied that the mind views some things directly, without the intervention of a bodily organ such as it requires for the exercise of other faculties. That was my own opinion, but I wanted you to agree.

THEAIT. Well, I'm quite satisfied it is so.

SOCR. [186] How then do you classify existence? For that belongs pre-eminently to all things.

THEAIT. Personally, I should rank it with those entities which the mind apprehends directly.

SOCR. And you would treat likeness and unlikeness, identity and difference in the same way?

THEAIT. Yes.

SOCR. How about 'honest' and 'dishonest', 'good' and 'bad'?

THEAIT. I look upon these too, above all, as things whose being is considered, one in comparison with another, by the mind, when it reflects within itself upon the past and the present with an eye to the future.

SOCR. Wait though. Will not the hardness or softness of what is hard or soft be perceived through touch?

THEAIT. Yes.

SOCR. But their existence and the fact that they both exist, their mutual opposition and, again, the existence of this opposition are things which the mind itself undertakes to judge for us, when it reflects upon them and compares them with one another.

THEAIT. Certainly.

SOCR. Is it not true then that all the impressions which reach the mind through the body are perceptible to animals (human and otherwise) by the very nature of these latter and from the moment of their birth, whereas notions about them with regard to their existence and usefulness are only acquired, if at all, with difficulty through a long and tedious process of training?

THEAIT. Assuredly.

SOCR. Is it possible then for a man to lay hold on truth when he cannot get as far as existence?

THEAIT. No.

SOCR. But can he possibly *know* a thing when its truth eludes him?

THEAIT. How can he, Socrates?

SOCR. In that case knowledge is not in the impressions but in our reflection upon them. It is there apparently, and not in the impressions, that one can apprehend existence and truth.

THEAIT. Clearly.

SOCR. Then are you going to call two such widely different things by the same name?

THEAIT. That would definitely not be right.

SOCR. What name do you give then to the first—to seeing, hearing, smelling, feeling cold and feeling warm?

THEAIT. Perceiving. What other name can I give it?

SOCR. Collectively then you call this perception?

THEAIT. Unavoidably.

SOCR. And perception, we are agreed, has no function in apprehending truth, since it has none in apprehending existence.

THEAIT. No, none at all.

SOCR. And therefore it has no part in knowledge either.

THEAIT. No.

SOCR. Then, Theaitetos, perception and knowledge cannot possibly be identical.

THEAIT. Evidently not, Socrates. It is now quite obvious that knowledge is something other than perception.

SOCR. [187] But when we embarked on this discussion it was certainly not in order to find out what knowledge is *not*, but what it *is*. However, we have progressed so far as to realize that we must not look for it in sense-perception at all, but in what takes place when the mind is engaged with things by itself, whatever name one gives that function.

THEAIT. Well, Socrates, I suppose one would call it 'making judgments'.

SOCR. You suppose rightly, my friend. Now start again from the beginning. Wash out all we have been saying, and see if you can get a clearer view from the point where you now stand. Once again, tell us what knowledge is.

THEAIT. It cannot be defined simply as judgment, Socrates, because there is such a thing as false judgment; but one might describe *true* judgment as knowledge. That, at any rate, is my answer. If, as we go along, it proves to be false, I will try to give you another.

SOCR. Well said, Theaitetos; much better be forthright than hesitate as you did at first. By so doing either we shall find what we are looking for, or we shall be less inclined to fancy we know something of which in fact we know nothing whatever; and that is surely no mean recompense. But now, what is it you say: that there are two kinds of judgment, one true, the other false, and you define knowledge as *true* judgment?

THEAIT. Yes; that is now my view.

SOCR. Then, had we better go back to a point we have already met in connection with judgment? [1]

THEAIT. What point is that?

SOCR. I refer to a question which troubles me now, as often before, and has much perplexed me both in my private

---

[1] The reference is to Protagoras' assertion that false judgment is impossible because 'it is impossible either to think what is not or to think anything except what one experiences, and all experiences are true'.

reflections and in conversation with others. I cannot explain the nature of this experience of ours, or how it comes about.

THEAIT. What experience?

SOCR. Making a false judgment. I am still in doubt and wondering whether we should by-pass that question or follow it up, not as we did before, but along fresh lines.

THEAIT. Why not, Socrates, if it seems at all necessary. A little while ago, when you and Theodoros were talking about leisure, you rightly observed that in a discussion of this sort the time factor does not count.

SOCR. You do well to remind me of that fact; for this may be the right moment to retrace our steps. It is better to perform a small task well than to bungle a big one.

THEAIT. Indeed it is.

SOCR. How shall we proceed, then? What do we really mean? Do we maintain that in every case and in the very nature of things there is a false judgment, and that one of us thinks what is false, another what is true?

THEAIT. Yes, we do.

SOCR. [188] And, in each and all cases, it is possible for us to know a thing or not to know it? I am not troubling, for the moment, about becoming acquainted with things and forgetting them, two intermediate processes between knowing and not knowing. Just now they are irrelevant to the argument.

THEAIT. Quite, Socrates; one knows or one does not know— there is never a third alternative.

SOCR. And does it not follow immediately that when a man thinks, he must be thinking either of something he knows or of something he does not know?

THEAIT. Certainly it does.

SOCR. Moreover, if he knows a thing he cannot possibly *not* know it, and vice versa.

THEAIT. Of course.

SOCR. Then does a man who thinks what is false imagine that things he knows are not those things but other things he knows? Does he, in other words, while knowing both, fail to recognize either?

THEAIT. No, Socrates, that is impossible.

SOCR. Well then, does he imagine that things he does *not* know are other things he does not know? Can a man, for example,

who knows neither Theaitetos nor Socrates conceive the idea
that Socrates is Theaitetos or vice versa?

THEAIT. How could he?

SOCR. But surely a man does not imagine that things he knows
are things he does not know, or the other way about?

THEAIT. No, that would be a reversal of nature.

SOCR. In that case, how can one judge falsely? On the assumption that all things are either known or not known, it must
surely be impossible to judge outside these alternatives; and
within them there is clearly no room for false judgment.

THEAIT. Quite true.

SOCR. What do you say, then, to approaching our quarry by
some other route? Instead of 'knowing or not knowing', let
us follow the line of 'being or not being'.

THEAIT. How do you mean?

SOCR. It may simply be that a man who thinks *what is not* about
anything must inevitably be thinking what is false, no matter
what the state of his mind in other respects.

THEAIT. That seems not altogether unlikely, Socrates.

SOCR. Then what are we to say, Theaitetos, if someone asks us:
'But who on earth can do what you describe? Can anyone
think what is not, either with or without reference to something that is?' Our reply, I suppose, will be: 'Yes, when he
believes something and that something is not true.' Is there
anything else we can say?

THEAIT. No, nothing.

SOCR. And is the same sort of thing possible in any other field?

THEAIT. What sort of thing?

SOCR. I mean, is it possible, for instance, that a man should see
something, and yet what he sees should be nothing?

THEAIT. Quite impossible.

SOCR. But surely if what he sees is something, it must be something that is. Or do you imagine that 'something' can be
counted among things utterly devoid of being?

THEAIT. No, I do not.

SOCR. Then a man who sees something sees a thing that is.

THEAIT. Evidently.

SOCR. [189] And when he hears a thing, he hears something, i.e.
hears a thing that is.

THEAIT. Yes.

SocR. And when he touches a thing, he touches something, which, being something, is.

THEAIT. True again.

SocR. And when he thinks, he thinks something, does he not?

THEAIT. Of course.

SocR. And when he thinks something he thinks a thing that is?

THEAIT. Granted.

SocR. So to think what is not is to think nothing.

THEAIT. Obviously.

SocR. But you must admit that to think nothing is equivalent to not thinking at all.

THEAIT. I can't deny that.

SocR. It is therefore impossible to think what is not, either with or without reference to anything that is.

THEAIT. Manifestly.

SocR. Then to think falsely must be something different from thinking what is not.

THEAIT. So it seems.

SocR. Accordingly, we can no more judge falsely on this basis than on the one we adopted a short while ago.

THEAIT. No, we certainly cannot.

SocR. Well, there is another way in which the thing we call false judgment may arise.

THEAIT. What is that?

SocR. We do acknowledge the existence of false judgment as a kind of misjudgment. The latter takes place when a person interchanges in his mind two things, both of which are, and says that the one is the other. On these occasions he is always thinking of something which is, but of one thing instead of another; he thereby misses the mark, and may fairly be said to judge falsely.

THEAIT. I believe you have at last hit the nail on the head. When a man thinks 'ugly' instead of 'beautiful', or vice versa, he is really and truly thinking what is false.

SocR. I see you no longer stand in awe of me, Theaitetos; I have begun to sink in your estimation.

THEAIT. Why, exactly?

SocR. I believe you expect to pass unchallenged with your 'truly thinking what is false'. You think I shall fail to ask whether a thing can be slowly quick or heavily light, or indeed whether *any* contrary can step outside its own nature to behave like its contrary. However, I don't wish to discourage you, so I will let that pass. You are satisfied, are you, that false judgment is mistaking?

THEAIT. Yes, I am.

SOCR. In your opinion then it is possible for the mind to take one thing for another, and not for itself.

THEAIT. Quite so.

SOCR. Now when the mind does this, must it not be thinking either of both things together or of one of them?

THEAIT. Certainly, both at once or each in succession.

SOCR. Excellent. And I wonder whether your description of the thought-process agrees with mine?

THEAIT. How do you describe it?

SOCR. As a discourse that the mind carries on with itself about any subject it has under consideration. I put forward this explanation without the least claim to expert knowledge; but I have an idea that when the mind is thinking, it is simply conversing with itself, asking and answering questions, [190] and affirming or denying. When it arrives at a decision (whether slowly or by a sudden leap), when doubt is resolved and agreement is reached, we call that its 'judgment'. I therefore describe thinking as discourse, and judgment as a statement expressed, not aloud to someone else, but in silence to oneself. What do you say?

THEAIT. I agree.

SOCR. Apparently, then, whenever a man thinks of one thing as another, he is telling himself that the one is the other.

THEAIT. Naturally.

SOCR. Now try to remember ever having said to yourself: 'Assuredly, what is beautiful is ugly', or 'what is unjust is just'. Ask yourself, in fact, the more comprehensive question: 'Have I ever tried to convince myself that one thing is assuredly another?' You will find, on the contrary, that, even when dreaming, you have never gone so far as to tell yourself that odd numbers must be even, or anything of that kind.

THEAIT. True enough.

SOCR. Do you imagine that anyone else, sane or insane, ever ventured in all seriousness and with full conviction to tell himself that an ox must be a horse or that two must be one?

THEAIT. Of course not.

SOCR. So, if telling oneself something is equivalent to making a judgment, then no one making a statement or judgment about two things at once, i.e. who has both in mind, can say or judge that one of those things is the other. Nor must you find fault with my language; I mean to convey that no one thinks 'the ugly is beautiful' or anything of that sort.[1]

THEAIT. I will not find fault, Socrates. I agree with you.

SOCR. A person, therefore, who is thinking of both cannot think of the one as the other.

THEAIT. Apparently not.

SOCR. Again, so long as he is thinking of one only, without any thought of the other, he will never think that the one is the other.

THEAIT. True; for that would entail his having in mind the thing he is not thinking of.

SOCR. Consequently, whether he thinks of both things or of one alone, he cannot possibly 'mistake'. Hence it is futile to define false judgment as 'misjudgment'. It appears that false judgment considered as 'mistaking' is no more a function of our minds than are those forms of mental activity we have already examined and repudiated.

THEAIT. It would seem not.

SOCR. On the other hand, Theaitetos, if it turns out that there is no such thing as false judgment we shall be forced to admit a whole host of absurdities.

THEAIT. Such as what?

SOCR. I will not tell you until I have tried exploring the ground along every line of approach. I should feel rather ashamed of our having to make such admissions before the difficulty has been resolved. [191] But if we find a means of escape then, as soon as we are out of the wood we shall not hesitate to speak of others as involved in the absurdities which we ourselves shall have escaped; though, if we are completely at a loss then, I suppose, we must accept our humiliation and allow the argument to do with us anything it pleases, like seasick passengers

[1] Socrates is warning Theaitetos against being misled by his saying that no one thinks *one thing* (τὸ ἕτερον) *is another* (ἕτερον) on the verbal ground that the same Greek word is used to denote each. He means all the individual cases (of which 'the ugly is beautiful' is but one example) that fall within the general statement.

lying about to be trampled on by members of the crew. Listen then while I tell you of an opening that seems to offer us a chance.

THEAIT. Yes, do tell me.

SOCR. I shall say we were wrong in agreeing that it is not possible for a man to think that things he knows are things he does not know, and thus be deceived. No, in a way it *is* possible.

THEAIT. Have you in mind something that occurred to me even while we were declaring it impossible? I suddenly realized that there are times when, despite my being well acquainted with Socrates, I see in the distance someone unknown to me and take him for the Socrates whom I do know. There you certainly have a case of 'mistaking'.

SOCR. And we fought shy of that statement, because it would have implied that we both knew and knew not what we know?

THEAIT. Just so.

SOCR. Well, let us put the matter somewhat differently. A path may open up, though it may come to a dead end. At any rate, our position is such that we must turn over every argument and examine it thoroughly. See what you think of this. Can a man become acquainted with something he did not previously know?

THEAIT. Of course.

SOCR. And he can do the same with a whole succession of things?

THEAIT. Certainly.

SOCR. I will ask you to imagine then, for the sake of argument, that our minds contain a tablet of wax, varying in size from one individual to another, and consisting of wax that is comparatively pure or adulterated, and harder in some, softer in others, and elsewhere of the right quality and condition.

THEAIT. And then?

SOCR. Let us call it the gift of Memory, mother of the Muses, and say that whenever we wish to remember something we see or hear or conceive in our minds, we hold this wax under the perceptions or ideas and impress them on it just as we stamp the markings of a signet ring. Whatever is thus impressed we remember and know so long as the image remains; whatever

is rubbed out or has failed to leave its mark we have forgotten
and do not know.

THEAIT. Very good.

SOCR. Now consider a man who knows things in this fashion,
and fixes his attention upon something that he sees or hears:
don't you think there is a possibility here of his making a false
judgment?

THEAIT. In what way?

SOCR. By thinking that things he knows are other things he
knows, or sometimes things he does not know.

THEAIT. What do *you* feel about it now?

SOCR. [192] We must begin with the following schedule.

　　1. *In the case of neither object being here and now perceived:*
you cannot mistake (*a*) a thing of which you have a memory-
image before your mind, and therefore know, for another such
thing; (*b*) a thing you know for another thing of which you
have no memory-image before your mind, and therefore do
not know; (*c*) a thing you do not know for something else you
do not know, or vice versa.

　　2. *In the case of present perception only:* you cannot confuse
(*a*) two things which you here and now perceive; (*b*) a thing
which you are perceiving with a thing which you are not;
(*c*) two things neither of which you are perceiving; or (*d*) a
thing which you are not perceiving with something you do
here and now perceive.

　　3. *Where both knowledge and perception are concerned:* you
cannot confuse (*a*) two known things both of which you here
and now (i) perceive and (ii) recognize as conforming to the
right memory images; (*b*) one such thing as described in (*a*)
with another which you know but do not now perceive; (*c*) one
such thing as described in (*a*) with another which you perceive but do not recognize; (*d*) two things which you neither
know nor perceive; (*e*) a thing such as described in (*a*) with
a thing you perceive but do not recognize; or (*f*) a thing such
as described in (*d*) with a thing you know but do not perceive.

　　In all these instances false judgment is absolutely out of the
question. There remain then certain cases in which, if anywhere, it may arise.

THEAIT. What are they? Let's hope they throw more light upon
the subject, for up to now I have not followed you.

SOCR. The cases to which I refer make another section of our schedule:

    4. *A man can mistake* (*a*) things he knows for others that he both knows and perceives; (*b*) things he knows for things which he does not know but does perceive; (*c*) a thing he both knows and perceives for another that he also knows and perceives.

THEAIT. Now I am more than ever adrift!

SOCR. Let me go back then and put it in a different way. I know Theodoros, I know Theaitetos, and I entertain a memory of what each is like. Now and then I see or touch or hear or otherwise perceive them; at other times I have no perception whatever of either, and yet I remember you both and have you present to my mind. Is not that so?

THEAIT. Certainly.

SOCR. That then is the first point I want to make clear: it is possible either to perceive or not to perceive something with which one is acquainted.

THEAIT. Agreed.

SOCR. So too in the case of something with which one is not acquainted: it is often possible not to perceive it either, and often *merely* to perceive it.

THEAIT. True.

SOCR. See if you understand me better now. [193] If Socrates knows Theodoros and Theaitetos, but sees neither and has no other present perception of them, he can never think to himself that Theaitetos is Theodoros. Does that make sense?

THEAIT. Yes, that is true.

SOCR. Well, that was an example of 1 (*a*) in my schedule.

THEAIT. I follow.

SOCR. Here now is an example of 1 (*b*): If I know one of you but not the other and perceive neither, again I could never think that the one I know is the other whom I do *not* know.

THEAIT. Correct.

SOCR. And an example of 1 (*c*): If I neither know nor perceive either of you, I could not mistake one unknown for the other unknown. And now pretend that I have gone over the whole of section 1 again—cases in which I shall never judge falsely about you and Theodoros, whether I know both or neither or only one of you. And the same applies to section 2, if you follow me.

THEAIT. Ah yes, now I see what you mean.

SOCR. So the possibility of false judgment remains in cases like these: 4 (*a*) Knowing you and Theodoros, possessing mental images of you both like impressions of two signet-rings in the waxen tablet, I may happen to see you indistinctly in the distance; then, being in a hurry to assign the proper imprint of each to the proper visual perception (like fitting a foot into its own footmark for the purpose of identifying someone), I may fall into the error of interchanging them, like a man who puts his feet into the wrong shoes, and apply the visual image of each to the imprint of the other. Or you may compare my lapse with the sort of thing that happens in a mirror when the visual current transposes right to left. In such cases mistaking or false judgment does occur.

THEAIT. I think it does, Socrates. That is a remarkably fine account of what happens to judgment.

SOCR. There is also the case 4 (*b*), where, knowing both of you, I perceive only one, and do not get the knowledge I have of him to square with my perception. That was a point I was trying to make before, but you did not then understand me.

THEAIT. No, I did not.

SOCR. Well, that is what I was saying: if I know one of two men and also perceive him, then, so long as I get my knowledge to accord with my perception of him, I shall never think he is someone else whom I both know and perceive, provided my knowledge of him is likewise got to correspond with the perception. That was so, was it not?

THEAIT. Yes.

SOCR. But, 4 (*c*), there remains the case of false judgment implied in what I have been saying. [194] It arises when you know both and see or otherwise perceive both, but do not get the two imprints to correspond each with its proper perception. Like a bad archer, you shoot wide and miss the target, which is in fact another way of saying you err.

THEAIT. And rightly so.

SOCR. Again, when there is present a perception belonging to one of the imprints, but not one belonging to the other, and the mind fits the imprint belonging to the absent perception to the present one, it errs in every such instance.

To sum up: if our present account is reliable, it would seem there can be no question of error or false judgment in the case of objects one does not know and has never perceived; but it is precisely in the sphere of objects we both know and perceive that judgment turns and twists, emerging false or true—true when it brings impressions fairly and squarely together with the appropriate imprints, false when it slips up and misapplies them.

THEAIT. Well, Socrates, I should call that a pretty good account of the matter.

SOCR. You'll consider it even more so when you have heard the rest. True judgment is a splendid thing; error is contemptible.

THEAIT. I quite agree.

SOCR. Now they say these differences originate as follows. Where the wax in a man's mind forms a good thick tablet, smooth and properly kneaded, and the images that come through the senses are stamped on this 'heart' of the mind— Homer's expression hints at the mind's similarity to wax [1]— then the imprints are clear and sufficiently deep for permanence. Such men learn quickly and also have good memories; nor do they interchange the imprints of their perceptions, but judge truly. These imprints, being distinct and not crowded together, are quickly fitted to their respective stamps ('real things' as they are called), and such men are described as clever. Perhaps you don't agree?

THEAIT. I most certainly do.

SOCR. On the other hand a man may have what the poet-sage praises as a 'shaggy heart', or the tablet may be dirty or of impure wax, or perhaps too soft or too hard. In such cases, those with soft wax are quick in the uptake but forgetful, those with the hard wax the reverse. Where it is shaggy or rough, a coarse material mixed with a lot of earth or filth, the imprints it receives are indistinct; so are they also when it is hard, because they have no depth. Impressions in soft wax are likewise indistinct, [195] because they fuse and quickly become blurred. And if, in addition, they overlap one another owing to the narrow space available in a miserable petty mind, they are yet more indistinct. All such people, therefore, are liable to judge falsely. When they see or hear or think of anything, they cannot quickly assign things to their respective

[1] κέαρ (heart), κηρός (wax).

imprints. Because they are so slow and sort things out so clumsily they never see or think or hear properly, and we describe them as mistaken about things and stupid.

THEAIT. You could not have put it more aptly, Socrates.

SOCR. We must therefore conclude that false judgments do exist in us?

THEAIT. Assuredly.

SOCR. But true ones also, I presume.

THEAIT. Yes indeed.

SOCR. At last then we may claim to have reached a satisfactory agreement that both these kinds of judgments exist beyond any doubt whatever?

THEAIT. Indubitably.

SOCR. Theaitetos, I think we can safely say that a garrulous man is a queer and unpleasant creature!

THEAIT. What on earth makes you say that?

SOCR. Annoyance with my own stupidity. Garrulous I am, to be sure: how else can you describe a man who is for ever disputing this way and that because he's such a bufflehead that he cannot be convinced and will not abandon a single one of his arguments?

THEAIT. But why be annoyed with yourself?

SOCR. I am not merely annoyed but apprehensive about what answer I shall give if someone asks me: 'Now, Socrates, have you realized that false judgment is found neither in our perceptions among themselves nor in our thoughts, but in the squaring of perception with thought?' Presumably I shall say 'Yes', and preen myself on this fine discovery of ours.

THEAIT. Well, Socrates, I don't think there's anything of which to be ashamed in that last conclusion.

SOCR. 'Do you go on', he will then ask, 'to assert that we can never imagine that a man whom we merely think of but do not see is a horse which we likewise do not see or touch but merely think of without perceiving it in any way?' I suppose I shall again reply in the affirmative.

THEAIT. And you will be quite right.

SOCR. 'In that case', he will continue, 'it is surely impossible to imagine that the number 11, of which one merely thinks, is the number 12, of which one likewise merely thinks?' Come now, Theaitetos, you must answer that.

THEAIT. Well, my answer will be that if a man saw or handled eleven concrete things he might mistake them for twelve; but he could never make that judgment about the eleven and twelve which are simply the objects of his thought.

SOCR. Tell me now, does anyone ever consider in his own mind 5 and 7—I do not mean five men and seven men or anything of that sort, but just 5 and 7 themselves, which [196] we describe as records imprinted on our waxen tablet, and in regard to which we say there can be no false judgment—does anyone, I say, ever consider them and ask himself, in the course of his interior conversation, what is their sum total; and does one man believe and openly proclaim that they add up to 11, another that they amount to 12, or is everyone agreed that they add up to 12?

THEAIT. By no means; many say 11. And the larger the numbers under consideration the more likelihood there is of error; for I take you to be speaking generally of any numbers.

SOCR. You understand me correctly. Now in the case of 5 and 7 what happens is surely this: the 12 itself imprinted on the waxen tablet is mistaken for 11.

THEAIT. So it would seem.

SOCR. Then have we not arrived back at proposition 1 (a) of our schedule? For when this happens to someone he is imagining that one thing he knows is another thing he knows—which we said was impossible. It was precisely in order to avoid concluding that the same man must at the same time know and not know the same thing that we were led to deny the possibility of false judgment.

THEAIT. Exactly.

SOCR. Like that, we must explain false judgment in some other way than as the misapplication of thought to perception. If it were that we should never go astray among our thoughts themselves. In point of fact, either there is no such thing as false judgment, or it is possible not to know what one knows. Which alternative is your choice?

THEAIT. I have no possible choice, Socrates.

SOCR. But there is no likelihood of the argument admitting both. However we must not shirk the issue: how about a stroke of derring-do?

THEAIT. In what way?

SOCR. By undertaking to describe what knowing is like.

THEAIT. Why call that 'derring-do'?

SOCR. You seem not to realize that our whole discussion from the very start has been an inquiry into the nature of knowledge, on the assumption that we did not know what it was.

THEAIT. I am well aware of that.

SOCR. Then do you not regard it as a piece of reckless daring to explain what knowing is *like*, when we don't know even what knowledge *is*? In point of fact, Theaitetos, our talk has all along been seriously tainted. Over and over again we have said 'we know', 'we do not know', 'we have knowledge', 'we have no knowledge', as if we were able to understand one another while we still know nothing whatever about knowledge. Only a few seconds ago, mark you, we again uttered the words 'know nothing' and 'understand', as if we had any right to use them while we are still devoid of knowledge!

THEAIT. But how do you propose to carry on the discussion, Socrates, if you fight shy of those words?

SOCR. [197] Being myself, I cannot, though I might if I were an expert in debate. If such a man were with us now he would claim to avoid them and say some hard things about my phraseology. Seeing, then, that we are so helplessly incompetent, shall I venture to describe what knowing is like? I believe such a course may be to our advantage.

THEAIT. By all means; and if you cannot avoid the words in question you shall not be blamed.

SOCR. You have heard, no doubt, what 'knowing' is commonly said to be?

THEAIT. Perhaps; but I don't remember at the moment.

SOCR. They say it is 'having knowledge'.

THEAIT. Ah, yes.

SOCR. Let us make a slight alteration and say '*possessing* knowledge'.

THEAIT. What difference do you see between the two expressions?

SOCR. Maybe there is none; but listen while I tell you what is in my mind and then help me test it.

THEAIT. Certainly, if I can.

SOCR. 'Having' seems to me different from 'possessing'. For example, if a man buys a cloak and owns it, but does not wear it, we should say he *possesses* it, not that he *has* it in the sense of having it about him.

THEAIT. We should be right too.

SOCR. Now ask yourself whether you can possess knowledge in that way without having it about you, like a man who has trapped a number of wild birds—pigeons or what you will—and keeps them in a home-made aviary. In a sense we might of course say that he 'has' them because he possesses them, what?

THEAIT. Yes.

SOCR. But in another sense we must admit that he 'has' none of them, although he has brought them under his control by imprisoning them in an enclosure which belongs to him; he can take and hold them whenever he likes by catching any bird he pleases, and let go of them again; and he can do this as often as he sees fit.

THEAIT. True.

SOCR. Once more then, just as a while ago we imagined as it were a waxen tablet in the mind, let us now think of every mind as containing an aviary stocked with birds of every sort, some in flocks apart from the rest, others in small groups and others again solitary, flying about at random among them all.

THEAIT. So what?

SOCR. We must suppose that during babyhood this enclosure is empty, and consider the birds as representing items of knowledge. Whenever someone acquires any such item and shuts it up in his enclosure, we must say he has learnt or discovered the thing of which this is the knowledge, and that is what 'knowing' means.

THEAIT. Granted.

SOCR. [198] Next, think of him hunting once more for some particular item of knowledge that he happens to require, catching and holding it, and then letting go of it again. What terms are we to employ in order to describe this process: the same that we applied to the original mode of acquisition, or different ones? An illustration will throw more light on what I mean. You admit there is a science called arithmetic?

THEAIT. Yes.

SOCR. Imagine arithmetic then as a hunt for items of knowledge about all the numbers, both odd and even.

THEAIT. Well?

SOCR. It is by virtue of this science, I believe, that a man has in his control items of knowledge about numbers and can transmit them to others.

THEAIT. Yes.

SOCR. And we describe their transmission as 'teaching', their reception as 'learning' and the having of them in the sense of possessing them in the aviary as 'knowing'.

THEAIT. Certainly.

SOCR. Now observe the sequel. A perfect arithmetician knows all numbers, does he not? There is no number of which there is no knowledge in his mind.

THEAIT. Assuredly.

SOCR. And he may sometimes count either the numbers themselves in his own head or some group of external objects that have number.

THEAIT. Indeed yes.

SOCR. And by 'counting' we shall simply mean trying to discover the sum total of a particular number.

THEAIT. Exactly.

SOCR. Apparently, then, the man whom we have recognized as knowing all numbers is trying to discover what he already knows as if he didn't know it all. You have doubtless heard riddles of that kind discussed.

THEAIT. Yes, I have.

SOCR. Very well then, our simile of hunting pigeons and getting possession of them enables us to say that the method of hunting is twofold: first, before and with a view to possession of the pigeon; secondly, after possession has been obtained, with a view to catching and holding the bird you have already long possessed. In the same way, if a man has long possessed items of knowledge about things he has learnt and knows, he can still get to know the same things again by going after the knowledge of some particular thing and getting hold of it— the knowledge, I mean, of which he long since obtained possession, but which was not lying handy in his mind.

THEAIT. True.

SOCR. That was the point of my question: what terms should we employ to describe the method of hunting when an arithmetician proceeds to count or a literate person to read? It rather looked in such cases as if the man were out to learn again from himself what he already knew.

THEAIT. [199] What an extraordinary idea, Socrates!

SOCR. Yes, but surely we are not entitled to say he is going to read or count what he does *not* know, when we have already granted that he knows all the letters or all the numbers?

THEAIT. No, that is equally absurd.

SOCR. Shall we say, then, that we are not interested in words, if it amuses anyone to juggle with the expressions 'knowing' and 'learning'. Having recognized a clear distinction between possessing knowledge and having it about one, we agree that it is impossible not to possess what one actually possesses, and thereby avoid the otherwise inescapable conclusion that a man may be ignorant of what he knows; but we say that it is possible for him to get hold of a false judgment about it. For he may not have about him the knowledge of that thing, but some other item of knowledge instead, if, while hunting among the whole fluttering flock for one such item in particular, he happens to miss it and grabs a different one. In the case of 11 and 12, you see, he mistakes the former for the latter, because he has seized the knowledge of 11 that is in his mind, instead of his knowledge of 12—a ring-dove instead of a pigeon, so to speak.

THEAIT. Yes, there is something in that.

SOCR. On the other hand, when he catches the item of knowledge he is out to catch, he is not mistaken but thinks what is true. Thus there can exist both true and false judgments, and the obstacles that formerly stood in our way are removed. You'll agree with me, no doubt—or won't you?

THEAIT. I will.

SOCR. Yes; for we are now clear of the difficulty about not knowing what one does know. We are no longer faced with the problem of not possessing what we do possess, whether we are mistaken about something or not. But I seem to descry an even stranger consequence.

THEAIT. What is that?

SOCR. That the interchange of items of knowledge should ever give rise to a false judgment.

THEAIT. How do you mean?

SOCR. In the first place isn't it most unreasonable that a man who has knowledge of something should fail to recognize that very thing, not through ignorance but on account of his own knowledge; and secondly that he should judge that thing to be something else and vice versa? Is it not, I say, beyond the bounds of reason that when an item of knowledge presents itself to the mind, the latter should fail to recognize anything and know nothing? Once admit that knowledge can ever make us fail to know, and there is nothing to prevent the presence of ignorance making us know something, or the presence of blindness causing us to see.

THEAIT. We may have been wrong, Socrates, in making the birds represent items of knowledge only; perhaps we should have pictured bits of ignorance flying about with them in the mind. Then, as he runs in chase of them, our friend would catch sometimes an item of knowledge, sometimes a piece of ignorance; and the ignorance would lead him to judge falsely, the knowledge truly, about one and the same thing.

SOCR. It is not easy, Theaitetos, to disparage anything you say; but take another look at your suggestion. Suppose you are right; [200] then the man who catches the piece of ignorance will, according to you, judge falsely. Is that it?

THEAIT. Yes.

SOCR. But he will not of course think he judges falsely.

THEAIT. Certainly not.

SOCR. No; he will believe himself to be judging truly; his attitude of mind will be the same as if he knew the thing about which he is mistaken.

THEAIT. Of course.

SOCR. So he will fancy that his chase has yielded him an item of knowledge, not a piece of ignorance.

THEAIT. Inevitably.

SOCR. Then after a long and roundabout journey we are back again face to face with the original difficulty. Our stern critic will laugh at us and say: 'My dear good people, do you ask me to believe that a man who knows an item both of knowledge and of ignorance actually imagines that one of these things he knows is the other which he likewise knows? Or does he, without knowing either, judge that one of these unknown things is the other? Or, again, does he know only one and identify this with the unknown thing, or vice versa? Or, finally, are you going to tell me there are further pieces of knowledge *about* your items of knowledge and ignorance, and that their owner keeps them shut up in or impressed upon yet another of your ridiculous "aviaries" or "waxen tablets", knowing them so long as he possesses them, even though they may not be lying handy in his mind? If that is what you maintain you will inevitably find yourselves running round in circles and never getting any further.' What shall we reply to that, Theaitetos?

THEAIT. Honestly, Socrates, I don't know what we are to say.

SOCR. Well, dear boy, can it be that we deserve this censure, and that the argument shows we were wrong in turning our backs on knowledge and trying first to explain false judgment? It is impossible to understand the latter until we have given a satisfactory account of what knowledge is.

THEAIT. In the circumstances your conclusion seems unavoidable, Socrates.

SOCR. Starting all over again then, we must try to define knowledge. For surely we are not going to call off the search as yet, are we?

THEAIT. That's entirely up to you.

SOCR. Tell me then: what definition is least likely to involve us in self-contradiction?

THEAIT. The one we tried before, Socrates; I have no other to put forward.

SOCR. What was that?

THEAIT. That true belief is knowledge. At any rate, there can surely be no mistake in believing what is true, and the consequences are always above suspicion.

SOCR. Well, Theaitetos, 'we can but try', as the man said when asked if the river could be forded. So in this case, if we go ahead with our inquiry we may come across something [201] that will reveal the object of our search; we shall discover nothing by just standing still.

THEAIT. You are perfectly right; let us go forward and see.

SOCR. One thing, at any rate, does not take much finding out: you have a whole profession to show that true belief is not knowledge.

THEAIT. How so? What profession?

SOCR. The profession of those intellectual eminences, the orators and lawyers, who, as you well know, employ their skill in persuasion, not by instruction, but by convincing people of whatever they wish them to believe. You can hardly imagine teachers so clever that they can, in the short time allowed them by the clock, instruct a court thoroughly in the true facts of a case of robbery, or other form of violence, at which the jurors themselves were not present.

THEAIT. No, I certainly can't imagine that; but they can convince them.

SOCR. By 'convincing' you mean making them believe something, don't you?

THEAIT. Indeed yes.

SOCR. So when a jury is rightly convinced of facts which can be known only by witnessing them and in no other way, then, judging by hearsay and accepting a true belief, they are judging *without knowledge*, despite the correctness of their conviction if they return the right verdict?

THEAIT. Undoubtedly.

SOCR. But, my dear fellow, if true belief and knowledge were identical, the best of jurors could never entertain a true belief without knowledge. So it is now clear that they are two different things.

THEAIT. Ah yes, I'd forgotten. I *have* heard someone distinguish the two. He said that true belief coupled with an account or explanation is knowledge, while belief without such an account is beyond its scope. Things of which no account can be given are 'unknowable'—that was his expression—but those which admit of one are knowable.

SOCR. Not a bad way of putting it. But tell me how he distinguished these 'knowables' from 'unknowables'. It may transpire that what you were told squares with something I have heard said.

THEAIT. I don't know that I can remember exactly; but I'm pretty certain it will come back to me if I hear it restated.

SOCR. Listen then while I tell you 'a dream for a dream'. I seem to have heard some people allege that what may be described as the first elements of which we and all else consist admit of no account. Each by itself can only be named; nothing further can be attributed to it, even to the extent of saying that it does or does not exist—[202] which would immediately involve the addition to it of existence or non-existence, whereas nothing at all should be added if one is to express just it alone. As a matter of fact, one ought not to add so much as 'just' or 'it' or 'each' or 'alone' or 'the' or anything else from a whole vocabulary of such terms. These loose terms are attached to everything, and they are distinct from the things to which they are attached. If it were possible for an element to be expressed in any formula exclusively belonging to it, it should be so expressed without the introduction of any other terms. Actually, however, no element can be expressed by a formula; it can only be named, for a name is all that belongs to it. But as regards things composed of these elements, just as they are themselves complex, so the names of the elements are combined into a description which is of its very nature a compound of names. Thus, elements are inexplicable and unknowable, but they can be perceived. Complexes, on the other hand, are knowable and explicable, and it is possible to have a true notion of them. Accordingly, when a man obtains the true notion of something without an account, he does not know it, although his mind thinks truly about it; for unless one can give and receive an account of a thing, one is without knowledge of that thing. But once he has also obtained an account, all this is within his power and he has everything required for knowledge. Is that the dream as you heard it, or were you given some other version?

THEAIT. No, that's exactly what I was told.

SOCR. So you approve it and maintain that true belief coupled with an account is knowledge?

THEAIT. Exactly.

SOCR. Is it possible, Theaitetos, that in the course of a few minutes conversation today we have discovered what generations of wise men have grown grey in seeking but have not found?

THEAIT. As far as I'm concerned, Socrates, our present statement is quite satisfactory

SOCR. Yes, the statement in itself may well be so; for it is difficult to see how there can ever be knowledge without an account and right belief. But there is one point in the theory as stated which does not attract me.

THEAIT. What is that?

SOCR. The very point that might appear its most telling feature
—that whereas the elements are unknowable, any and every
complex (e.g. a syllable) is knowable.

THEAIT. But isn't that correct?

SOCR. We must find out. The example just used to illustrate our
statement will serve as a kind of hostage for the theory.

THEAIT. You mean——?

SOCR. The syllable, a complex made up of letters, which are the
elements of writing. Or do you think the author of the theory
we are discussing had some other prototype in mind?

THEAIT. Oh no.

SOCR. [203] Then let us grab hold of that example and put it to
the question, or rather put this question to ourselves: Was it
on that principle we learnt our letters, or not? First, is it true
that one can give an account of syllables but not of the letters
forming them?

THEAIT. Maybe.

SOCR. I think so too, decidedly. Take the first syllable of
'Socrates'. Suppose you were asked to explain what SO is:
what would you say?

THEAIT. S and O.

SOCR. And in saying that you have given an account of the
syllable?

THEAIT. Yes.

SOCR. Go on now, and give us an account of the letter S.

THEAIT. How can one enunciate the elements of an element? In
point of fact, Socrates, S is one of the consonants, a mere
noise, as of the tongue hissing. B, on the other hand, and
indeed most of the letters, not only lack articulate sound but
are not even noises. So it is quite right to call them inexplicable, seeing that the clearest of them, the seven vowels themselves, have only a sound, and no account whatever can be
given of them.

SOCR. Well, then, that is one step towards an accurate definition
of knowledge.

THEAIT. Yes, I think it is.

SOCR. Wait though: had we any right to declare that while the
syllable can be known the letter cannot?

THEAIT. I don't see why not.

SOCR. See here now; do we mean by 'syllable' both the letters or (if there are more than two) all of them? Or do we refer to a single entity which arises the instant they are put together?

THEAIT. I should say we mean both (or all) the letters.

SOCR. Then take the case of those two letters S and O. The two together are the first syllable of my name. Anyone who knows the syllable knows the pair of letters, eh?

THEAIT. Of course he does.

SOCR. That is to say, he knows S *plus* O.

THEAIT. Yes.

SOCR. But has he then no knowledge of *each* letter? In other words, does he know the pair without knowing either of its constituents?

THEAIT. That, Socrates, is utterly absurd.

SOCR. And yet, if it is necessary to know each of two things before one can know the pair, it is absolutely indispensable that he should know the letters first, if he is ever to know the syllable; and so our splendid theory will take to its heels and leave us standing.

THEAIT. It certainly will—in double quick time.

SOCR. Yes, because we are not keeping a strict watch upon it. Perhaps we ought to have recognized the syllable not as the letters but as a single entity arising out of their juxtaposition with a unitary character all its own and distinct from the letters.

THEAIT. Perhaps we ought. Indeed it may well be so rather than the other way about.

SOCR. Let us look into that. It will never do to abandon so impressive a theory without putting up some sort of fight.

THEAIT. Definitely not.

SOCR. [204] Suppose then that the truth is as we now suggest, namely that the syllable is a single entity arising from any group of letters which can be combined; and that the same is true of every complex as well as in the case of syllables formed of letters.

THEAIT. Very well.

SOCR. Like that, it must be devoid of parts.

THEAIT. Why?

SOCR. Because if a thing has parts, the whole thing must be the same as all the parts. Or do you say that any whole, as well as the syllable, is a single entity arising out of the parts and different from their aggregate?

THEAIT. Yes, I do.

SOCR. Then is the sum, in your view, the same thing as the whole, or are they different?

THEAIT. I don't feel too sure about that; but you tell me to answer boldly, so I will take a chance on it and say they are different.

SOCR. Your boldness is right, Theaitetos; whether your answer is so remains to be seen.

THEAIT. Yes, it does.

SOCR. Well then, according to our present view the whole will be different from the sum.

THEAIT. Yes.

SOCR. But how about this? Is there any difference between the sum and all the units it contains? For example, when we say 'one, two, three, four, five, six' or 'twice three' or 'three times two' or 'four and two' or 'three and two and one', are we in all these instances expressing the same thing or different things?

THEAIT. The same thing.

SOCR. In other words, six and nothing else?

THEAIT. No, just six.

SOCR. In each form of expression, therefore, we have expressed all the six.

THEAIT. Yes.

SOCR. But when we express them all, is there no sum that we express?

THEAIT. Of course there is.

SOCR. And is that sum anything but 'six'?

THEAIT. No.

SOCR. Then at all events in the case of things that are made up of number, when we use the expressions 'sum' and 'all the things' we refer to the same thing.

THEAIT. Apparently.

SOCR. Well now, let us put the argument in this way. The number of square yards in an acre and the acre itself are the same thing, are they not?

THEAIT. Yes.

SOCR. And so too with the number of yards in a furlong?

THEAIT. Yes.

SOCR. And again with the number of troops in an army and the army itself, and so on and so forth. The total number is always the same as the total thing.

THEAIT. Yes.

SOCR. But you don't mean to say that the number of units in any aggregate can be anything but parts of it?

THEAIT. No.

SOCR. Now doesn't everything that *has* parts *consist of* parts?

THEAIT. Obviously.

SOCR. But we have agreed that, if the total number is to be the same as the total thing, all the parts are the same as the sum.

THEAIT. Yes.

SOCR. Then the whole does not consist of parts; if it were all the parts it would be a sum.

THEAIT. I agree.

SOCR. But can a part be part of anything but the whole to which it belongs?

THEAIT. Yes, of the sum.

SOCR. [205] You put up a fine show, Theaitetos; but is not the sum precisely something from which nothing is missing?

THEAIT. Naturally.

SOCR. And is not a whole just the same thing, i.e. something which lacks absolutely nothing? On the other hand, when something is removed, the thing ceases to be a whole or a sum; it changes at the same instant from being both to being neither.

THEAIT. I now recognize that there is no difference between a sum and a whole.

SOCR. Well, the sum or whole of anything that has parts will be the same thing as all the parts. Isn't that what we were saying?

THEAIT. Exactly.

SOCR. Once again then, as I was trying to explain just now, if the syllable is not the same thing as the letters, are we not bound to admit that it cannot include the letters as parts of itself; otherwise, being the same thing as the letters, it would be just as knowable as they are?

THEAIT. That is true.

SOCR. It was in order to avoid that very conclusion that we posited the syllable as different from the letters.

THEAIT. Yes.

SOCR. Well, if the letters are not parts of the syllable, can you mention any things, other than its letters, which *are* parts of a syllable?

THEAIT. I certainly cannot, Socrates. If I conceded that it had any parts, I should be making a fool of myself in ignoring the letters and looking for something else in place of them.

SOCR. So according to our present view, Theaitetos, the syllable will be a single and absolutely indivisible entity?

THEAIT. Apparently.

SOCR. Now do you remember our admitting a little while ago a statement we believed to be well grounded? It urged that no account was possible of the primary elements of which other things are composed, because each of them, taken just by itself, was non-composite: and that one could not rightly attribute even existence to it or refer to it as 'this', because these terms denoted things other than, i.e. extraneous to, it; and that this was the reason for acknowledging the primary element as inexplicable and therefore unknowable.

THEAIT. Yes, I remember.

SOCR. Then is not this the one and only reason for its being simple and indivisible? I can see no other.

THEAIT. Of course; there *is* no other.

SOCR. Well, if the syllable has no parts and is a single entity, it turns out to be the same sort of thing as the letter or primary element. What do you say?

THEAIT. I entirely agree.

SOCR. To sum up now: If (1) a syllable is (*a*) the same thing as a number of letters and (*b*) a whole of which those letters are the parts, then the letters must be just as knowable and explicable (or unknowable and inexplicable) as are syllables, since we have shown that all the parts are the same thing as the whole.

THEAIT. Quite true.

SOCR. But if (2) a syllable is one and indivisible, then, for the same reason, syllable and letter likewise are equally inexplicable and unknowable.

THEAIT. I can't deny that.

SOCR. In which case we cannot agree with anyone who maintains that the syllable can be known and explained, whereas the letter cannot.

THEAIT. No, not if we stand by our argument.

SOCR. [206] I should think not. On the contrary, wouldn't your own experience of learning to read incline you rather to the opposite view?

THEAIT. How do you mean?

SOCR. I mean that all the time you were learning your whole purpose was to distinguish, by means of eye or ear, each letter by itself, so as not to be confused by any series of them in the written or the spoken word.

THEAIT. That is perfectly correct.

SOCR. Nor of course were you given full marks in the music school, unless you were able to pick out each single note and tell which string produced it; and notes, as everybody is aware, are the elements of music.

THEAIT. Precisely.

SOCR. Then if we are going to make deductions from what we have learned about elements and complexes, we shall find that elements in general admit of much clearer knowledge than does the complex, a knowledge also which is far more remunerative in any branch of study. If ever we are told that the complex is by its nature knowable and the element un-knowable, we shall presume that our informant is trifling with us, wittingly or otherwise.

THEAIT. Fair enough.

SOCR. As a matter of fact I believe I could find other ways of proving that point. But we must not allow them to lure us from the main question: What is really meant by saying that knowledge in the fullest sense is provided by an account added to true belief?

THEAIT. Yes, that is the question.

SOCR. To begin with, what are we meant to understand by the term 'account'? I think it must signify one of three things.

THEAIT. What are they?

SOCR. The first will be manifesting one's own thought in vocal sound by means of nouns and verbs, throwing an image of what one has in mind upon the stream that flows through the lips, like a reflection in a mirror or in water. Do you agree that such expression is an account?

THEAIT. I do. It is what we call expressing ourselves through the spoken word.

SOCR. That, however, is something anyone can do more or less fluently. Provided a man is not born deaf or dumb he can reveal whatever is in his mind. In this sense, accordingly, anyone and everyone who has a correct notion will obviously have it *with an account*, and it will never be possible to have a correct notion without knowledge.

THEAIT. True.

SOCR. Then we must pause before charging the man who framed the definition of knowledge now under review with talking nonsense. He may not have meant that. He may have meant being able to answer the question, [207] What is so-and-so, by stating the several elements of which it is composed.

THEAIT. An example, please, Socrates.

SOCR. Well, take what Hesiod says about a wagon: 'There are a hundred pieces of wood in a wagon.' I could not name them all, and I don't suppose you could either. If we were asked what a wagon is, we should be quite pleased with ourselves if we could mention wheels, axle, body, rails, yoke.

THEAIT. Certainly.

SOCR. But he would no doubt think us just as ridiculous as if we answered a similar question about your name by enumerating the syllables. We might think and express ourselves accurately enough, but it would be absurd for us to look upon ourselves as grammarians and able to give an account of the name Theaitetos such as a grammarian would produce. He would declare it impossible to give a scientific account of anything unless one added to one's true notion a full list of the elements, as, I believe, was said earlier.

THEAIT. Yes, it was.

SOCR. So too, he would say, we may have a right notion of the wagon, but the man who can provide an exhaustive statement of its nature by listing those hundred parts has thereby added an account to his true notion and, instead of mere belief, has achieved a technical knowledge of the wagon's nature by describing the whole in terms of its elements.

THEAIT. Don't you agree with that, Socrates?

SOCR. Tell me if *you* agree, my friend. In other words, tell me whether you accept the view that an exhaustive enumeration of elements is an account of any given thing, but that description in terms of syllables or still larger units leaves it unexplained. Tell me that, and we will try to find out what your answer is worth.

THEAIT. Yes, I do accept that view.

SOCR. Do you believe that anyone has knowledge of a particular object when he thinks that one and the same thing is sometimes part of one object, sometimes part of another; or again when he regards now one and now another thing as part of one and the same object?

THEAIT. Good heavens, no!

SOCR. Have you forgotten, then, that when you began learning to read and write, that was just what you and your fellow pupils did?

THEAIT. Are you alluding to the times when we thought that now one and now another letter was part of the same syllable, and when we put the same letter now into the correct syllable, now into the wrong one?

SOCR. Yes.

THEAIT. Oh, I remember well. No, I don't think anyone at that level can be said to have knowledge.

SOCR. Here's an instance. If at that stage in his progress a child is writing 'Theaitetos' [208] and thinks he ought to write T and H and E and does so, but when he is trying to write 'Theodoros', he thinks he should write T and E and does so, can we say that he knows the first syllable of those two names?

THEAIT. No; we have just agreed that one still lacks knowledge at that level.

SOCR. And is there any reason why a person should not be at the same level with respect to the second, third and fourth syllables.

THEAIT. None at all.

SOCR. May we take it, then, that whenever he writes down in their proper order all the letters of the name 'Theaitetos' he posseses the full list of elements coupled with true belief?

THEAIT. Evidently.

SOCR. Being still, as we agree, devoid of knowledge, though he believes correctly?

THEAIT. Yes.

SOCR. Notwithstanding that when he writes he possesses the 'account' (i.e. the list of elements), together with right belief.

THEAIT. True.

Socr. And so, my friend, there is such a thing as right belief together with an account, which cannot as yet properly be called knowledge.

Theait. I can scarcely deny it.

Socr. Apparently then our supposition that we had reached a completely accurate definition of knowledge was but a golden dream. Or shall we wait a bit before finally condemning the theory? Maybe the real meaning of 'account' is not this at all, but the remaining one of the three, one of which we said must be intended by anyone defining knowledge as 'correct belief coupled with an account'.

Theait. A timely warning; there is of course one other left. The first was a kind of vocal image of thought; and the one just discussed was a progress through the elements to the whole. What is the third?

Socr. The meaning that would satisfy most people: being able to name some particular characteristic which marks off the thing in question from everything else.

Theait. Could you give me an example of an 'account' in this sense?

Socr. Well, I take it you'll be prepared to accept the following account of the sun: it is the brightest of the heavenly bodies in orbit round the earth.

Theait. Certainly.

Socr. I want you to understand the significance of this example. It is to illustrate what we were saying just now, that if you get hold of the characteristic which differentiates any given thing from all others, then, as some hold, you will have an 'account' of it; but so long as you batten on something that is common to other things, your account will include all those things by which it is shared.

Theait. I follow. It seems to me that 'account' is just the right word for what you have described.

Socr. And if, in addition to a right notion about any given thing, a man also grasps its difference from all else, he will have raised an erstwhile notion into knowledge of that thing.

Theait. Exactly.

Socr. On the other hand, Theaitetos, now that I get a close-up of this statement, it is like a piece of stage scenery: so long as I stood well back it appeared to represent something, but I can no longer make anything of it.

THEAIT. What do you mean? Why do you say that?

SOCR. [209] I will do my best to explain. Suppose I have a correct notion about you: if I couple with it the account of you, then I am taken to know you; otherwise I have no more than a notion.

THEAIT. Quite.

SOCR. And 'account', we have agreed, is the verbal expression of your different-ness.

THEAIT. Just so.

SOCR. So long, therefore, as I had only a notion, my mind did not grasp any of the characteristics which differentiate you from others?

THEAIT. Apparently not.

SOCR. Then there must have been present to my mind one of those common characteristics which belong to anybody else quite as much as to you?

THEAIT. Evidently.

SOCR. Half a minute, though! How on earth, in that case, could I be having a notion of you as distinct from anyone else? Suppose I was thinking: Theaitetos is one who is a man and has a nose and eyes and a mouth, and so on, naming each and every part of the body. Will thinking along those lines produce a notion of Theaitetos rather than of Theodoros or, indeed, of the proverbial Man in the Street?

THEAIT. No, I don't see how it can.

SOCR. Next, suppose I think not simply of a man with nose and eyes, but one with a *snub* nose and *protruding* eyes: shall I even then have a notion of *you* rather than of myself or anyone else of similar appearance?

THEAIT. No.

SOCR. In fact, I do not believe I shall possess any notion of Theaitetos until this particular snubness has impressed upon and laid up in my mind a record distinct from all the other examples of snubness I have seen; and so with each of your physical features in turn. Then, if I come across you tomorrow, that record, by stirring my memory, will provide me with a correct notion about you.

THEAIT. Very true.

Socr. Consequently the right notion of anything must itself include the different-ness.

Theait. Obviously.

Socr. Then I should like to know what meaning can possibly be attached to 'couple an account with the correct notion'. If on the one hand it means 'add the notion of how a thing differs from other things', the words make no sense at all.

Theait. How so?

Socr. Having a correct notion of the way certain things differ from others, we are then told to add thereto a correct notion of the way they differ from other things—an order that reduces the most vicious circle to comparative nothingness! Such an order might more justly be described as the sort of direction a blind man might give; for a man who tells us to get hold of something we already have, so that we may get to know something already in our minds, would seem to be living in a state of abysmal darkness.

Theait. And on the other hand—what? The beginning of your statement suggested an alternative.

Socr. I was going on to say that if the order to 'add an account' bids us get to *know* the different-ness, as distinct from merely have a notion of it—why, what a pretty pickle our crowning definition of knowledge turns out to be! 'Getting to know' is acquiring knowledge, [210] isn't it?

Theait. Yes.

Socr. So our definition, if asked what knowledge is, will apparently reply: 'Correct belief *together with knowledge of a different-ness*'; for that, in its view, is what one means by 'adding an account'.

Theait. So it seems.

Socr. Exactly; and when we are investigating the nature of knowledge it is the very height of stupidity to say that it is correct belief coupled with a *knowledge* of different-ness or of what you will.

Therefore, Theaitetos, neither perception nor true belief, nor an account coupled with true belief can be knowledge.

Theait. I suppose not.

Socr. Now, my friend, are we in labour with a fourth child, or have we brought to birth all we have to say about knowledge?

THEAIT. We certainly have, Socrates; and your efforts have enabled me to express a good many more ideas than were in me.

SOCR. And has not my skill as a midwife declared the whole lot of them to be mere wind-eggs, not worth the rearing?

THEAIT. Most decidedly.

SOCR. Well then, Theaitetos, if you ever again set about conceiving, and manage to become pregnant, your embryo thoughts will be all the better for this inquiry; and if you remain barren, you will be gentler and more agreeable to your associates, having the good sense not to imagine you know what you don't know. That much and no more my art can accomplish; nor have I any of that knowledge possessed by the intellectual giants of yesterday or of today. But my mother and I received the art of midwifery from God: she for the sake of women, I for the benefit of glorious youth and of all in whom virtue resides.

Now I must go to the Porch of the King Archon to answer the indictment which Meletus has lodged against me. But let us meet again here, Theodoros, tomorrow morning.

THE SOPHIST

PERSONS OF THE DIALOGUE

Theodoros.
Socrates.

A Stranger from Elaia.
Theaitetos.

THEOD. [216] Here we are, Socrates, to keep yesterday's appointment; and we have with us a guest. Our friend here is a native of Elaia; he belongs to the school of Parmenides and Zeno, and is a keen student of philosophy.

SOCR. I see. But are you certain, Theodoros, he *is* an ordinary guest and not some divinity whom you have brought along unawares? Homer tells us that gods attend the footsteps of mortal men who tread the paths of mercy and of righteousness; and that the God of Strangers in particular keeps watch upon the obedience or insubordination of mankind. It may be that your companion is one of those higher powers—a spirit of refutation, so to speak—who comes to observe and show up our weak points in debate.

THEOD. Our friend is not made like that, Socrates; he is more reasonable than your carping critics. I am far from calling him a god; but there is something divine about him—as I maintain there is about any philosopher.

SOCR. And rightly, my friend. One might almost say, on the other hand, that the type you mention—the genuine as opposed to the sham philosopher—is not much easier to recognize than is a god. These men, as they travel from one city to the next, surveying from on high the life below, appear (such is human ignorance) in every sort of guise. Some look on them as of no consequence, others as beyond all praise; now they are taken for statesmen, now for mere sophists; and sometimes they give the impression of being just plain crazy. But I should like to ask our guest, if he doesn't mind, what his own countrymen thought and in what sense they used these names.

THEOD. [217] What names?

157

Socr. Sophist, statesman, philosopher.

Theod. What exactly are you getting at? What is your difficulty about those names?

Socr. This: did they think of all three as one type, or as two; or did they distinguish three types and assign to each of them one of the three corresponding names?

Theod. So far as I am aware, there is no objection to your question. What do you say, sir?

Str. I agree with you, Theodoros; the question is welcome and the answer not far to seek. They distinguished three types; but it is no short and easy task to give a clear definition of each.

Theod. It so happens, Socrates, that you have hit on a subject very much akin to one about which we were questioning him before we came along to join you. He made the same excuse to us then as he has just offered you, though he admits he has had a good schooling and has not forgotten what he learned.

Socr. In that case, sir, 'refuse us not the favour first we ask. Tell us this much': [1] which do you generally prefer—to discourse on your own, without interruption, on any subject you wish to explain, or to use the method of question and answer, as I once heard Parmenides himself do in the course of a brilliant exposition? I was young at the time and he was quite an old man.

Str. Dialogue is the easiest way, Socrates, when the other party is tractable and gives no trouble; otherwise it is better to do all one's own talking.

Socr. Then you may choose anyone you like from the present company; you will find them all tractable, and they will answer as required. But you will be well advised to select one of the younger men—Theaitetos here or someone else of about his age, just as you prefer.

Str. Well, Socrates, I am meeting you and your friends for the first time, and I feel rather shy at the prospect of spinning out a lengthy discourse on my own, or even addressing it to another, as if I were giving an exhibition of rhetoric. I would prefer to exchange ideas with you in the normal course of conversation. For indeed your question is not so easy a matter as its form might suggest; it needs discussion at great length.

[1] Probably a quotation from a lost tragedy.

On the other hand, to disappoint you and your friends, especially when you make the request in the way you have done, seems to me an act of discourtesy quite unbecoming in a guest. In view of my previous conversation [218] with Theaitetos and of your own advice, I shall be delighted to accept him as my opposite number.

THEAIT. That is all very well, sir; but are you going to satisfy the whole company by doing what Socrates recommends?

STR. I'm afraid there is nothing more to be said about that, Theaitetos; from now on, it seems, the discussion must run its course between you and me. If its length tires you—well, that is your friends' fault, not mine.

THEAIT. Oh, I don't feel at the moment as if I shall have to call it off. But if anything of the sort does happen we will call in Socrates' namesake here; he's about my own age and quite used to tackling any problem with me.

STR. Very well, you can please yourself as we go along; from now onwards the discussion must be one between our two selves. I think we had better start by studying the Sophist, and try to embody his nature in a clear formula; all that you and I so far apprehend in common is the mere name 'Sophist'. Each of us may have his own mental image of the thing to which he gives that name; but it is always desirable to have agreed about the thing itself by way of positive statements, instead of merely using a word without explicit formulation of its meaning. It is not the easiest thing in the world to comprehend this group we are going to study, or to say what exactly a sophist is. However, it has long been recognized that any major project is best undertaken in the light of experiment on something comparatively small and easy to handle. This is the course I suggest we now follow, Theaitetos. We regard the Sophist as a difficult sort of creature to track down; so let us first practise the method of hunting him on some easier form of prey, unless you can think of a more satisfactory procedure.

THEAIT. No, I certainly cannot.

STR. You are prepared then to take someone less exalted and try to use him as a model of our more important quarry?

THEAIT. Yes.

STR. What shall we choose now that is quite familiar and small but no less capable of definition than anything large? What about an angler? He is quite well known to everyone and of no great consequence to anybody.

THEAIT. True.

STR. [219] I'm fairly sure the process of defining him can help us to what we require.

THEAIT. Let's hope so.

STR. I shall begin by asking you whether we should consider him as possessed of an art, or as someone without an art but having some other potency.

THEAIT. He certainly has an art.

STR. Right. Now every art falls under one of two heads.

THEAIT. How so?

STR. A single epithet might fairly be applied to agriculture and the whole business of tending plants and animals, to every form of craftsmanship or manufacture and to the whole field of imitative skill.

THEAIT. On what grounds do you say that, and what is this epithet?

STR. When a man brings into being something that did not exist before we describe him as 'producing' it, and the object thus brought into being as 'produced'.

THEAIT. True.

STR. And all the activities I have just mentioned are directed to production.

THAIT. They are indeed.

STR. Then we may classify them under one head as 'productive' art.

THEAIT. Fair enough.

STR. Next, you have the spheres of learning and knowing, money-making and capture. None of these produces any-thing; they merely employ words or deeds to get hold of things that already exist or to prevent others from getting hold of them. We may therefore classify the whole lot of them as 'acquisitive' art.

THEAIT. Yes; that is quite acceptable.

STR. Well now, Theaitetos, there you have all the arts classified as 'acquisitive and productive'. To which class do you think angling belongs.

THEAIT. To the acquisitive, surely.

STR. But are there not two sorts of acquisitive art, one consisting of exchange between voluntary agents by way of gifts, wages, or purchase; the other, getting hold of things by word or deed, and therefore to be described comprehensively as 'capture'?

THEAIT. It appears so, at any rate, from what you have said.

STR. Wait, though; haven't we yet to make a twofold division of capture?

THEAIT. How are we to do that?

STR. By calling that part of it which is conducted openly 'contention', and its more secret manifestation 'hunting'.

THEAIT. Yes.

STR. Then reason demands a subdivision of hunting.

THEAIT. Tell us how that is to be effected.

STR. By distinguishing the hunting of inanimate and that of living things.

THEAIT. Certainly, if both exist.

STR. [220] Of course they do. Now leaving aside the first of those, which has no special name, except as regards some kinds of diving and the like, which are of small importance, let us call the pursuit of living things 'animal hunting'.

THEAIT. Very well.

STR. We may recognize, further, two kinds of animal hunting: the hunting of land animals (those which go on feet) in all its manifold variety, and the hunting of water animals, i.e. of those that swim.

THEAIT. Certainly.

STR. And water animals may be classified in turn as 'winged' and 'subaqueous'?

THEAIT. Agreed.

STR. Now the whole business of hunting the winged class is known to us as 'fowling'.

THEAIT. It is.

STR. And of the subaqueous class as 'fishing'.

THEAIT. Yes.

STR. Again, might I not distinguish two main kinds of fishing?

THEAIT. On what basis?

STR. In one the fish are caught by trapping, in the other by striking.

THEAIT. How do you mean? How do you distinguish the two?

STR. Well, in the first case, whatever catches anything and holds it so that it cannot get away is properly called a 'trap'.

THEAIT. Certainly.

STR. May we not then apply the word 'trap' to all such things as nets, eel-baskets, lobster-pots and so forth?

THEAIT. Yes.

STR. The other, done with a fish-spear or with hook and line, we may include under the single term 'striking'—unless you can think of a better one, Theaitetos.

THEAIT. Never mind the word; 'striking' will do well enough.

STR. Furthermore, I believe fishermen themselves refer to what they do at night with the aid of flares as 'fire-fishing'.

THEAIT. That's right.

STR. And to their daytime activities as 'barb-fishing', because their spears and hooks are tipped with barbs.

THEAIT. Perfectly correct.

STR. Again, the 'barb-fishing' type of 'striking', in which the stroke is delivered from above, is called 'spearing', presumably because the usual weapon is a three-pronged spear.

THEAIT. Yes; some people, at any rate, call it that.

STR. Then, one may say, there is only one other kind of fishing.

THEAIT. You mean——?

STR. That in which the stroke is delivered from the opposite position, i.e. from below; a stroke made with a hook suspended from a rod and line, [221] directed exclusively at the fish's head and mouth—not, as in using a spear, at any random part of its body. Now, Theaitetos, what do you say is the proper name for this?

THEAIT. At last, it seems, our search is ended; we have discovered what we set out to find.

STR. So you and I are not only agreed as to the word 'angling'; we have also given a satisfactory account of the thing itself. Taking Art as a whole, we found one half of it to be the acquisitive branch. One half of the latter we named 'capture', with the following as one line of its derivatives: hunting; animal hunting; water-animal hunting; fishing; striking; barb-fishing; and angling. This last, the object of our search, in which the stroke is directed upwards *at an angle*, is named accordingly.

THEAIT. That certainly requires no further explanation.

STR. Good then, let us try to discover the nature of the Sophist by working along those lines.

THEAIT. Very well.

STR. Our first question as regards the angler was whether we should recognize him simply as a man, or as a man with an art.

THEAIT. Yes.

STR. Now, Theaitetos, take our friend the Sophist: shall we put him down as just a man, or as really and truly a man of wisdom.

THEAIT. Certainly not as just a man. I see though what your question is intended to suggest: he is far from being what his name represents.

STR. But we must surely allow that he possesses *some* kind of art.

THEAIT. Yes, but *what* kind?

STR. Good heavens! have we overlooked the likeness between the two men?

THEAIT. Between which two men?

STR. The angler and our Sophist.

THEAIT. How are they alike?

STR. They both look to me very much like a pair of hunters.

THEAIT. We've dealt with the angler in that respect; but what does the Sophist hunt?

STR. A little while ago, you remember, we recognized two kinds of hunting, according as the quarry swims or goes on foot.

THEAIT. Yes.

STR. Now we dealt with the first type, so far at any rate as fish are concerned; but we made no subdivision of hunting on land, except to notice that it has many forms.

THEAIT. [222] Quite so.

STR. Up to this point the Sophist and the angler are parallel practitioners of acquisitive art.

THEAIT. Yes, I suppose they are.

STR. Animal hunting, then is the point after which they begin to diverge. One of them now turns to hunt those creatures which live in the sea, in rivers, or in lakes.

THEAIT. Exactly.

STR. Meanwhile the other turns toward the land, to rivers of a different kind—everlasting meadows, as it were, of youth and riches—whose denizens he means to catch.

THEAIT. What do you mean?

STR. There are two main types of hunting on land.

THEAIT. Name them, please.

STR. One the pursuit of tame, the other of wild creatures.

THEAIT. But are tame creatures hunted?

STR. Oh yes; man is a tame animal. But choose your own ground. Either you assume (1) that tame animals do not exist; or (2) that although there are such things, they are something other than man, who is in fact wild; or again (3) you say that although man is a tame animal you don't think he is ever hunted. Tell us plainly which of these positions you adopt.

THEAIT. No, sir, I think man *is* a tame animal, and that there is such a thing as man-hunting.

STR. In that case we may say the hunting of tame animals is twofold.

THEAIT. How do you make that out?

STR. First I distinguish *violent* man-hunting. This includes piracy, slave-trading, tyranny and all forms of warfare.

THEAIT. Good.

STR. Forensic and political oratory, on the other hand, and displays of rhetoric in private, I class together as *persuasive* man-hunting.

THEAIT. Correct.

STR. Now the latter may be subdivided into two kinds.

THEAIT. How so?

STR. One is concerned with individuals, the other with the community at large.

THEAIT. Quite a fair distinction.

STR. The hunting of individuals, in turn, may be subdivided according as it involves taking fees, or making presents.

THEAIT. I don't understand.

STR. Apparently you've never studied the art of hunting as employed by a lover.

THEAIT. In what respect?

STR. His efforts include the giving of presents to his prey.

THEAIT. Ah, of course!

STR. That may be called the 'erotic' art.

THEAIT. Certainly.

STR. Now for the subdivision in which fees are taken. When the hunter offers his companionship as a means to gratification, using pleasure alone as his bait and asking simply for maintenance in return, I think [223] we should all agree to call it the art of flattery.

THEAIT. Fair enough.

STR. But when he professes to seek the company of his victim for the latter's improvement and in return for hard cash then, surely, he deserves another name.

THEAIT. He certainly does.

STR. And what is that name? See if you can tell me.

THEAIT. Why, it's obvious. I believe we have tracked down the Sophist, and in uttering that word I think I've called him by his rightful name.

STR. It would seem then, according to our present line of argument, that sophistic is a form of hunting, which is itself a branch of acquisitive art employing the method of capture. It is a mode of animal-hunting; its quarry is tame land-animals of the species Man; and it operates privately, offering rich and likely young men a so-called education in return for cash payment.

THEAIT. An admirable summary.

STR. However, let us look at the thing from another angle. Not only has the class of persons we are now studying a very complicated system that deserves careful examination, but our previous remarks themselves suggest that it is something rather different from what we have just declared it to be.

THEAIT. How so?

STR. There is a distinction between the sale by a manufacturer of his own products and the business of exchanging what others have produced.

THEAIT. Certainly.

STR. Further, that department of exchange which amounts to about one half thereof, and is carried on within the city walls, is known as local retail trade.

THEAIT. Yes.

STR. Contrasted with which we have mercantile trade, i.e. the buying of goods in one city for sale in another.

THEAIT. Quite so.

STR. Now, as we know, there is one branch of such trade that sells (i.e. exchanges for cash) whatever supplies bodily needs, and another branch that does likewise for the soul.

THEAIT. I don't follow you.

STR. We know all about the first of these branches; the second is perhaps not so familiar.

THEAIT. No.

STR. [224] Well, take education as a whole. Its various accomplishments are traded from city to city, bought in one place, and carried off for sale in another. Such are painting, puppet-showmanship and the like, which are acquired and sold partly for the soul's entertainment and partly for its more serious needs. We must admit that a man who trades in these commodities is no less a merchant in the proper sense of that word than one who offers food and drink for sale.

THEAIT. I quite agree.

STR. And do you also agree that the same name is applicable to one who buys up knowledge and hawks it about from city to city in return for cash?

THEAIT. Certainly I do.

STR. Well, one division of this trade in commodities that are to nourish the soul might properly be called 'displays', mightn't it? The other division, though just as comical, is nevertheless traffic in knowledge, and ought therefore to be given a name in keeping with its activity.

THEAIT. Of course.

STR. Traffic in knowledge, furthermore, is itself twofold; and that branch which has to do with goodness should be named differently from that concerned with other kinds of accomplishment.

THEAIT. Yes, indeed.

STR. The name 'craft-merchant' would fit the dealer in this latter branch; but what do you think we should call a man who trades in goodness? See if you can tell me.

THEAIT. Why, surely the only possible name is that belonging to the object of our present inquiry—the sort of man we call a 'Sophist'.

STR. Exactly. In a nutshell then sophistic appears this time as an offshoot of that branch of the acquisitive art which operates by exchange, and from which it is derived as follows: Selling —mercantile trade—mercantile trade in words and knowledge that are to nourish the soul—the sale of goodness.

THEAIT. That's right.

STR. But suppose, in the third place, a man were to settle down here at Athens and propose to live by selling these same articles of knowledge, buying some of them and making others himself: I don't imagine you would call him by any other name than the one you just now mentioned.

THEAIT. Certainly not.

STR. Again, I presume you will apply the name 'sophistic' to any branch whatsoever of acquisitive art in the form of exchange by sale (whether it functions as retail trade or as the sale of one's own products), provided only that it is a sub-division of mercantile trade in knowledge.

THEAIT. I can do nothing else; your reasoning compels me.

STR. Then let us go a step further and see if we can get another, though kindred, view of the class now under investigation.

THEAIT. [225] What view.

STR. We recognized 'contention' as a branch of acquisitive art.

THEAIT. We did.

STR. There is also good reason for subdividing it into two.

THEAIT. What are those subdivisions?

STR. We may call one of them 'friendly competition' and the other 'fighting'.

THEAIT. I see.

STR. Then, as regards fighting, in the shape of physical conflict, it may fairly be described by some such name as 'violence'.

THEAIT. Yes.

STR. And can you think of a better word than 'controversy', Theaitetos, for describing verbal contest?

THEAIT. No, I can't.

STR. But now we have to recognize two sorts of controversy.

THEAIT. What are they?

STR. Well, first, whenever one long speech is opposed to another in public about rights and wrongs, there you have forensic oratory.

THEAIT. Yes.

STR. Whereas controversy that is carried on privately in the small change of question and answer is commonly known as disputation, isn't it?

THEAIT. Yes.

STR. There is a kind of disputation concerned with business agreements. It has the character of disputation, to be sure, and must be considered a distinct branch, because our method of classification has shown it to differ from other branches. But it is an informal process, carried on at random; so we need not trouble to give it a special name, any more than did our predecessors.

THEAIT. True; its subdivisions are too miscellaneous and unimportant.

STR. That kind of disputation, on the other hand, which is subject to rules of art and deals with right and wrong in themselves, or with any other abstract notion, we usually call 'eristic'.

THEAIT. We do.

STR. Now we find that one sort of eristic *wastes* money, while another *makes* money.

THEAIT. I thoroughly agree.

STR. Then let us try to find the distinctive name of each.

THEAIT. Yes, we must do that.

STR. First as to the kind which leads one to neglect one's own affairs for the pleasure of spending time in that way, but which is carried on in a style that gives no pleasure to the average hearer: this can only be called 'babbling'.

THEAIT. And so it is.

STR. Then what about the opposite kind—the one that *makes* money from private disputes. Take your turn now and see if you can tell me what it is called.

THEAIT. Only one answer is possible: once again and for the fourth time we've run across that extraordinary fellow we've been tracking down—the Sophist. [226]

STR. Exactly. The Sophist then appears to represent the money-making side of eristic, which is derived, as we have just shown, from acquisitive art through contention—fighting—controversy—disputation.

THEAIT. Clear enough.

STR. Do you see the truth of my statement that this creature has many sides? He is not to be caught with one hand, as the saying goes.

THEAIT. Very well then, we must try to get hold of him with both.

STR. We must, indeed, and for all we are worth. Come on, let's follow another of his tracks. Tell me: there are certain terms, are there not, used in connection with a variety of household occupations?

THEAIT. Oh, a great many; but to which of them do you refer?

STR. We speak, for instance, of 'filtering', 'sifting', 'winnowing', 'dividing the warp'.

THEAT. We do.

STR. And again of 'carding', 'combing', 'beating the web' and countless other technicalities with which we are all familiar. Isn't that so?

THEAIT. Yes; but what's your point in bringing up these examples? What are your questions intended to show?

STR. Well, in every one of those I have mentioned some sort of separation is involved.

THEAIT. Yes.

STR. Then in my view they are all branches of one art, which calls for a distinctive name.

THEAIT. What name shall we give it?

STR. The 'separative' art.

THEAIT. Very good.

STR. Now see whether we can recognize two forms of this art.

THEAIT. You ask for some quick thinking on my part!

STR. Not at all. In my first set of examples good is separated from bad, and in the second like from like.

THEAIT. Ah, now I begin to see your point, when you state it in that way.

STR. I know of no common name for this latter kind of separation; but I do know of one for the kind that retains the good and gets rid of the bad.

THEAIT. Tell us what it is.

STR. Every such process, I believe, is recognized universally as a form of 'purification'.

THEAIT. Yes, it is.

STR. And anyone can see that purification is twofold.

THEAIT. So he might, given time. At the moment, quite frankly, I don't.

STR. Well, there are many forms of bodily purification, which may be grouped together under one name.

THEAIT. What forms, and under what name?

STR. I mean (1) the purification of living creatures, that gets rid of (a) impurities *inside* the body (e.g. by gymnastic or medicine), and (*b*) those on the *outside* of the body, [227] which are best left unmentioned and which it is the business of a bath attendant to remove; (2) the purification of inanimate objects, which is the province of laundering and exterior decorating in general, and which, according to its various branches, has been given many names that seem of trifling consequence.

THEAIT. Yes, that is just what they seem.

STR. Exactly, Theaitetos. But on the other hand, our method of classification takes as much account of external cleaning as of medicine, notwithstanding the greater benefit we derive from the latter. It is for the purpose of knowledge that our method tried to draw up a pedigree of all the arts, every one of which, therefore, it holds in equal honour, without invidious comparisons. If a man puts forward generalship as an example of the art of hunting, it considers him not one whit more dignified than another who does the same with flea-catching —generally, in fact, as rather more pretentious!

And now for your question about the name under which we should include all those functions that are directed to the purification of bodies, animate or inanimate. It is no part of our method to look for the neatest and most expressive term; any word or phrase will do, so long as it unites all processes of bodily purification and marks them off clearly from the purification of the soul. The aim of our method so far, if rightly understood, has been to isolate that branch of purification which has to do with the soul.

THEAIT. Oh, I do understand; and I admit there are two separate kinds of purification, one dealing with the soul and another with the body.

STR. Excellent. Now I will ask you to try a further subdivision.

THEAIT. I'll try to help you in whatever way you suggest.

STR. Is it true to say that good and evil in the soul are quite distinct?

THEAIT. Of course.

STR. And we agreed that purification of anything consists in retaining the former and getting rid of whatever is bad.

THEAIT. Yes, we did.

STR. So if we discover any process that removes evil from the soul we shall be right in calling it 'purification'.

THEAIT. Certainly.

STR. Now we must recognize two sorts of evil in the soul.

THEAIT. What are they?

STR. [228] One is comparable with bodily disease, the other with physical deformity.

THEAIT. I don't understand.

STR. Perhaps it has never occurred to you that disease and discord are the same.

THEAIT. Again, I don't know quite what to say.

STR. Maybe you reckon discord as something other than warfare between things naturally akin, due to a process of corruption.

THEAIT. Oh no, I don't.

STR. And what is deformity but a species of disproportion, ugly in whatever it resides?

THEAIT. Nothing else at all.

STR. Now don't we find in the souls of worthless men judgment at variance with desire, courage with pleasure, reason with pain and so forth?

THEAIT. We certainly do.

STR. And yet they must all be naturally akin.

THEAIT. Why, yes.

STR. Then it will be true to say that wickedness is psychological discord or disease.

THEAIT. It will.

STR. Very good. Now consider a missile repeatedly aimed at a certain target, but swerving and missing the mark every single time: are we to attribute this failure to the right proportion of its parts, or rather to their lack of proportion.

THEAIT. To their lack of proportion, obviously.

STR. We know too that a soul's ignorance is always involuntary.

THEAIT. Yes.

STR. And ignorance of course is just the swerving aside of the soul's impulse towards truth; its understanding flies wide of the mark.

THEAIT. Perfectly true.

STR. In which case we must regard an ignorant soul as deformed, that is to say lacking in proportion.

THEAIT. Apparently.

STR. It seems then there are two kinds of evil in the soul. One of them is commonly known as 'wickedness', which is quite clearly a disease.

THEAIT. Yes.

STR. The other is called 'ignorance', which is not, however, readily identified with 'vice' when it occurs only in the soul.

THEAIT. Despite my failure just now to grasp your meaning, I must admit that there are two kinds of evil in the soul; that cowardice, intemperance and injustice must all alike be considered a disease in man; and that ignorance in its infinite variety must be regarded as deformity.

STR. Right. Now physical deformity and disease are the province respectively of two arts, are they not?

THEAIT. Explain.

STR. [229] Deformity is the province of gymnastic, medicine of disease.

THEAIT. Oh yes, I follow.

STR. The most suitable remedy then for overweening pride, unfairness and cowardice, is the justice that chastises, don't you think?

THEAIT. I suppose it is, from the human standpoint at all events.

STR. And can you think of a more appropriate antidote for ignorance in all its forms than instruction?

THEAIT. No, I can't.

STR. Now then, what are we to say: that there is only one sort of instruction, or that it has several branches, of which two are the most important?

THEAIT. Let me see——

STR. I think I know a short cut to the answer.

THEAIT. What is that?

STR. By finding out whether it is possible to subdivide ignorance. If the latter turns out to be twofold, instruction must likewise consist of two parts, each corresponding to one sort of ignorance.

THEAIT. Can you by any chance see what you are looking for?

STR. Well, I think I can at any rate see one large and formidable subdivision. It is distinct from other kinds, and massive as all the rest together.

THEAIT. What is it?

STR. Thinking one knows something when one doesn't. I believe this to be responsible for every single error into which the human mind falls.

THEAIT. True.

STR. I believe, moreover, that this is the only kind of ignorance to be called 'stupidity'.

THEAIT. You are quite correct.

STR. Now what name are we to give that branch of instruction which removes it?

THEAIT. Well, sir, in Athens we call it moral education, as opposed to what I think is known as technical instruction.

STR. That is what most Greeks call it, Theaitetos; but we must go a step further and see whether it is one and indivisible or whether it is capable of division into branches that deserve a special name.

THEAIT. Indeed we must.

STR. It seems to me there *is* a way in which it can be so divided.

THEAIT. On what grounds?

STR. There is verbal instruction with its more severe and its gentler way.

THEAIT. What name shall we give to each?

STR. The time-honoured practice of our ancestors in dealing with their sons is not altogether uncommon nowadays: it consists in alternate [230] reprimand and gentler exhortation, both of which together we shall best call 'admonition'.

THEAIT. That is so.

STR. Some people, on the other hand, appear to have convinced themselves that all inability to understand is involuntary, that a man who believes himself wise is never ready to learn any subject in which he considers himself an expert, and that education by reprimand and exhortation yields little result in return for much pains.

THEAIT. How right they are too.

STR. They ply a man with questions about some matter on which he fancies he has something important to say when in fact he is talking nonsense. Then when such people begin to waver they have no difficulty in marshalling their opinions, collecting them in argument and confronting them with one another, and thereby showing them to contradict one another on the same subjects, at the same moment, from the same standpoint. When the others see this they are annoyed with themselves, and become gentler towards others; so by this means they are delivered from their lofty and obstinate opinion of themselves—of all deliverances the most pleasant to behold and of most permanent advantage to the patient. Just as doctors hold that the body can derive no benefit from taking food until it has been voided of obstructions, so too those who profess to purify the soul maintain that it can never profit by the instruction it receives until cross-examination has reduced its owner to a modest frame of mind by clearing away the vain conceits that are an obstacle to understanding, and thus purged him and convinced him that he knows only what he does know and nothing more.

THEAIT. That is indeed the best and most enlightened state of mind.

STR. For all these reasons, Theaitetos, we must consider cross-examination as the highest and most sovereign form of purification; we must recognize that a man who has never been subjected to the ordeal—though he be the King of Persia himself—is not yet purified of his worst defects; he is therefore uneducated and has grown deformed inasmuch as he lacks unsullied purity of soul, the prerequisite of bliss.

THEAIT. True, true.

STR. Well then, what name shall we give those who practise this art? [231] For my part I hesitate to call them Sophists.

THEAIT. Why?

STR. For fear of attaching too high a dignity to their function.

THEAIT. And yet you have described something that bears a resemblance to that type.

STR. So does the wolf to the dog, the fiercest of animals to the tamest. But caution dictates that we should be on our guard against resemblances; they are very slippery customers. However, let these folk pass for Sophists; if they ever attempt an adequate defence of their territory, the disputed frontier will be of great importance.

THEAIT. Fair enough.

STR. Right. Then let us accept the following pedigree: Separative art—Purification—Purging of the soul as distinct from that of the body—Instruction—Education—Cross-examination. This last, which has drifted into the present argument on a side-wind, banishes the vain conceit of wisdom, and we can let it pass simply under the name high-born Sophistry.

THEAIT. Agreed. But we have already had glimpses of the Sophist in so many guises that for my part I am at a loss to know what one is to say he really is, with any assurance that one is speaking the truth.

STR. I don't wonder you are puzzled. But the Sophist himself must by now be wondering how on earth he can once again slip through the net of our argument; there is a true saying that it is not easy to evade *all* the wrestler's holds. So now, if ever, we must pounce on him.

THEAIT. I'm with you.

STR. First, then, let us stop for a breather, and meanwhile let us recall in just how many guises the Sophist has appeared. First, I think, we saw him as the paid hunter of rich young men.

THEAIT. Yes.

STR. And secondly as a merchant, so to speak, of learning as food for the soul.

THEAIT. Certainly.

STR. Thirdly, he turned up as a retail dealer in the same commodities, didn't he?

THEAIT. Yes; and fourthly as selling the products of his own manufacture.

STR. You have a good memory; but I myself will remind you of his fifth appearance. It was as an athlete in debate, making his own that subdivision of contention which we have called the art of eristic.

THEAIT. That's right.

STR. The sixth appearance was a little hazy; all the same, we agreed to allow his claim as a purifier of the soul from conceits that are an obstacle to understanding.

THEAIT. Exactly.

STR. [232] Has it occurred to you that, if someone is called after a single art but appears to be master of several, this appearance is not genuine? If any particular art strikes you in that way it is evidently because you have no clear view of that one of its features in which all these kinds of skill meet, and therefore you call a man who possesses them by many names rather than by one.

THEAIT. No doubt that is about the truth of the matter.

STR. Well then, we must be on the alert against any such thing happening to us in our inquiry. We may start by going back to one of those features we recognized in the Sophist—one that impressed me particularly as indicating his character.

THEAIT. What was that?

STR. Did we not say that he was a controversialist?

THEAIT. Yes.

STR. And also that he appears as one who instructs others in controversy?

THEAIT. We did.

STR. Let us then ask ourselves in what field are such people found as controversialists. Here perhaps is the way to the heart of this matter: does the competence of their pupils extend to things divine that no common eye beholds? What do you think?

THEAIT. It is said to do so, at all events.

STR. And how about the visible world of sky and earth and so forth?

THEAIT. Oh yes, to that as well.

STR. And in private company, whenever any general statement is made on the subject of becoming or reality, we know full well how cleverly they can dispute it and enable others to do likewise. Isn't that so?

THEAIT. Indeed it is.

STR. And again, don't they promise to produce men capable of debating laws and public affairs in general?

THEAIT. They do; otherwise hardly anyone would take part in their discussions.

STR. As for the crafts in general and each one in particular, the arguments to be used in controversy with any practising craftsmen have been published and widely circulated for all who may care to learn.

THEAIT. I suppose you are referring to Protagoras' books on wrestling and other arts.

STR. Yes, my good friend, and on many other subjects. The art of controversy in fact seems to claim competence for disputation on any and every subject.

THEAIT. There certainly appears to be little or nothing of which it does not take account.

STR. But do you really believe that is possible? You young people may perhaps see more clearly; we older men have poor sight.

THEAIT. [233] Is what possible? What exactly am I supposed to see? I don't quite understand your question.

STR. I mean, is it possible for any man to know everything?

THEAIT. Indeed, sir, if that were possible our race would be more than happy.

STR. Then if a man without knowledge enters into controversy with one who knows, how can there be anything worth while in what he says?

THEAIT. There can't be.

STR. In that case, what is so extraordinary about this magical power of Sophistry?

THEAIT. In what respect?

STR. I mean, how are they able to create in the minds of young men an illusion that they are the wisest of mortals on every subject? For clearly unless they were in the right as controversialists or appeared to be so in the eyes of their youthful hearers, and unless that appearance strengthened the belief that they are wise because they can dispute, then, to quote your own words, it is difficult to see why anyone should be anxious to pay for tuition in this subject.

THEAIT. Difficult it certainly is.

STR. But in point of fact there is such a demand.

THEAIT. Very much so.

STR. That, I imagine, is because the Sophists are believed to have specialized knowledge of the matters about which they dispute.

THEAIT. Most probably.

STR. And, as we said, there is no subject that escapes their disputation.

THEAIT. None at all.

STR. Then their pupils look upon them as wise in every subject.

THEAIT. Certainly.

STR. Although they are not really so; for that, we have agreed, is quite impossible.

THEAIT. Of course it's impossible.

STR. In other words the Sophist has turned out to possess a kind of attributed knowledge on all subjects, but not the real thing.

THEAIT. I quite agree; and that is probably the truest thing yet said about him.

STR. Let us, then, have recourse to an analogy that will make his position clearer.

THEAIT. What sort of analogy?

STR. I will tell you. Try to give me your undivided attention when answering.

THEAIT. Ask away.

STR. Suppose a man claimed to know, not how to speak or dispute about everything, but how to do, i.e. to produce, all things by a single art.

THEAIT. What do you mean by 'all things'?

STR. There now, you fail to grasp my meaning at the very start! So you don't understand the phrase 'all things'.

THEAIT. No.

STR. I mean it to cover you and me, the whole animal kingdom, and every plant as well.

THEAIT. I see; go on.

STR. Well suppose a man undertook to produce you and me and all creatures.

THEAIT. [234] What sort of production have you in mind? You can't be thinking of him as some kind of farmer, because you referred to him as producing animals as well.

STR. Oh yes, and sea and earth, sky and gods, and everything else into the bargain. Furthermore, having produced each one of them by lifting his little finger he sells them for quite a small sum.

THEAIT. You mean in some kind of game?

STR. Well, a man who says he knows everything and can teach it to another for a small fee in a very short time can hardly be taken seriously.

THEAIT. No, that's true.

STR. And can you think of any more skilful or entertaining sort of game than imitation?

THEAIT. No; when you consider that one sort, with all its possible implications, it covers an enormous variety.

STR. Well, this much we know about the man who professes to be able, by virtue of a single art, to produce all things: if he employs his brush to create representations which have the same names as real things, he will be able to deceive the ingenuous minds of children, by showing them his pictures at a distance, into believing him capable of producing, *in actual fact*, anything he chooses to make.

THEAIT. Certainly.

STR. Then may we not expect to find a corresponding art in the domain of speech, whereby it is possible to beguile young men, who are still a long way off from the reality of things, by means of words that deceive the ear, displaying every sort of image in a shadow-play of talk, with the result that they think they hear the truth and that the speaker is the wisest of mortals in every field?

THEAIT. I think it very likely there is some such art.

STR. With the passage of time these young pupils grow older and, coming into closer touch with realities, are led by experience to apprehend things clearly as they are. Surely at this point most of them will put away their earlier beliefs; so that what seemed important will now appear trivial and what seemed easy, difficult, and all the illusions begotten in discourse will be completely overthrown by the stark realities of life from day to day.

THEAIT. Yes, that is true, so far as I can see at my age; but I suppose I'm one of those who are still a long way off.

STR. And that is exactly why all of us here are trying, and will go on trying, to bring you as near the realities as possible without your having first-hand experience. But as regards the Sophist: [235] are we now satisfied that he is a kind of illusionist, who imitates real things; or have we still a lurking suspicion he may possess genuine knowledge of all those things which he seems able to make the subject of dispute?

THEAIT. How can he, sir? It is obvious enough from what has been said that he is one of those whose business is mere entertainment.

STR. Then he may be classed as an illusionist—in other words as an imitator of some sort.

THEAIT. Certainly he may.

STR. Very good then, it is now up to us to see that our quarry does not get away again. It is not untrue to say we have him in the kind of net provided by argument for hunting of this sort. He will never wriggle out of this.

THEAIT. Out of what?

STR. From his belonging to the class of illusionists.

THEAIT. I'm with you so far.

STR. That means we must quarter the ground without further delay by dividing the art of Image-making; then if we go down into our enclosure and immediately find the Sophist at bay, we must arrest him on a warrant issued by King Reason, report his capture and deliver him to His Majesty. But if he finds cover among the various subdivisions of the imitative art, we must keep up the chase by repeatedly quartering the area in which he lurks until we catch him. It is quite certain that neither he nor any other kind of creature will ever boast of having eluded so close and so comprehensive a process of investigation.

THEAIT. You are right; that's what we must do.

STR. Following the same analytical method as before, I seem once again to recognize two forms of Imitation; but as yet I can't quite make out in which of them the type of person we seek to identify is to be found.

THEAIT. Never mind. First distinguish the two forms and tell us what they are.

STR. One art that I see in Imitation is 'Likeness-making'. You have a perfect example of this when an artist produces a copy that follows the proportions of the original in length, breadth and depth, and gives each part of it its proper colour.

THEAIT. But isn't that what all imitators try to do?

STR. Not those sculptors and painters who work on a colossal scale. If they reproduced the true proportions of a well-made figure, the upper parts would, as you know, [236] look too small and the lower too large, because we see the former at a distance and the latter close at hand.

THEAIT. Perfectly true.

STR. Artists then, in point of fact, leave truth to look after itself, and give the images they make, not the proportions of the original, but those which will *appear* beautiful. Isn't that so?

THEAIT. It is.

STR. The first kind of image, then, being like the original, may fairly be called a likeness.

THEAIT. Yes.

STR. And the corresponding branch of the art of imitation may be given the name of Likeness-making, which we used a moment or two ago.

THEAIT. Quite.

STR. Now what shall we call the class of image which seems to

be a likeness of a well-made figure only because it is viewed at
a deceptive angle, but which to a man whose vision was fully
adapted to so large an object would not even resemble the
original of which it claims to be a copy? Since it *appears* to
be a likeness, without *being* so, may we perhaps call it a
'semblance'?

THEAIT. Just the word.

STR. And this is a very comprehensive class, both in the field of
painting and in all kinds of imitation.

THEAIT. It certainly is.

STR. The most appropriate name, therefore, for the art which
creates a semblance, as distinct from a likeness, will be
Semblance-making, will it not?

THEAIT. Yes indeed.

STR. There, then, you have the two forms of image-making to
which I referred just now: likeness-making and semblance-
making.

THEAIT. I follow.

STR. Yet even now I cannot quite see the solution to that doubt
of mine: in which of the two divisions we should place the
Sophist. It is indeed extraordinarily hard to get a clear view of
the fellow; this very moment, and with consummate skill, he
has taken refuge in a class which defies exploration.

THEAIT. So it seems.

STR. You agree with me, but do you understand what class I
mean, or has the stream of argument swept you along through
sheer force of habit to so ready an assent?

THEAIT. How? To what do you refer?

STR. To tell you the truth, my friend, we have reached an
extremely difficult problem. This 'appearing' or 'seeming'
without actually 'being', and the saying of things which are
not in fact true—all these expressions are, and always have
been, matters of the utmost obscurity. It is mighty hard,
Theaitetos, to find words in which one can rightly say or
think that falsehoods have real existence, without the very
[237] speaking of such words involving us in contradiction.

THEAIT. Why is that?

STR. The statement implies a daring assumption that what is not
has being; for that is precisely what the existence of a false-
hood implies. But when we were lads, dear boy, the great

Parmenides consistently proclaimed the impossibility of this; time and again he would quote his own poem:

> Never shall this be proved, that things which are not, are;
> And do thou, in thy inquiry, deter thy thought from this way.

Such is his testimony, and the surest way of extracting an admission of the truth will be to subject the statement itself to a mild dose of torture. So if it's all the same to you, let us make a start by examining the proposition on its own merits.

THEAIT. Just as you please. Choose whatever you think the most satisfactory form of argument, and take me along with you.

STR. Very good. Tell me now: do we or do we not hesitate to use the phrase 'that which has no sort of being'.

THEAIT. Of course we don't.

STR. Then apart from eristic debate and mere playing with words, imagine that one of us were pressed to concentrate his mind and tell the company to what this phrase, 'that which is not', can be applied. Of what or what sort of thing do you think he would use it himself, and what would the questioner take him to indicate?

THEAIT. That is a difficult question; you can scarcely expect a fellow like me to find the answer.

STR. Well, one thing at any rate is clear: we cannot apply the term 'what is not' to anything that exists.

THEAIT. Indeed no.

STR. And that being so, it cannot properly be applied to 'something'.

THEAIT. Why not?

STR. Surely it is obvious that this word 'something' is always used of a thing that exists. It cannot be used just by itself, a naked object, so to speak, isolated from everything that exists, can it?

THEAIT. No.

STR. Do you say 'No' because you realize that to speak of 'something' is to speak of 'some *one* thing'?

THEAIT. Yes.

STR. Because you will allow that 'something' denotes one thing, just as 'some things' denotes two or more things?

THEAIT. Certainly.

STR. It seems then to follow inevitably that to speak of what is not 'something' is to speak of no thing whatever.

THEAIT. Yes, inevitably.

STR. Surely we cannot even admit that in such a case a man says anything significant, though he may be speaking of nothing. Surely we must assert that he is talking mere nonsense when he pronounces the words 'a thing that is not'.

THEAIT. There the argument reaches a point of almost insoluble difficulty.

STR. [238] 'Boast not too soon!' We have still, my friend, to face the greatest of all difficulties—and indeed the first, striking as it does at the very root of the matter.

THEAIT. How do you mean? Don't fight shy of telling me.

STR. When a thing exists, something else that exists may, presumably, be attributed to it.

THEAIT. Of course.

STR. But are we entitled to say that something which exists can be attributed to what has no existence?

THEAIT. Certainly not.

STR. Well, number generally is to be reckoned among things that exist.

THEAIT. Yes, that, if anything, must be held to do so.

STR. In which case we must not even attempt the attribution of either plurality or unity in number to the non-existent.

THEAIT. Our argument would certainly appear to forbid it.

STR. How then can anyone utter the words 'things which are not' or 'that which is not', or even entertain a notion of such, apart from number?

THEAIT. How do you mean?

STR. When we speak of 'things that are not', are we not attempting the attribution of plurality?

THEAIT. Yes.

STR. And unity when we speak of 'that which is not'?

THEAIT. Clearly.

STR. And yet we maintain that it is neither correct nor in any way justifiable to attempt the attributing of a non-existent to something that exists.

THEAIT. Very true.

STR. Then you see what follows: one cannot rightfully utter the words, or speak or think of what has absolutely no existence; it is beyond conception, speech, utterance or expression.

THEAIT. That is perfectly correct.

STR. Then perhaps I was mistaken just now in saying I was going to propound the greatest difficulty involved; we can state another which is even worse.

THEAIT. What is that?

STR. Why, my dear fellow, do not the very phrases I have just been using show that the non-existent brings even one who would refute it to such a pass that as soon as he attempts to do so he is obliged to contradict himself?

THEAIT. How do you mean? Explain more clearly.

STR. Don't look to me for enlightenment. I declared that the non-existent could never be associated with unity or plurality, and yet just now—an instant ago, in fact—I spoke of it as one thing by saying '*the* non-existent'. You see my point?

THEAIT. Yes.

STR. And again not long ago I spoke of its *being* a thing beyond speech, utterance or expression. Do you follow?

THEAIT. Yes, of course.

STR. Very well, in trying to attach that participle 'being' to it, [239] was I not contradicting what I said before?

THEAIT. Evidently.

STR. Next, in attaching that particular form of the definite article was I not treating it as singular?

THEAIT. Yes.

STR. And when I spoke of it as 'a thing beyond expression, speech or utterance', I did so as if with reference to a single thing.

THEAIT. Certainly you did.

STR. We have agreed, on the other hand, that one should not, strictly speaking, designate it either as one thing or as many, or even call it 'it' at all; for the use even of this designation means attributing to it the character of singleness.

THEAIT. Exactly.

STR. In that case what is there left to be said for me? I shall be found at a disadvantage from start to finish in my criticism of the non-existent. Consequently, as I said, we must not look for an adequate description of the non-existent in anything *I* have to say; we must rely upon you for that. Come along.

THEAIT. But I——

STR. Now, now, you are a young man; show some spirit, and do your best. Try to describe the non-existent in some correct formula, without attributing to it either being, unity or plurality.

THEAIT. Considering your own fate, I should have to be more than ambitious before undertaking such a task.

STR. Well, if you agree, let's not bother about our two selves; until we run across someone who can perform this feat, let us say that the Sophist, with remarkable cunning, has found an inaccessible hiding-place.

THEAIT. It certainly looks like it.

STR. Consequently if we are going to say he possesses the art of 'semblance-making', he will easily take advantage of these our methods of argument in this way to counter-attack and use them against us. When we call him an image-maker he will inquire what exactly we mean by an image. So we must ask ourselves, Theaitetos, how we are to answer the fellow's challenge.

THEAIT. Obviously we shall say we mean images in water or in mirrors, as well as paintings, statues and everything else of that kind.

STR. Ah, Theaitetos, it's clear you've never met a Sophist!

THEAIT. What makes you think so?

STR. He will behave as though his eyes were shut or he had no eyes at all?

THEAIT. How so?

STR. When you give him an answer of that sort, referring him to something in a mirror or a work of art, he will laugh at your words, as implying that he can see. [240] He will pretend to know nothing about mirrors or water, or even about eyesight, and will question you exclusively upon what can be gathered from discourse.

THEAIT. What is that?

STR. The character common to all these things, which you say are many but which you saw fit to call by one name when you employed the word 'image' as a single term applicable to them all. Say what it is then, and stand your ground. Don't yield the man an inch.

THEAIT. Well, sir, how can one define an image, except as another thing of the same kind, copied from a real original?

STR. What do you mean by 'of the same kind'—another real thing, or what?

THEAIT. No, not real of course, but *like* it.

STR. Meaning by 'real' a thing that actually exists?

THEAIT. Quite.

STR. And by 'not real' the opposite of real?

THEAIT. Naturally.

STR. Then by 'like' you signify something that has no real existence, if you are going to call it 'not real'.

THEAIT. It does have some kind of existence.

STR. But not real existence, according to what you say.

THEAIT. No, except that it is really a likeness.

STR. Therefore, although it has no real existence, it really *is* what we call a likeness?

THEAIT. Strange to say the real does seem to have become entangled in some such manner with the unreal.

STR. Yes, most extraordinary. You see that once again, by combining them in this way, our hydra-headed Sophist has driven us into admitting that 'what is not' has some kind of being.

THEAIT. Yes, I do.

STR. Well, how can we possibly, I wonder, define his art without contradicting ourselves?

THEAIT. How do you mean, contradicting?

STR. When we say he deceives with that 'semblance' of which we spoke and that his art is one of deception, shall we mean that his art misleads our minds into thinking what is false, or what?

THEAIT. There is surely nothing else we could mean?

STR. And false thinking, in turn, will be thinking things contrary to the things that are, won't it?

THEAIT. Yes.

STR. By false thinking then you mean thinking things that are not?

THEAIT. Obviously.

STR. Does that mean thinking that things which are not, are not, or that things which have no existence at all in some way are?

THEAIT. It must at least mean thinking that things which are not, are in some way; unless no statement can ever be described as in the slightest degree erroneous.

STR. And also of course thinking that things which certainly are, are not in any way whatever?

THEAIT. Yes.

STR. This too is error?

THEAIT. It is.

STR. And a false statement, I suppose, is to be regarded likewise, [241] as stating that things which are, are not, and vice versa.

THEAIT. Yes; in what other way could a statement be false?

STR. Virtually in no other way. But our Sophist will say No to that, on the ground that no intelligent person could accept it in the light of our earlier admissions. Do we understand, Theaitetos, to what he is referring?

THEAIT. Of course we understand. He will accuse us of contradicting what we said only a little while ago, when we dare to say that falsehoods exist in thoughts and in statements; for we are obliged over and over again to attribute what exists to what does not, despite our having just admitted that this is absolutely impossible.

STR. You do well to remind me. But it is now time to consider what should be done about the Sophist; for you see how wide we open the door to many awkward objections if we conduct our search by classifying his art with that of illusionists and creators of error.

THEAIT. I do.

STR. Objections of that kind are almost innumerable and we have mentioned only a very few of them.

THEAIT. Like that, it seems quite impossible to catch the Sophist.

STR. What, are we then to despair and call off the hunt?

THEAIT. I'm not saying we should, as long as we have the smallest chance of being able to get our hands on the fellow by some means or other.

STR. You will bear with me then, and, as you now say, be satisfied if we manage to free ourselves even partially from the grip of so cogent an argument?

THEAIT. Certainly I will.

STR. Well, I have another and still more urgent request.

THEAIT. What is it?

STR. That you will not think I am turning into a sort of parricide.

THEAIT. What on earth do you mean?

STR. It will be necessary, by way of self-defence, to stretch

Parmenides' dictum on the rack. He is my spiritual father; but we shall have to use violence in order to establish that what is not, in some sense is, and vice versa.

THEAIT. Our argument clearly requires us to take a stand on that.

STR. Even a blind man, as they say, could see as much. These propositions must be either disproved or accepted; otherwise a man who talks about false statements or false judgments as being 'images' or 'likenesses' or 'copies' or 'semblances', or about any of the arts that have to do with such things, will almost inevitably contradict himself and thereby hold himself up to ridicule.

THEAIT. True enough.

STR. [242] For this reason we must now pluck up courage and attack the Founder's dictum, or else, if we cannot bring ourselves to do so, abandon the whole subject for good and all.

THEAIT. Oh no, nothing whatever must deter us.

STR. In that case, and for the third time, I want to ask you a small favour.

THEAIT. Ask away.

STR. I told you a little while ago, did I not, that on this point I have never been able to accomplish the task of refutation, and that I remain so incapable to this hour?

THEAIT. Yes, you told me that.

STR. Well, I'm afraid such an admission may make you think me crazy, shifting my position backward and forward at every turn. It is for your sake that we shall attempt a refutation of the dictum, if it is at all possible to do so.

THEAIT. I shall certainly never look upon you as guilty of the least impropriety if you go ahead with your refutation and proof. You need have no qualms whatever so far as that is concerned.

STR. Come then, what's the best point from which to start upon so perilous a journey? I believe I know beyond any doubt the road we shall have to take.

THEAIT. What road is that?

STR. We must begin by studying things that are at present supposed to be perfectly clear; it may be that in point of fact we are in some confusion about them and jump to conclusions too readily on the assumption that we understand them well enough.

THEAIT. Tell us more precisely what you mean.

STR. It seems to me that not only Parmenides but all those who have undertaken to decide how many real things there are, and the nature of those things, have given us their view in a somewhat discourteous fashion.

THEAIT. How so?

STR. Each and all of them appear to be telling us a story, as if we were mere children. One says there are three real things, some of which are now, so to speak, at war among themselves, and then, having settled their differences, proceed to marriage and the begetting and rearing of children. According to another there are two—Moist and Dry, or Hot and Cold— whom he pairs off as husband and wife. The Eleatic school, in my part of the world, looking back to Xenophanes and even earlier, base their account on the assumption that what we call 'all things' are really one thing. Later, certain Muses in Ionia and Sicily came to the conclusion that it was safest to combine the two accounts and say that the real is both many and one, being held together by Strife and Love. The stricter of these Muses [1] hold that in parting asunder it is always being drawn together. The milder [2] relax the rule that such is always the case: they maintain that the universe is now one and at peace through the power of Love [243] and now many and at variance with itself owing to some kind of Strife. It is not easy to tell whether or not any of these theories is correct, and it would be unfair of us to indulge in carping criticism of men whose brilliant reputations have endured through the ages. But one assertion can be made without offence.

THEAIT. What is that?

STR. That they have made insufficient allowance for ordinary people like ourselves by talking over our heads. Each school pursues its own way to the bitter end, regardless of whether or not we can follow its argument or get left behind.

THEAIT. How do you mean?

STR. When one of them in discourse uses the expressions 'there really are' or 'have come to be' or 'are coming to be' 'many things' or 'one thing' or 'two', or when another speaks of 'Hot being mixed with Cold', 'combining' and 'separating',

[1] The school of Heracleitos (Ionia).
[2] Empedocles (Sicily).

do you honestly, Theaitetos, understand a word of what they say? Personally, when I was a younger man I used to think I understood quite clearly when someone spoke of this thing which now perplexes us—'the unreal'. But now you see the difficulty in which we find ourselves on that subject.

THEAIT. Yes, I do.

STR. It may be then that our minds are equally confused about reality. We claim that the real does not worry us and that we understand the word when it is spoken (though we may not be able to grasp the unreal), when all the time perhaps we are just as much at sea about both.

THEAIT. Maybe.

STR. And the same can be said of those other expressions which I have just noted.

THEAIT. Certainly.

STR. We may have occasion later on to consider the whole series. We must start now with the most important, i.e. the most fundamental of them all.

THEAIT. Which——? Oh, of course, you mean we should begin by studying 'reality' and finding out what those who use the word believe it signifies?

STR. You've hit the nail right on the head, Theaitetos; that is precisely the method I say we must follow. Let us imagine representatives of every school here before us, and ask them this question: 'Now then, you who say that Hot and Cold or some such pair really are all things, what exactly do you intend to convey by this expression you apply to both when you say that *both are* real or *each* of them *is* real? How are we to understand this "reality" of which you speak? Are we to suppose it is a third thing alongside the other two, and that the All is no longer, as you say, two things, but three? For surely you don't give the name "reality" to one of the two and then say both alike are real; for in that case there will be only one thing (either one or other of the two) and not two.'

THEAIT. They will agree to that.

STR. 'Well then, do you intend to give the name "reality" to the pair of them?'

THEAIT. To that they will answer: 'Perhaps'.

STR. [244] 'Come, gentlemen,' we shall reply, 'even then you will clearly be referring to the two things as one.'

THEAIT. Perfectly right.

STR. 'We are altogether at a loss then, and you must tell us plainly what you mean when you utter the word "real". Clearly you must be well aware of what you mean, whereas we, who formerly imagined we knew, are now bewildered. First, therefore, throw some light on this particular point, so that we may not fancy we understand what you tell us, when the exact opposite is the case.'

If we thus approach these people and anyone else who maintains that the All is more than one thing, shall we, my friend, be overstepping the mark at all?

THEAIT. Not in the least.

STR. And what about those who say that the All is one thing: must we not do our best to discover what *they* mean by 'reality'?

THEAIT. Indeed we must.

STR. Then let them answer this question: 'You say, don't you, that there is only one thing?' They will of course reply: 'We do.'

THEAIT. Yes.

STR. 'And there is something which you call "real"?'

THEAIT. Their answer will be in the affirmative.

STR. 'Is it the same thing as that which you call "one"? Do you apply two names to the same thing, or what?'

THEAIT. How will they reply to that?

STR. Obviously, Theaitetos, it is not the easiest thing in the world for one who adopts their fundamental proposition to answer this latest question or any other.

THEAIT. Why not?

STR. To start with, no intelligent person admits the existence of two names after postulating that there is no more than one thing.

THEAIT. Of course.

STR. Moreover it is just as ridiculous to admit the statement that a name has any existence, when that is inexplicable.

THEAIT. Inexplicable? In what way?

STR. Well, anyone who assumes that the name is different from the thing is surely speaking of two things.

THEAIT. Yes.

STR. If he maintains, on the other hand, that the name is identical with the thing, either he will be obliged to say it is not the name of anything, or if he says it is the name of something, the name will turn out to be merely a name of a name and of nothing else.

THEAIT. Exactly.[1]

STR. And what about 'the whole'? Will they declare it to be other than the 'one real thing' or identical therewith?

THEAIT. Identical of course; they already say as much.

STR. Then if the 'one real thing' is a whole—as indeed Parmenides says: 'Every way like the mass of a perfect sphere, evenly poised from the centre in every direction; for neither more nor less must needs be here than there'—then the real being, like that, has a middle and extremities, and therefore must certainly have parts. Am I right?

THEAIT. Yes indeed.

STR. [245] Now if a thing is divided into parts, there is no reason why it should not have unity by virtue of its being an aggregate of those parts, and be thus one, i.e. as a sum or whole.

THEAIT. I quite agree.

STR. It is impossible, however, for a thing in the condition described to be absolute Unity, isn't it?

THEAIT. Why?

STR. Well surely Unity in the true sense, i.e. as properly defined, must be altogether devoid of parts.

THEAIT. Yes, it must.

STR. But the sort of thing now in question, consisting of a number of parts, will not fit that definition.

THEAIT. I understand.

STR. Then (1) is the Real one and a whole in the sense that it has the property of unity, or (2) are we to say that it is in no sense a whole?

THEAIT. You offer a hard choice.

STR. Too true. For if we admit the first of those propositions the Real will clearly not be identical with Unity, and the All will be more than one.

THEAIT. Yes.

STR. And again if we admit the second but at the same time

[1] The text of the Stranger's next remark is hopelessly corrupt and unnecessary to the argument. It has therefore been omitted together with Theaitetos' reply.

assert (*a*) that Wholeness itself is real, it will follow that the Real falls short of itself.

THEAIT. Indeed it will.

STR. So this line of argument too shows that the Real, being devoid of reality, will not be a thing that is.

THEAIT. Yes.

STR. Moreover, once again the All will be more than one, because Reality and Wholeness will each be found to have its own distinct nature.

THEAIT. Yes.

STR. On the other hand if, while still admitting the second proposition, we say (*b*) that there is absolutely no such thing as Wholeness, not only will the same things be true of the Real, but it will also be true to say that, besides not being a truly existent thing, it can never even become such.

THEAIT. Why not?

STR. Whenever a thing reaches the stage of being, it has then and there come to be as a whole; so unless you reckon unity or wholeness among real things, you cannot very well speak either of 'being' or of 'coming into being' as having existence.

THEAIT. There seems no doubt at all about that.

STR. Nor indeed can that which is not a whole have any definite quantity; for anything having a definite quantity must amount to that quantity, whatever it be, *as a whole*.

THEAIT. Precisely.

STR. And if you say that the real is either two things or only one, you will be face to face with countless other problems, each hopelessly insoluble.

THEAIT. That is pretty clear from those which have just cropped up. One leads to another, each carrying us further into an increasingly complicated maze of doubt about every theory as it is put forward.

STR. We have not considered all those who give an exact account of what is real or unreal, but let this suffice. Now we must deal with those who put the matter differently, so that, from a complete review of all philosophers, we may see that reality is just as hard to define as non-reality.

THEAIT. Very well, we had better move on to them.

STR. [246] And what do we find? Why, something like a Battle of Gods and Giants fought over the subject of reality.

THEAIT. How so?

STR. One group is trying to drag down everything to earth from heaven and the invisible, literally grasping rocks and trees in their hands; for they lay hold of all such things and stoutly maintain that real existence belongs only to what can be touched and handled. They define reality as identical with body, and if one of their opponents asserts that anything incorporeal is real, they show the utmost contempt and will not hear another word.

THEAIT. Terrible fellows! I myself have already come across a good number of such people.

STR. Yes, and consequently their adversaries are very cautious in defending their position somewhere up above in the invisible world, urging for all they are worth that true reality consists in certain intelligible and incorporeal Forms. Their arguments annihilate those material bodies advanced by their opponents, and what the latter put forward as true reality they call, not real being, but a kind of moving process of becoming. On this question, Theaitetos, there is always a tremendous battle in progress between the two sides.

THEAIT. True.

STR. Let us then try to get from each party in turn some account of the reality they proclaim.

THEAIT. How shall we do that?

STR. Such an account will be comparatively easy to obtain from those who place reality in Forms, because they are more civilized; but not so readily (if at all) forthcoming from those whose aim is to drag everything down to the material level. However I think I know the right way to approach them.

THEAIT. What is that?

STR. Preferably, if it were at all possible, to effect an improvement in their character; but if this cannot be done, we must *imagine* this improvement and assume them willing to answer our questions in a more law-abiding spirit. The better a man's character the more force there is in any agreement one makes with him. However, we are less concerned with the character of these people than with our search for the truth.

THEAIT. Quite right.

STR. Assuming such an improvement, now tell these people to

hand you their replies to my questions so that you can do the
answering for them.

THEAIT. I will.

STR. We should like to know, then, whether they admit there is
such a thing as a mortal living creature.

THEAIT. Naturally they do.

STR. And will they agree that it is a body animated by a soul?

THEAIT. Certainly.

STR. Recognizing the soul as something real?

THEAIT. [247] Yes.

STR. Next, will they allow that one soul is just and another
unjust, one wise and another foolish?

THEAIT. Of course.

STR. And that any soul comes to be just or wise (or the reverse)
by the possession of justice or wisdom (or the reverse) which
is present in it?

THEAIT. Again the answer is Yes.

STR. But surely they will concede that whatever is capable of
coming to be present or absent is certainly a real thing.

THEAIT. Yes.

STR. Allowing then that justice or wisdom, or any other kind of
goodness or badness, is real, and also that a soul in which they
come to exist is real, do they hold that any of these things can
be seen and touched, or that they are all invisible?

THEAIT. They are pretty well bound to say that none of them is
visible.

STR. And do they honestly suggest that anything invisible has a
body?

THEAIT. There are two sides to that question, and they do not
answer it without drawing a distinction. The soul itself, in
their view, does have a sort of body; but as regards wisdom
and the various other things about which you asked, they do
not venture either to conclude that they have no place in the
order of reality or to insist that all of them are bodies.

STR. That, Theaitetos, is clear evidence of an improvement in
their character. The Giants among them, true earth-born sons
of the dragon breed, would stick at nothing; they would cling
to the assertion that whatever they cannot grasp tightly in
their hands is absolutely nothing at all.

THEAIT. That is a fair summary of their attitude.

STR. Then let us ask them some more questions; we shall be satisfied if they are ready to admit that even the smallest particle of reality is incorporeal. Here we go now: when they say that (a) these incorporeal things and (b) other things, which have body, are alike 'real', what character do they look upon as covering both (a) and (b)? In case they cannot find an answer to that, please ask them whether they would allow us to put forward a description of the real in the hope that it may prove acceptable.

THEAIT. Perhaps we shall be able to tell you, if you will let us know what that description is.

STR. Well, I suggest that real being belongs to anything that is so constituted as to possess any sort of power either to produce a change in anything else or to be affected, however slightly, even by the most inconsiderable agent, though it be only once. I am proposing that the mark whereby to distinguish real things is nothing else than active and passive potency.

THEAIT. Well, they accept that, because here and now they can think of nothing better to suggest.

STR. Fair enough; later on perhaps both they and we may take a different view. For the present then [248] let us take it that this agreement stands as between ourselves and the one school.

THEAIT. It does.

STR. Good; now let us approach the other school, those who uphold the existence of Forms. I will invite you once again to answer on their behalf.

THEAIT. I'll do that.

STR. Is it not true that you distinguish between 'Becoming' and 'Real being' and speak of them as separate?

THEAIT. Yes.

STR. And you say that our association with Becoming is by means of the body through sense, and with Real being by means of the soul through reflection. You maintain further that Real being is permanently unchanging, whereas Becoming varies from one moment to the next.

THEAIT. We do.

STR. Splendid! But how are we to understand your use of the word 'association', which you apply in both cases? Surely you mean what we just now described.

THEAIT. What was that?

STR. The experiencing or the production of an effect, arising, in consequence of some potency, from an encounter of two things. Maybe, Theaitetos, you don't quite get their reply; perhaps I can, though—I'm used to them.

THEAIT. What do they say?

STR. They reject our proposition about reality which we put up to the earth-born Giants a little while ago.

THEAIT. Would you mind repeating it?

STR. Don't you remember: we established as a satisfactory mark of real things the presence in a thing of the power of being acted upon or of acting in relation to something, no matter how inconsiderable it may be.

THEAIT. Ah yes.

STR. Well, to this they reply that Becoming is endowed with active and passive potency, but that neither is compatible with Real being.

THEAIT. Isn't there something in what they say?

STR. Yes, something to which we in turn must reply with a request for further information. Do they agree also that the soul knows and Real being is known?

THEAIT. They do indeed.

STR. Well, do you acknowledge that knowing or being known is (a) an action, or is it (b) experiencing an effect, or (c) both? Or is one of them (b) and the other (a)? Or does neither of them fall under any of these three heads?

THEAIT. The answer is clearly that neither falls under any of the three; otherwise those whom I represent would be going back upon what they said earlier.

STR. I see what you mean. They would be saying this: 'If knowing is to be acting on something, then what is known must necessarily be affected thereby; in which case Reality, when being known by the act of knowing, must, in so far as it is known, be changed by the mere fact of its being thus affected; and that, we say, cannot happen to the changeless.'

THEAIT. Precisely.

STR. God above! Are we honestly going to be so easily convinced that there is no place for change, life, soul or understanding in what is perfectly real: [249] that what is perfectly real neither lives nor thinks, but stands immutable, solemn and remote?

THEAIT. That, sir, would be a curious admission.

STR. But are we entitled to say it has intelligence without life?

THEAIT. Hardly.

STR. Then if we grant that it contains both, can we deny it soul in which they reside?

THEAIT. No; that is the only way it could possess them.

STR. Very good. Now if we say it is endowed with intelligence, life and soul, can we maintain that this living thing remains immobile and absolutely changeless?

THEAIT. Oh no, that is surely unreasonable.

STR. So it must be allowed that what changes and change itself are real things.

THEAIT. Certainly it must.

STR. It follows, however, Theaitetos, that, if all things are unchangeable intelligence cannot really exist anywhere in anything with regard to any object whatever.

THEAIT. Exactly.

STR. And on the other hand, if we admit that all things are in flux and changing, on that theory we shall likewise be excluding intelligence from the order of real things.

THEAIT. How so?

STR. Do you think that, without a state of rest, there could ever be anything that remains permanently in the same condition and in the same respects?

THEAIT. Indeed I don't.

STR. Right; and without these objects can you picture intelligence existing or coming into existence anywhere?

THEAIT. I certainly can't.

STR. Well then, we shall have to muster all the forces of reason against anyone who supports any assertion about anything while doing away with knowledge, understanding or intelligence.

THEAIT. Most definitely.

STR. It seems, in consequence, that the philosopher, who values knowledge and so forth above all else, has one sovereign duty. He must refuse to accept from the advocates either of the One or of the many Forms the dogma that all Reality is changeless; nor must he listen to the other school which depicts Reality as everywhere changing. Echoing the children's prayer, he must

pronounce Reality or the sum of things to be both at once [1]—
all that is unchangeable and all that is undergoing change.

THEAIT. Very true.

STR. At last then, by means of our description, we seem to have
reality well and truly caught.

THEAIT. Indeed we do.

STR. And yet—— Alas, Theaitetos! I think it's just at this point
that we're going to discover how difficult the problem of
reality turns out to be.

THEAIT. How so? Why do you say that?

STR. My dear fellow, don't you see that the question has now
got us hopelessly baffled, though we fancy our remarks make
good sense.

THEAIT. I certainly imagined they did, and I just can't understand how we can be deceived as to our situation.

STR. Then take another look and ask yourself whether, in
reaching these last conclusions, [250] we might not in fairness
be asked the same question we put earlier on to those who
said that the sum of things 'really is' Hot and Cold.

THEAIT. What question? You will have to remind me.

STR. Certainly; and I will try to do so by questioning you in the
same way as I did them. Maybe we shall make a little progress
at the same time.

THEAIT. Just as you wish.

STR. Listen now: in speaking of Movement and Rest, you do so,
presumably, as of two things diametrically opposed to one
another.

THEAIT. Of course.

STR. You say also, of both together and of each severally, that
they are real.

THEAIT. I do.

STR. And when you acknowledge them as real. do you mean that
either or both of them are in motion?

THEAIT. By no means.

STR. Well, in saying both are real, do you mean that both are at
rest?

THEAIT. How can I?

STR. So you envisage reality as a third thing distinct from these

[1] The allusion is to the child's answer, 'Both', when asked: 'Which hand
will you have?'

two; in other words, when you speak of movement and rest as being real, you mean you are considering both of them together as embraced by reality and concentrating on their common association therewith.

THEAIT. It certainly appears that we visualize reality as a third thing when we say that movement and rest are real.

STR. Reality then is not motion and rest 'both at once', but something else distinct from them.

THEAIT. So it seems.

STR. By virtue of its own nature then reality is neither at rest nor in motion.

THEAIT. Presumably.

STR. Where then is the mind to turn in its desire for some clear-cut and firmly established notion of reality?

THEAIT. Where indeed?

STR. It seems there is no ready source of help. If a thing is not in motion, how can it be otherwise than at rest. And again, if a thing is in no way at rest, surely it must be in motion. Yet now we find reality to be outside both these classes. Is that possible?

THEAIT. Impossibility could go no further.

STR. Then here is something that must be borne in mind at this juncture.

THEAIT. Namely——?

STR. That we were hopelessly at sea when asked to what the term 'unreal' should be applied. Do you remember?

THEAIT. Of course.

STR. Well, are we now any the less perplexed about reality?

THEAIT. Even more so, sir, I'ld say, if that were possible.

STR. So much then for a full statement of our problem. But since reality and unreality are wrapped alike in obscurity, there is for that reason some hope that any light, however much or little, cast on the one may likewise reveal the other. [251] If on the other hand we fail to catch a glimpse of either, we will make the best of a bad job and elbow our way through the argument.

THEAIT. Good.

STR. Let us explain then how it is that we so often call a thing by several names.

THEAIT. What, for instance? Give us an example.

STR. Well, as you know, we speak of a man under many additional names; we attribute to him colours, shapes, sizes, defects and good qualities. Now in all these and in countless other statements we say he is not only a 'man' but also 'good', and so on and so forth. The same applies in every other case: we regard any given thing as one, yet we call it by many names and therefore speak of it as many.

THEAIT. True.

STR. Yes, and in doing so I fancy we have provided a splendid entertainment for the young as well as for a number of older men who have turned to study late in life. Anyone can join in and object straight away that many things cannot possibly be one, nor one thing many. Indeed they thoroughly enjoy telling us we must not speak of a man as 'good'; according to them we should only speak of the good as good, and of the man as man. I imagine, Theaitetos, you must often run across fanatics of this kind, sometimes elderly gentlemen whose poor little minds are thrilled with such discoveries, and who believe themselves to have struck a perfect mine of wisdom.

THEAIT. I certainly have.

STR. By way then of addressing ourselves to all alike who have ever expressed any view on the subject of existence, let it be clear that the questions we shall now ask are directed not only to these people but to all those others with whom we have been conversing earlier.

THEAIT. What are the questions?

STR. Are we not to attach Existence to Motion and Rest, nor anything else to anything else, but to assume, on the contrary, in our dis ourse that they can neither blend with nor participate in c e another? Or are we to treat them as an aggregate, each member of which is capable of associating with the others? Or shall we say that this applies to some but not to others? Which of these alternatives should we say they prefer, Theaitetos?

THEAIT. I am not in a position to reply on their behalf.

STR. Then why don't you answer the questions individually and see what the result is in each case?

THEAIT. A good idea.

STR. First, if you don't mind, let us suppose they say that nothing has any capacity for association with anything else for any purpose whatever. Then Motion and Rest will have no share in Existence, will they?

THEAIT. [252] No.

STR. Well then, will either of them exist, if it has no association with Existence?

THEAIT. No, it will not.

STR. That admission seems to demolish all theories; at one stroke it upsets those who stand for a universe in motion, those who argue in favour of an immobile unity, and all who say their realities exist in Forms that are in all respects invariable; for every one of these schools attributes existence to things, some holding that they really *are* in motion, and some that they really *are* at rest.

THEAIT. Exactly.

STR. Yes, and now for those who teach that all things at one time come together and at another separate out. Whether they bring an indefinite number of things into and out of a unity, or divide things into or combine them out of a limited number of elements—regardless of whether they imagine this to take place alternately or to be continually going on—all such theories will be mere idle talk if there is no blending whatsoever.

THEAIT. You are right.

STR. Then again, the most fantastic consequence of all will arise if we adopt the theory of those very people who will not allow one thing to participate the quality of another and therefore to be called by its name.

THEAIT. How is that?

STR. Surely because they are obliged, in speaking of anything, to use such words and phrases as 'being', 'apart', 'from the others', 'by itself' and countless more into the bargain. They cannot steer clear of these expressions or avoid connecting them in their pronouncements, and therefore have no need of others to refute them. Their enemies, as the saying has it, are those of their own household, and, like our droll friend Eurycles, they bear within them wherever they go a voice of contradiction.

THEAIT. True; a most appropriate simile.

STR. What now if we suppose that all have the capacity to combine with one another?

THEAIT. Even I can refute that suggestion.

STR. How?

THEAIT. Well. Motion itself would come to a complete stand-still, and Rest would be in motion if each supervened on the other.

STR. And it is, of course, absolutely impossible that Motion should come to rest and Rest be in motion?

THEAIT. Absolutely.

STR. Then the third alternative alone remains.

THEAIT. Yes.

STR. And therefore one of the following must necessarily be true: either (a) all will blend, or (b) none, or (c) some will and others will not.

THEAIT. Of course.

STR. But the first two have proved impossible.

THEAIT. They have.

STR. So anyone who desires to answer correctly must take his stand on the third and only alternative.

THEAIT. Precisely.

STR. Now, in view of the fact that some Forms will blend and others not, [253] we may consider them subject to the same limitations as the letters of the alphabet, some of which cannot be conjoined while others can.

THEAIT. Quite true.

STR. And the vowels in particular run like a sort of cement through the whole series of letters, which cannot be fitted one to another except through the medium of a vowel.

THEAIT. Agreed.

STR. Now does everyone know which letters can be combined with which, or does one need an art in order to do so correctly?

THEAIT. One needs an art.

STR. What is that art?

THEAIT. Grammar.

STR. And is not the same true of high-pitched and low-pitched sounds? He who possesses the art of recognizing those sounds which do or do not blend is a musician, while he who does not understand that is unmusical.

THEAIT. True.

STR. And we shall find similar differences between qualification and lack thereof in any other art?

THEAIT. Of course.

STR. We have now agreed that the Kinds [1] stand likewise towards one another in the matter of blending. Very well then, surely one must travel the road of discourse with the aid of some science, if one is going (1) to pinpoint the kinds of Forms that are (*a*) consonant and (*b*) incompatible with one another, also (2) to make it clear (*a*) whether there are some kinds which pervade them all and link them up so that they can blend, and (*b*), where there are separations, whether there are certain others that run through wholes and give rise to the separation.

THEAIT. One definitely needs *some* science—perhaps the very greatest science of all.

STR. What shall we call this science? Or—why, good heavens, Theaitetos, have we stumbled unwittingly upon the knowledge that belongs to free men and, while looking for the Sophist, run across the Philosopher first?

THEAIT. How do you mean?

STR. Is not dialectic the science whose function is to divide according to Kinds, not believing that the same Form is a different one or vice versa?

THEAIT. Yes, it is.

STR. Then he who can do that intuitively perceives (*a*) one Form extended everywhere throughout many, where each one lies apart, and (*b*) many Forms differing from one another, included within one Form; and again (*c*) one Form connected in a unity through many wholes, and (*d*) many Forms entirely marked off apart. Thus he knows how to distinguish, Kind by Kind, in what ways the several Kinds are or are not able to combine.

THEAIT. Most certainly.

STR. And I imagine you will allow this mastery of Dialectic to none but the pure and rightful lover of wisdom.

THEAIT. Impossible to do otherwise.

STR. Then it is in this kind of country that we shall find the Philosopher, if we get round to hunting him. [254] He too is difficult to see clearly, but for a reason different from that which makes the Sophist so hard to detect.

THEAIT. What is the difference?

[1] 'Kinds' (γένη), synonymous in this dialogue with 'Forms'.

STR. The Sophist runs to earth in the darkness of Not-being, where long practice has taught him to feel his way about; and the very darkness of the place makes it hard to discern him.

THEAIT. Quite likely.

STR. Our Philosopher, on the other hand, whose mind is ever concentrated upon the nature of reality, is difficult to see because his dwelling is so bright; for the eyes of an average soul cannot for long endure the sight of the divine.

THEAIT. That seems equally probable.

STR. We'll study the Philosopher more closely later on, perhaps, if we still feel that way inclined. As for the Sophist, make no doubt about it, we must not let up until we have him in full view.

THEAIT. Hear, hear!

STR. Well, we are now agreed (1) that some of the Kinds will combine with one another and some will not, and (2) that some will combine with a very limited number, others with a great many, while others again pervade all and there is nothing to prevent their being combined with everything. Let us therefore proceed with the argument as follows. In order not to lose our way in the whole vast multitude of Forms, we will select only a few of those that are generally acknowledged as highly important; we shall next consider (1) their respective natures and (2) whether or not they are capable of combination with one another. By so doing, though we may fail to understand Being and Not-being with perfect clarity, we shall at any rate give as satisfactory account of them as is possible within the limited scope of our present inquiry, and see whether we may with impunity assert that what is not, *really is*.

THEAIT. Yes, that is the best course we can take.

STR. Now as regards the Kinds, those we were discussing a little while ago, viz. Existence itself and Rest and Motion, are undoubtedly of high importance.

THEAIT. Indeed they are.

STR. And let me remind you that two of them, as we have agreed, will not blend with one another.

THEAIT. Quite so.

STR. Existence, on the other hand, can be blended with both; for the very good reason that they both exist.

THEAIT. Of course.

STR. So all together they make three.

THEAIT. Beyond a doubt.

STR. Each one of them then is different from the other two and the same as itself.

THEAIT. That's right.

STR. But what on earth do we mean by these words we have just used: 'same' and 'different'? Are they a pair of Kinds distinct from the aforesaid three, though always of necessity combining with them, so that we have to consider the Forms as totalling five instead of three? Or when we say 'same' or 'different' [255] are we unconsciously referring to one or another of those three?

THEAIT. Perhaps.

STR. Well, Motion and Rest at all events cannot be identical with Difference or Sameness?

THEAIT. Why not?

STR. Because if they were, Motion would be at rest and Rest in motion; for whichever of the two becomes applicable to both will force the other to change to the contrary of its own nature, by virtue of thus coming to participate in its contrary.

THEAIT. Just so.

STR. But both do participate in Sameness and Difference.

THEAIT. Yes.

STR. Then we must not identify Sameness or Difference with Motion or with Rest.

THEAIT. No.

STR. But should we think of Existence and Sameness as identical?

THEAIT. Maybe.

STR. But if 'Existence' and 'Sameness' mean exactly the same thing, then once again, when we say that Motion and Rest both 'exist' we shall in effect be speaking of them as identical.

THEAIT. But that of course is impossible.

STR. In which case Sameness and Existence cannot be one thing.

THEAIT. Hardly.

STR. Then we may recognize Sameness as a fourth Form, along with the initial three.

THEAIT. Certainly.

STR. And should we call Difference a fifth? Or must we think of it and of Existence as two names for a single Kind?

THEAIT. Possibly.

STR. But you will surely allow that some existing things are always spoken of as being what they are simply in themselves, and others as being what they are in relation to other things.

THEAIT. Yes indeed.

STR. And a thing that is different is always so called with reference to something else. Isn't that so?

THEAIT. It is.

STR. It wouldn't be, if Existence and Difference were not totally different things. If Difference, like Existence, participated in both characters, the class of differents would sometimes contain something that was different without reference to something else. Actually, however, we find beyond any doubt that whatever is different, by that very fact is what it is with reference to another thing.

THEAIT. That is perfectly correct.

STR. Then we must recognize the nature of Difference as a fifth among the Forms we are selecting.

THEAIT. Yes.

STR. And we shall also say that it permeates them all; for each one is different from the others, not by virtue of its own nature, but owing to its participation in the character of Difference.

THEAIT. Exactly.

STR. Good; now taking each of the five Kinds in turn, let us say something about them.

THEAIT. Say what?

STR. First as regards Motion: we may say it is totally different from Rest. Isn't that right?

THEAIT. It is.

STR. Motion, therefore, is not Rest.

THEAIT. Not in any sense whatever.

STR. [256] But Motion exists by virtue of participating in Existence.

THEAIT. Yes.

STR. And again, it is different from the Same.

THEAIT. Undoubtedly.

STR. So it is not the Same.

THEAIT. No.

STR. And yet we agreed that Motion is the same as itself, because everything partakes of the Same.

THEAIT. Certainly.

STR. We have to admit then, quite frankly, that Motion is both the same and not the Same. For we don't use those two phrases in an identical sense: when we say it is 'the same', we do so because of its participation in the Same with reference to itself; but when we say it is 'not the Same', that is because of its combination with Difference, whereby it becomes distinct from the Same and is rendered not the Same but different, so that we are entitled this time to speak of it as 'not the Same'.

THEAIT. Very true.

STR. Likewise, even if Motion itself partook in any way of Rest, there would be nothing paradoxical in referring to it as stationary. As a matter of fact, however, it does *not* partake of Rest.

THEAIT. No.

STR. It does, on the other hand, partake both of Sameness and of Difference, so that we are quite in order when we speak of it as both the same and not the Same.

THEAIT. Perfectly in order, so long as we are ready to allow that some of the Kinds will blend with one another, and that others will not.

STR. That of course is a conclusion at which we arrived earlier on, when we proved that such was actually their nature.

THEAIT. So we did.

STR. Very well, returning now to our statements: is Motion different from Different, just as we found it to be other than the Same and other than Rest?

THEAIT. It must be.

STR. In a sense then Motion is not Different, and also is different, according to the argument we put forward a minute or two ago.

THEAIT. True.

STR. Now about the next point. Are we to say that Motion is different from three of the four Kinds, but not from the fourth, when we have already recognized five kinds as demanding investigation?

THEAIT. How can we? We cannot allow that they are fewer than they were shown just now to be.

STR. So we need not hesitate to say that Motion is different from Existence.

THEAIT. Certainly we need not.

STR. It is in fact plain that Motion really is a thing that is not and also a thing that is, since it participates in Existence.

THEAIT. Quite plain.

STR. Then it must be possible for 'what is not' to be. And this is true as regards not only Motion but all the other Kinds as well; for in the case of them all the nature of Difference operates so as to make each one different from Existence and consequently something that 'is not'. On the same principle, therefore, we are entitled to speak of them all as things that in this sense 'are not', and again, since they partake of Existence, as things that are, i.e. have being.

THEAIT. I suppose so.

STR. In the case of any Form whatsoever then there is much that that Form *is* and an indefinite number of things that it *is not*.

THEAIT. Apparently.

STR. [257] Furthermore, one must call Existence itself different from the rest.

THEAIT. Inevitably.

STR. We conclude then that Existence 'is not' in as many respects as there are other things; for, since it is not those others, although it *is* its sole self, it *is not* those indefinitely numerous other things.

THEAIT. That is so.

STR. We must not, therefore, hesitate to accept even that conclusion, assuming that Kinds are of such a nature as to allow of combination one with another. If anyone proposes to reject that, he must dispose of our previous arguments before attempting to rebut their consequences.

THEAIT. Fair enough.

STR. Here now is something else for our consideration.

THEAIT. What?

STR. When we speak of 'that which is not', I don't think we mean something contrary to what exists, but only something that is different.

THEAIT. How so?

STR. Well, when we speak for instance of something as 'not tall', do you fancy that expression necessarily implies something short rather than something of medium height?

THEAIT. I don't see why it should.

STR. So when we are told that a negative signifies a contrary, we shall not agree; we shall admit no more than that the adverb 'not' points to something different from the words which follow it, or rather from the things which those words denote.

THEAIT. Exactly.

STR. And now, by your leave, we have another question to ponder.

THEAIT. Yes?

STR. It seems to me that the nature of the Different is distributed, just as is knowledge.

THEAIT. How do you mean?

STR. Knowledge, like the Different, is of course one, but each part of it which deals with some particular subject is sharply defined and has a special name of its own. Hence the recognition of many arts and forms of knowledge.

THEAIT. Granted.

STR. And the same is true of the parts of the one nature of the Different.

THEAIT. I don't dispute that, but we might as well explain just how.

STR. There exists, doesn't there, a part of the Different contrasted with the Beautiful?

THEAIT. There does.

STR. Are we to say it is nameless, or has it a distinctive name?

THEAIT. It has one. For every time we use the phrase 'not Beautiful', we are referring precisely to that which is different from the nature of the Beautiful.

STR. Tell me something, then.

THEAIT. Tell you what?

STR. Isn't it true to say that the existence of the not-Beautiful consists in its being marked off from one determinate Kind among existing things and contrasted in turn with something that exists?

THEAIT. Yes.

STR. Apparently then the not-Beautiful is a case in point of one existing thing being set in contrast to another.

THEAIT. Perfectly correct.

STR. Where do we go from there? Has the Beautiful, then, any stronger claim than the not-Beautiful to be recognized as a thing that exists?

THEAIT. Most certainly not. [258]

STR. So we must admit that the not-Tall exists just as truly as the Tall itself.

THEAIT. Just as truly.

STR. We must likewise rank the not-Just with the Just in so far as neither has any more existence than the other.

THEAIT. Certainly.

STR. And we shall say the same of all the rest, since the nature of the Different is proved to be one of the things that exist, and, because it exists, we are no less bound to ascribe existence to its parts.

THEAIT. Of course.

STR. Apparently then, if there are set in contrast a part of the nature of the Different and a part of the nature of the Existent, that contrast is, if one may say so, no less a reality than Existence itself; it does not signify what is contrary to 'existent', but simply and solely what is different from the Existent.

THEAIT, I see exactly what you mean.

STR. Then what are we to call it?

THEAIT. It is obviously that very 'what-is-not' we were looking for in connection with the Sophist.

STR. Does it then, as you say, exist no less really than the rest? May we now boldly assert that 'that which is not' indubitably *is* a thing having its own peculiar nature (just as the Tall was tall and the Beautiful was beautiful, so also with the not-Tall and the not-Beautiful), and in that sense 'that which is not' also, on the same principle, both was and *is* what-is-not, a single Form to be counted among the many realities? Or have we, Theaitetos, any remaining doubts?

THEAIT. None whatever.

STR. You see, therefore, that having turned our backs on Parmenides, we have gone far beyond what he forbade.

THEAIT. In what way?

STR. Going ahead with our search, we have taught him something about a country he would not have us so much as to explore.

THEAIT. How?

STR. You will remember his words:

Never shall this be proved, that things, which are not, are;
And do thou in thy inquiry, deter thy thought from this way.

THEAIT. Yes, that is what he says.

STR. Against that we have not only discovered that things which are not, are, but we have also explained the true character of not-being. We have shown that the nature of the Different has existence and is distributed throughout the realm of existent things in relation to one another; and we have ventured to declare that every part thereof which is contrasted with 'that which is', *is really* 'not-being'.

THEAIT. Exactly, sir, and I think what we have said is quite true.

STR. Very well; in that case, when we venture to assert that 'what is not' exists, let no one say that by 'what is not' we mean the contrary of the existent. With regard to the question whether or not there is such a thing as a contrary of the existent, and whether or not any account can be given of it, we have long since put it aside. [259] But as for the what-is-not, which we have now said exists, our account of it must either be refuted so as to convince us it is wrong, or, if that proves impossible, the following statements must be accepted as true:

(*a*) The Kinds blend one with another. (*b*) Existence and Difference permeate them all and one another. (*c*) Difference, participating in Existence, *is* by virtue of that participation, and yet *is not* that in which it participates, but is different; and since it is different from Existence, it is of necessity possible for it to *be* a thing that *is not*. (*d*) Since Existence participates in Difference, it will be different from all the remaining Kinds, and therefore it *is not* any one of them nor all of them together, but is itself alone; so that, once again beyond a shadow of doubt, Existence *is not* thousands and thousands of things, and all the other Kinds in the same way, whether individually or collectively, in many respects *are* and in many others *are not*.

THEAIT. True.

STR. And anyone who is beset with doubt as to these apparent contradictions had better make a study of the question and improve on the explanation we have just put forward; but if he imagines himself to have found an awkward puzzle and enjoys treating argument as a mere bandying of words, he is wasting his efforts in an occupation that is simply not worth while, as our present argument makes clear. It is neither

clever nor difficult to make such a discovery; but I will tell
you what *is* hard and worth a good deal of trouble.

THEAIT. You mean——?

STR. What I said earlier on: ignoring all such word-play as
profitless, to be able to follow stage by stage what we assert
and, while criticizing the statement that in one sense a different
thing is the same or the same thing different, to bear in mind
the exact sense, i.e. the precise respect, in which we declare
them to be one or the other. Simply to demonstrate that in
some undetermined way the same is different or vice versa,
the tall short, the like unlike, and to delight in continually
brandishing such contradictions in argument, is not legitimate
criticism; no indeed, it is the new-born babe of a mind that
has only recently made contact with reality.

THEAIT. I couldn't agree more.

STR. Yes, dear boy, and the endeavour to separate everything from
everything else is not only out of place, but is also the mark of
a man who has no link whatever with the Muse of Philosophy.

THEAIT. Why?

STR. To isolate every single thing from everything else is to do
away with discourse lock, stock and barrel; for all discourse
originates in the weaving together of Forms.

THEAIT. True.

STR. [260] Observe then how timely was our struggle with the
isolationists, when we compelled them to recognize that one
Form blends with another.

THEAIT. Timely in what way?

STR. By its establishment of discourse as among the kinds of
existing things. Deprived of discourse, we should be de-
deprived of philosophy. That would be the most disastrous
result; but, in addition, we have here and now to agree as to
the nature of discourse, and had we been robbed of its very
existence, we should obviously not be able to discourse any
further. And robbed we should certainly have been if we had
allowed that no Form blends with another.

THEAIT. True enough; but I don't understand why it is that we
must agree here and now on the subject of discourse.

STR. Don't you? Well, perhaps the easiest way out of your difficulty will be to follow a line of thought which I am going to
suggest.

THEAIT. What is that?

STR. We saw that 'not being' is one of many Kinds, spread out over the whole domain of realities.

THEAIT. Yes.

STR. The next question is, whether it blends with thinking and discourse.

THEAIT. Why?

STR. Unless it does so blend, everything must be true. But if it does, we shall have false thinking and discourse; for you will doubtless admit that thinking or saying 'what is not' amounts to falsity in thought or speech.

THEAIT. It does.

STR. And if there is such a thing as falsity then deception is possible.

THEAIT. Yes.

STR. And if deception exists, the world will be littered with images, likenesses and appearances.

THEAIT. Inevitably.

STR. And we said that the Sophist had gone to earth somewhere in that region, and had then denied that falsity so much as exists, maintaining that no one could either think or say 'what is not', because what is not must be totally devoid of being.

THEAIT. That is what he declared.

STR. But 'what is not' has now been found to share in being; therefore perhaps he will no longer oppose us on that ground. He may, however, urge that while there are some things which participate in not-being there are some which do not, and that speech and thinking are among the latter; and so again he might maintain that the art of making images and semblances, in which we have located him, has absolutely no existence, since thought and speech do not participate in not-being, without which participation there can be no such thing as falsity. It is for this reason we must first investigate the nature of discourse, thinking and appearance, in order [261] so to establish their combination with not-being as to prove the existence of falsity, and by so doing to corner the Sophist there, if it can be done, or else let him go and look for him in another Kind.

THEAIT. Well, sir, it appears we were perfectly right at the outset, when we described the Sophist as a difficult sort of creature to track down. He evidently possesses an interminable line of defences in the shape of problems, and every time he shelters behind one of them we have to take it by storm before we can come to grips with him. Why, here we are now, having only just overwhelmed his defence that 'what is not' cannot exist, when another is thrown up: we are required, it seems, to prove that falsity exists both in speech and thought, and after that perhaps something else, and so on—apparently *ad infinitum*.

STR. No one, Theaitetos, should lose heart so long as he can make steady progress, however slow it be. If he becomes discouraged then, what will he do in other circumstances when he can make no headway at all or even loses ground? It will be a long time, as the saying goes, before a man of that sort storms a city. And now, my friend, that we have passed the line you speak of it may well be that the highest wall is in our hands, and the rest may be less formidable and easier to take.

THEAIT. Good.

STR. Then, as I said just now, let us begin with statement and judgment, in order to clear up the question whether not-being touches them at any point, or both are entirely true and neither is ever tainted with falsity.

THEAIT. Very well.

STR. Bearing in mind what we said a while ago about Forms and letters, we will now proceed to consider words in the same way. The object of our present search appears to lie somewhere in that direction.

THEAIT. What is it we want to know about words?

STR. Whether they all fit together, or none of them, or some do while others do not.

THEAIT. The answer is clear: some do, and others do not.

STR. This, I suspect, is more or less what you are trying to say: those words which make sense when uttered in succession do fit together; those which mean nothing when strung together do not.

THEAIT. What do you mean?

STR. What I supposed you had in mind when you said: 'Some do, and others do not'. The vocal signs we use to signify being are surely of two kinds.

THEAIT. How?

STR. [262] One kind called 'nouns', the other 'verbs'.

THEAIT. Let us have a description of each.

STR. By 'verb' we mean an expression indicative of action.

THEAIT. Yes.

STR. And by 'noun' the vocal sign indicative of what performs such actions.

THEAIT. Exactly.

STR. Well, a statement is never composed entirely of nouns uttered in succession, nor indeed of verbs apart from nouns.

THEAIT. I don't follow that.

STR. You must have had something else in mind when you agreed with what I said a moment ago; because what I was trying to say was precisely this, that these words strung together in this way do not make a statement.

THEAIT. In what way?

STR. For example, 'walks runs sleeps', and so on with all other verbs that signify actions; if you utter them all in succession, you are not making a statement.

THEAIT. No, of course not.

STR. And again, if you say 'lion stag horse', and any other nouns representing things which perform actions, no juxtaposition of such words ever constitutes a statement. In neither example does the concatenation of sounds denote any action performed or not performed, or the nature of anything that does or does not exist; one has first to combine verbs with nouns. As soon as that is done the words fit together and the most elementary combination becomes a statement of what one might describe as the most elementary and shortest kind.

THEAIT. Then how do you make such a statement?

STR. Suppose one says 'A man understands'; do you agree that this is a statement of the most elementary and most simple kind?

THEAIT. Yes.

STR. Of course you do, because it now supplies information about facts or events in the present, past or future; it does more than just name something, it gets us somewhere by interweaving verbs and nouns. That is why we say it 'states' something, instead of merely 'names' something; and indeed it is to this complex that we apply the word 'statement'.

THEAIT. True.

STR. So then just as some things fit together while others do
not, so also with vocal signs: some do not fit together, but
those that do fit form a statement.

THEAIT. Yes, I see exactly what you mean.

STR. Now for another small point.

THEAIT. What is that?

STR. Wherever you have a statement, it must be a statement
about *something*; it cannot be about nothing.

THEAIT. Correct.

STR. And it must be of a certain quality, mustn't it?

THEAIT. Naturally.

STR. Now let us concentrate upon ourselves.

THEAIT. Very good.

STR. I am going to address a statement to you, combining a
thing with an action by means of a noun and a verb. It will be
your job to tell me what the statement is about.

THEAIT. I will do my best. [263]

STR. 'Theaitetos sits'—not a long statement, is it?

THEAIT. No, quite a short one.

STR. Now you have to say what it is about, in other words to
whom it applies.

THEAIT. Clearly to me; I am the subject.

STR. What about this next one?

THEAIT. Go ahead.

STR. 'Theaitetos (with whom I am now talking) flies.'

THEAIT. All would agree that I am again the subject, that the
statement is about me.

STR. And we have also admitted that any statement must have
a certain quality.

THEAIT. Yes.

STR. Then what quality should be ascribed to each of the foregoing statements?

THEAIT. The second is false, the first true.

STR. And the latter states about you the facts as they are.

THEAIT. Certainly.

STR. The false one, on the other hand, states about you things
different from the actual facts.

THEAIT. Yes.

STR. And therefore represents things that *are not* as *being*.

THEAIT. Undoubtedly.

STR. Yes, but it states things that exist, different from things that exist in your case. For we said that in the case of everything there are many things that are and many that are not.

THEAIT. Quite.

STR. So in the first place my second statement about you must, according to our definition of the nature of a statement, itself necessarily be one of the shortest possible.

THEAIT. We agreed as to that just now.

STR. And in the second place it must be about something.

THEAIT. Yes.

STR. And if it is not about you it is not about anything at all.

THEAIT. Of course not.

STR. And if it were about nothing, it would not be a statement at all; for we showed that there could not be a statement that was a statement about nothing.

THEAIT. Perfectly true.

STR. Therefore what is stated about you, but in such a way that what is different is stated as the same, or what is not as what is —well, a noun-verb combination of that sort seems to be really and truly a false statement.

THEAIT. It does indeed.

STR. Right then, is it now clear that thinking and judgment and appearing, all alike, occur in our minds both as false and as true?

THEAIT. How is that?

STR. You will understand more readily if you will first allow me to give you an account of their nature and of how each differs from the others.

THEAIT. By all means do so.

STR. Well, thinking and discourse are the same thing, except that what we call thinking is nothing else than an interior dialogue carried on between the mind and itself without the accompaniment of vocal utterance.

THEAIT. Certainly.

STR. But the stream that flows from the mind through the mouth is called discourse.

THEAIT. True.

STR. Moreover there is a thing which we know occurs in discourse.

THEAIT. You mean——?

STR. Assertion and denial.

THEAIT. Yes.

STR. [264] Now when this occurs in the mind during silent thought, can you call it anything but judgment?

THEAIT. No.

STR. And when such a state of mind occurs, not independently, but through perception, can it properly be called anything but 'appearing'?

THEAIT. No.

STR. Very good then, since we have found (a) that there is true and false statement; (b) that of the aforesaid mental processes thinking is a dialogue between the mind and itself; (c) that judgment is the final product of thinking; and (d) that what we mean by 'it appears' is a combination of perception and judgment; it follows that thinking, judgment and appearing, since they are of the same nature as statement, must likewise be, some of them and sometimes, false.

THEAIT. Oh yes, they must.

STR. So you see we have discovered the nature of false judgment and false statement sooner than we hoped to do a little while ago when we feared that our undertaking to search for them would prove an endless task.

THEAIT. I do.

STR. Then let us not lose heart in face of what has yet to be done. Having settled these points we may revert to our previous divisions by forms.

THEAIT. What divisions?

STR. We distinguished two forms of Image-making: the making of likenesses and the making of semblances.

THEAIT. Yes.

STR. And we declared ourselves at a loss to know under which heading we should include the Sophist.

THEAIT. So we did.

STR. And amidst our perplexity we were enveloped in an even darker cloud of unknowing by the emergence of an argument that disputed all these terms and challenged the very existence of any copy, image or semblance, on the ground that there can never be any such thing as falsity.

THEAIT. True.

STR. But now that we have proved the existence of false

statement and false judgment, it is possible that there should
be imitations of real things and that false judgment should
give rise to an art of deception.

THEAIT. Yes, it is possible.

STR. And we agreed some time ago that the Sophist comes
within one or other of the two forms of Image-making.

THEAIT. Yes.

STR. Right, then let us once again get down to work and, as we
make a twofold division of the kind proposed, keep to the
right-hand line at each stage.[1] By so doing we shall trace the
successive characters of which the Sophist partakes, but
gradually discard all that he has in common with others until
we are left only with his distinctive nature. So we shall reveal
that nature, first to ourselves [265] and secondly to others
temperamentally attuned to such procedure.

THEAIT. Very well.

STR. Now we began by dividing Art into (a) an Acquisitive and
(b) a Productive branch.

THEAIT. Yes.

STR. And under the heading Acquisitive we caught fleeting
glimpses of the Sophist in the arts of hunting, contention,
exchange and so forth.

THEAIT. We did.

STR. But having now brought him within an art of Imitation,
obviously our first step must be to subdivide the Productive
branch. For Imitation is of course a kind of production,
though it be only a production of images, as we say, and never
of originals. Do you agree?

THEAIT. I do, certainly.

STR. Then let us first recognize two kinds of Production.

THEAIT. What are they?

STR. (a) Divine, and (b) Human.

THEAIT. I don't yet understand.

STR. You remember what we said at the outset: we defined
Production as any power that can bring into existence what
did not exist before.

THEAIT. Oh yes, I remember.

STR. Well now, consider all mortal animals and also all things
that grow—plants that grow out of the earth from seeds and

[1] Each stage of the 'right-hand line' is indicated here by (b), the left by (a).

roots, and inanimate bodies, whether fusible or infusible, that are compacted below the surface. Is it not exclusively to divine craftsmanship that we must attribute their coming into being from not-being? Or are we to adopt another and commonly held theory?

THEAIT. What theory?

STR. That Nature brings them forth as a result of some spontaneous cause that generates without intelligence. Or shall we say that they arise from a cause which, employing reason and art, is divine and proceeds from divinity?

THEAIT. Owing perhaps to my youth, I often move from one opinion to the other; but here and now, looking into your eyes and believing you to hold that the things in question are of divine origin, I too am convinced.

STR. Good for you, Theaitetos. If I thought you were the kind of person to change your mind later on I would now try to make you accept that account by sheer force of persuasion. But it is quite clear to me that your nature, without any argument on my part, will come of its own accord to the conclusion which you tell me now attracts you. So I will not bother with that: it would be mere waste of time. I will merely emphasize that the so-called products of Nature are works of divine art, just as things made by man from these raw materials are works of human art; which means that there are two kinds of Production, one divine and the other human.

THEAIT. Fair enough.

STR. Now subdivide each of those two into two parts.

THEAIT. How?

STR. [266] You have just divided the whole field of Production horizontally; well now divide it vertically.

THEAIT. Very good.

STR. The division gives us four parts in all: two on our side, human; two on the side of the gods, divine.

THEAIT. Yes.

STR. And taking the horizontal divisions, one section (a) of each part will be the production of originals, and we can best describe the other two (b) as production of images. So, on that principle, there is a second division of Production.

THEAIT. Tell us again how the divine part and the human part are divided.

STR. We ourselves, presumably, and all other living creatures and the elements of natural things (fire, water and the like) are all originals, the offspring, as we are well aware, of divine craftsmanship. You agree?

THEAIT. Yes.

STR. And corresponding to each one of these products there are images which are not the thing itself, but for whose existence divine craftsmanship is equally responsible.

THEAIT. Such as——?

STR. Dream images, and by day all those naturally produced semblances which are called 'shadow' when a dark object interrupts the light, or a 'reflection' when the light from the eye fuses with light from something else on a bright and smooth surface and begets a shape giving rise to a perception that is the reverse of the normal direct view.

THEAIT. Yes, those are the two products of divine craftsmanship: the original and an image that invariably corresponds therewith.

STR. And how about human art? Is it not correct to say that in building it produces an actual house, and in painting another sort of house—a man-made dream, so to speak, for our waking hours?

THEAIT. Certainly.

STR. And so in every case, we find once again that there are twin offspring of our own production occurring in pairs: one is an actual thing and the other an image.

THEAIT. Now I see more clearly, and I recognize two branches of production, each of them capable of twofold subdivision: there are the divine and human branches, each of which produces actual things and some kind of likenesses.

STR. Let us recall then that there were to be two kinds of Image-making, producing respectively (*a*) likenesses and (*b*) semblances, provided falsity could be shown to be something that really *is* false or, in other words, of such a nature as to rank among existing things.

THEAIT. Quite right.

STR. Now that that condition has been fulfilled, shall we consider these two forms of Image-making as beyond dispute?

THEAIT. Yes.

STR. [267] Let us then go on to make a two-fold subdivision of Semblance-making.

THEAIT. How?

STR. One kind (*a*) works by means of tools; in the other (*b*) the producer obtains his effect through the medium of his own person.

THEAIT. How do you mean?

STR. When someone uses his own body or voice to represent your features or your speech, isn't the proper name for creating a semblance of that kind 'Mimicry'?

THEAIT. Yes.

STR. Well, let us give that branch of Semblance-making the general name of mimicry, leaving to someone else the trouble of unifying the other branch and giving it a suitable name.

THEAIT. As you wish.

STR. But there is still good reason to believe, Theaitetos, that mimicry is twofold. I will tell you why.

THEAIT. Please do.

STR. Some mimics know the thing they counterfeit, others do not; and could we point to a more fundamental distinction than that of knowing from not knowing?

THEAIT. Indeed no.

STR. The example I gave just now was of mimicry linked with knowledge; for a man who would imitate you would first have to be familiar with you and your features.

THEAIT. Naturally.

STR. And what about the features of Justice and of virtue in general? There must be many who, though they have no knowledge of virtue but only some kind of opinion about it, try their hardest to make it appear that virtue (such as they imagine it to be) is incarnate in themselves, mimicking it as best they can in word and deed?

THEAIT. Yes, there are only too many such folk.

STR. And do they invariably fail in their efforts to appear virtuous when they are not so at all? Is not the very opposite true?

THEAIT. It certainly is.

STR. In that case, we must distinguish the ignorant mimic from the one who has knowledge.

THEAIT. Yes.

STR. Where then is one to seek an appropriate name for each? It is doubtless no easy task to find one, because earlier thinkers, it would seem, were victims of a certain laziness and short-sightedness as regards the division of Kinds by forms; none of them even attempted to make such divisions, so that there is an inevitable dearth of names. However, though the expression may seem rather daring, for the sake of distinction let us call (a) mimicry founded upon knowledge 'scientific mimicry', and (b) that which is based on opinion 'conceit-mimicry'.

THEAIT. Yes, that will do.

STR. We are concerned then with the latter. Why? Because we agreed that the Sophist is not among those who have knowledge, but he does rank with those who practise mimicry.

THEAIT. Quite so.

STR. Now let us tap the 'conceit-mimic' as if he were a piece of metal, and see whether he rings true or whether there is a crack in him.

THEAIT. Let us do so.

STR. [268] Well, there is a very definite crack. You have the simple-minded type who imagines that he knows what he merely believes, and another type who is experienced in the rough and tumble of discussion, with the result that his attitude is one of uneasy suspicion that what the world regards as his knowledge is in fact ignorance.

THEAIT. Certainly both the types you have described exist.

STR. Shall we then put down (a) the second of these mimics as 'sincere', and (b) the first as 'insincere'?

THEAIT. Yes, I think we may.

STR. Are we to reckon the latter as of only one kind, or of two?

THEAIT. That is for you to say.

STR. And so I will: I can clearly make out a pair of them. I see one who can openly play the hypocrite at enormous length and before vast audiences, and another who employs brief arguments in private and forces the person with whom he is conversing to contradict himself.

THEAIT. You are quite right.

STR. And whom are we to recognize in (a) the more garrulous type—Statesman or demagogue?

THEAIT. Demagogue.

STR. And what shall we call (*b*) the other—sage or Sophist?

THEAIT. We cannot very well call him sage, having reckoned him as ignorant; but as a mimic of the sage he will clearly take to himself a title derived from his, and now I see that here at last we have the fellow who must indeed be described as the real and authentic Sophist.

STR. Shall we then as before retrace the various stages of his pedigree, starting at the bottom and proceeding upwards to the apex, and, so to speak, tie our threads together in a knot?

THEAIT. By all means.

STR. Here we go then: The art of making others contradict themselves, which stages a mere shadow-play of words, is a branch of insincere kind of conceit-mimicry, itself an off-shoot of Semblance-making. The latter is a branch of Image-making, which is in turn recognized as a part (not divine but human) of Production. Such is the pedigree which can be assigned with perfect truth to the genuine Sophist.

THEAIT. I entirely agree.

THE STATESMAN

PERSONS OF THE DIALOGUE

Socrates.
Theodoros.

The Stranger from Elaia.
Socrates the Younger.

Soc. [257] I am greatly indebted to you, Theodoros, for having introduced me to Theaitetos as well as to the Stranger.

Theod. You can take it from me, Socrates, that you will very soon owe me three times as much, when they have helped you to draw portraits of the Statesman and the Philosopher.

Soc. Come, come, Theodoros; what a remark from the leading expert on mathematical computation and geometry!

Theod. What do you mean, Socrates?

Soc. I mean, fancy treating these men as equal quantities when the difference between their respective values surpasses any proportion your art can express.

Theod. By our god Ammon, Socrates, that is a well-deserved criticism, and one which underlines my false computation with a fine sureness of memory. I'll repay you another time.

But do you, sir, continue to extend us your courtesy, and choose now without further delay with which of the two you prefer to deal first, the Statesman or the Philosopher.

Str. Yes, Theodoros, that must be done; having once set our hand to the work, we must not leave it until we have completed our programme. But in the circumstances what line am I to take as regards Theaitetos?

Theod. How do you mean?

Str. Well, shall we give him a rest and get his fellow student, young Socrates here, to take his place? Or what do you advise?

Theod. Do as you suggest, and replace him; for both of them are young and will more easily survive this test if we allow them breathing space.

Soc. Yes, and there's another point, sir: both lads would appear to be distantly related to me. After all, you yourself

227

have said that one of them resembles me. The other bears my
name, and the common appellative makes us somehow akin.
[258] We ought always to welcome an opportunity of getting
to know our relatives by means of discourse. I myself had
just such a conversation with Theaitetos, and I've just been
listening to him answering your questions; but with young
Socrates I've not made contact in either way. He too, however, must be examined. My turn to question him will come
later on; for the present *you* had best do so.

STR. Very well. Now, Socrates, you hear what Socrates says?

S. Y. Yes.

STR. And you agree with his suggestion?

S. Y. Certainly.

STR. There is evidently no objection on your part, and of course
there is still less on mine. Very good then, it is my opinion that
after the Sophist it is the Statesman to whom we should devote
our attention. So tell me, yes or no, ought we to rank him also
among those who have knowledge?

S. Y. Yes.

STR. Then we must distinguish the branches of knowledge, as
we did when considering the Sophist?

S. Y. I suppose so.

STR. But to my way of thinking, Socrates, the Statesman will
not be found in the same quarter.

S. Y. Then——?

STR. We must look for him in another.

S. Y. So it would seem.

STR. Whereabouts then shall we discover the Statesman's
hiding place? We must find it and distinguish it clearly from
others, by attaching to it some peculiar mark and including all
other regions under a single sign of specific difference, and
thus bring our minds to recognize the totality of knowledge as
divided into two kinds.

S. Y. As to that, sir, I think it is your business and not mine.

STR. All the same, Socrates, it will inevitably be yours too, once
we have clarified the matter.

S. Y. You are quite right.

STR. Very well then, is it not a fact that arithmetic and some
kindred arts have nothing whatever to do with action, but
simply enable one to know?

S. Y. It is.

STR. Those arts, on the other hand, which have to do with carpentry or any other form of manufacture possess knowledge that is rooted, so to speak, in action, and are linked therewith until the objects to which it gives existence have been produced.

S. Y. What exactly do you mean?

STR. Well, divide the sciences according to this principle, calling one branch practical science and the other purely theoretical science.

S. Y. Fair enough; let us recognize these as two forms of Science in general.

STR. Shall we then regard the Statesman as King, master of slaves, and head of a household, on the assumption that all three terms denote only one thing, or shall we rather say that there are three separate arts corresponding to those three terms? Look at it another way?

S. Y. What is that?

STR. [259] I mean, suppose a mere layman is competent to advise a qualified medical practitioner, ought one not to accord him the same professional style as the man to whom he gives advice?

S. Y. Why, yes.

STR. Good, then take the case of a man who reigns over a whole territory: if there happens to be a private individual sufficiently outstanding to act as his counsellor, shall we not say that this individual possesses the science of which the ruler himself should have at his disposal?

S. Y. Indeed we shall.

STR. But the science appropriate to the genuine king is the science of kingship (or kingly science)?

S. Y. Yes.

STR. And he who possesses it (whether he be actually in power or in a private station) will likewise be accorded the kingly title by virtue of his art?

S. Y. That will be only fair.

STR. And will not the same apply in the case of a master of slaves and of the head of a household?

S. Y. What then?

STR. Well, is there any difference, where the exercise of

authority is concerned, between a large household and the area of a small state?

S. Y. None.

STR. So, answering the question we asked ourselves just now, it is clear that one science is concerned with all those things; and we shall not mind whether it be called 'kingly science', 'political science' ('statecraft') or 'economic science'.

S. Y. There would be no point in doing so.

STR. But this much at least is clear: no king can afford to rest his authority upon his physical strength and dexterity as he can upon his intelligence and determination.

S. Y. That is quite plain.

STR. Then may we take it as agreed that the King is more familiar with theoretical sciences than with manual skill and practical science generally?

S. Y. Yes indeed.

STR. So we shall take statecraft and the science of kingship, the Statesman and the King, and treat each pair as the same thing.

S. Y. Evidently.

STR. The next thing to do, surely, is to subdivide theoretical science.

S. Y. Certainly.

STR. Pay careful attention now, and see if we do not discover there an original duality.

S. Y. Tell us what it is.

STR. I will explain. We have mentioned an art of mathematical computation.

S. Y. Yes.

STR. And you will agree that it is undoubtedly a branch of theoretical art.

S. Y. Most certainly.

STR. Good. Now, once a mathematician knows the difference between one number and another, can we expect him to do anything more than judge what he knows.

S. Y. What else is there for him to do?

STR. Again, no architect is himself a workman, but merely superintendent of the workmen——

S. Y. Yes.

STR. Because he supplies knowledge, not manual labour.

S. Y. Quite.

STR. [260] It is fair to say, then, that he partakes of theoretical science.

S. Y. Certainly.

STR. I imagine, however, that having once formed his judgment he should not consider his task accomplished and leave it at that, like the mathematician; he must supervise each of the workmen until the job is finished.

S. Y. Correct.

STR. Thus all such sciences are theoretical, as well as those that go along with mathematics; but the two kinds differ inasmuch as one merely judges whereas the other also directs.

S. Y. Clearly.

STR. So if we distinguished two branches of theoretical science, calling the one 'directive' and the other 'critical', might we not claim to have made a fair division?

S. Y. Yes, I think so.

STR. Now when two persons are engaged in a common task it is pleasant for them to be in full agreement.

S. Y. Of course it is.

STR. Well, seeing that you and I enjoy this pleasure, let us not worry about what others may think.

S. Y. Very well.

STR. With which of these two arts are we to associate the King —with the critical, as a mere spectator, or shall we decide that his is rather the directive art, since in fact he governs as a master?

S. Y. Obviously the latter.

STR. Very good then, we must now consider this directive art, and see whether it affords a basis of subdivision. I think we have such a basis in that the kingly type differs from the herald tribe in the same way as do retailers from those who trade their own products.

S. Y. How is that?

STR. Surely retailers begin by purchasing a commodity made by others, and then sell it at second hand.

S. Y. Certainly.

STR. Likewise, the class of persons known as heralds receives from elsewhere orders which it has not itself conceived, and duly passes them on to others.

S. Y. Perfectly true.

STR. What then? Shall we confuse the kingly art with that of an interpreter, of a bo'sun, of a seer, of a herald, or with the many arts kindred to these, all of which are truly directive? Or would you prefer that we should follow up the comparison we have just made and coin an analogous term, for there is at present none that can be used satisfactorily to designate this class of directors whose authority is derived from themselves alone? The character denoted by such a term will then serve the purpose of our division; we shall place the kingly class of persons in the 'self-directive' group, without troubling about the other class or delaying to give *it* a name, for our search is concerned with the ruler, [261] not with his opposite.

S. Y. Exactly.

STR. Well now, here we have the class in question fairly well distinguished from the others by this contrast of borrowed and inherent authority. We must now go on to subdivide the said class, if we can find in it some suitable line of cleavage. Agreed?

S. Y. Certainly.

STR. I think I see such a line. Come on then, and help me to make the division.

S. Y. How do you mean?

STR. Whenever we think of rulers exercising such direction, shall we not also find that they give orders with a view to some form of production?

S. Y. Of course we shall.

STR. And it is not so very difficult to divide all the various kinds of products into two.

S. Y. On what principle?

STR. Surely some of this total number are inanimate and others animate.

S. Y. Yes.

STR. Well, it is according to the same principle that the directive part of theoretical science must be divided, if at all.

S. Y. Exactly how?

STR. We shall recognize one branch as the production of inanimate beings, and the other as that of animate beings; in that way we shall achieve an initial division of the whole.

S. Y. Perfectly correct.

STR. Let us ignore one of these branches and concentrate upon the other—concentrate, I mean, with a view to its sub-division.

S. Y. Upon which do you propose that we should concentrate?

STR. Naturally, that which is concerned with living creatures. For it goes without saying that the kingly science does not, like architecture, control inanimate things; its function is more noble, it reigns among the living, and it is over them that it continually exercises dominion.

S. Y. Quite right.

STR. As to the production and rearing of living creatures, it is possible to distinguish (a) the rearing of individuals singly, and (b) that which cares for its charges collectively as flocks or herds.

S. Y. Right.

STR. As for the Statesman, we shall not find him rearing individuals, like a farm-hand who looks after his ox or a groom his horse. No, he is more like a breeder of horses or cattle.

S. Y. Put like that it is quite clear.

STR. Well, what name shall we give that branch of rearing animate creatures which rears whole groups collectively? Shall we call it the rearing of flocks and herds or collective rearing?

S. Y. Whichever is most fitting in the circumstances.

STR. Well done, Socrates! If you persevere in this detachment with regard to words, we shall find that you wax wiser with the passing years. Meanwhile let us do as you say: do you see how it is possible to show that the rearing of flocks and herds is of two kinds, and thus ensure that our inquiry, [262] instead of turning upon this twofold object, shall be confined to one half only thereof?

S. Y. Let me think now. Why, yes, I think one branch consists in the rearing of men, the other in that of brute beasts.

STR. Indeed that is a division made with the utmost courage and zest. All the same, let us do our best to avoid falling back into these errors.

S. Y. What errors?

STR. One should not isolate one small portion and contrast it with several large ones, without considering its kind; one ought, on the contrary, to make due allowance for the kind to which that part belongs. It is all very well to draw a single line of cleavage between the object of one's search and everything else, but one must be fair. You yourself, for example, thought just now that you had perceived the dividing line, but you were in an unreasonable hurry when you saw the whole human race on one side of it. In fact, my friend, it is dangerous to chop one little bit off a whole. The safer procedure is to divide the whole into halves; in that way one has a better chance of finding specific characters, which are the be all and end all of our search.

S. Y. What do you mean by that, sir?

STR. Your nature, Socrates, requires a clearer statement of the facts, which I must try to give. Here and now it is impossible to leave absolutely nothing obscure; but we must try to push the matter a little further forward for the sake of clarity.

S. Y. What was that fault of which you said we were guilty when making our division just now?

STR. It was as if a man, wishing to divide the human race into two, did so along the lines followed by most people here in Athens. They begin by isolating the Hellenic race as a unit distinct from all the rest. They then treat those others as a single bloc (though they are very numerous, have no contact with one another, and do not understand one another's languages), lump them all together under the one term 'Barbarians', and imagine that by giving them a single name they make of them a single kind. Or again, it is as if a man thought that, in order to divide numbers into two groups, he need only detach the number 10,000 from all the rest, isolate it as forming a single kind, and give the others a common name in the belief, once again, that this single appellation suffices to create a second kind in contrast to the first. I think there is a better way of making these divisions: he would keep closer to the kinds, and effect a truer dichotomy, if he divided numbers into odd and even, the human race into male and female, and if he refrained from detaching, say, the Lydians, the Phrygians or other groups, and contrasting them with the rest of men, until it were no longer possible to find a division of which each term were at once both a kind and a part. [263]

S. Y. That is quite right, but there is another point, sir: how exactly is one to know that the kind and the part are not the same but two distinct things?

STR. My dear Socrates, you're asking something there! We

have already wandered too far from our subject, and you suggest that we wander still farther. It will be better if we retrace our steps; like good hunters, we will undertake this new line of inquiry later on, when we have time. Still, take care not to go believing that I have given you a perfect explanation.

S. Y. Explanation of what?

STR. Of the distinction between kind and part.

S. Y. Well?

STR. Wherever there is a kind, it is inevitably part of that whereof it is said to be a kind, but it by no means follows that the part is at the same time a kind. There, Socrates, you have the explanation (it is one of two) that you must always quote as mine.

S. Y. I will do so.

STR. And now for something else.

S. Y. What is that?

STR. Where were we before we embarked on the digression which has brought us to this point? I think I had just asked you how to divide the art of rearing flocks and herds, and you had assured me that there are two kinds of living things, the human race on the one hand, and on the other a single group consisting of the rest of the animal kingdom.

S. Y. True.

STR. Yes; and I realized at once that, having isolated a part of the whole, you imagined that all the rest formed a single kind. I understood that much as soon as you applied the one name 'brute beasts' to them all.

S. Y. Right again.

STR. Now that, my fine fellow, is what might be done by any other animal we could conceive as endowed with reason; the crane will serve as one possible example. It too might distribute names as you do: having isolated the crane tribe and contrasted it with all other living creatures in order thus to glorify itself, it would lump together the remainder (man included) under some such generic name as 'brute beasts'. Let us try then carefully to avoid mistakes of this kind.

S. Y. How?

STR. By not dividing the whole animal kingdom into two; in that way we shall be less liable to such errors.

S. Y. Yes, they must certainly be avoided.

STR. But it was a division of that sort which gave rise to the mistake we made just now.

S. Y. Why so?

STR. We considered the entire directive branch of theoretical science as part of the rearing of animals, i.e. of animals in flocks and herds, did we not?

S. Y. Yes.

STR. [264] That was equivalent to dividing the whole animal kingdom into domestic and wild. For those animals which are by nature apt for domestication are called tame, and the others wild.

S. Y. Granted.

STR. But the science which we are trying to track down has always had tame animals as its province, and it is among those which are reared in flocks and herds that we must look for it.

S. Y. Yes.

STR. Well then, we must not follow our previous method of making an entire kind the object of division; we must not be in too much of a hurry to catch up with the Statesman. 'More haste less speed,' says the proverb, and we have recently discovered its truth.

S. Y. How so?

STR. Through delay in reaching the final term of our division, which was caused by our unwillingness to take the time in which to do it properly.

S. Y. A fortunate discovery, sir.

STR. Enough of that. Let us resume our attempt to subdivide collective rearing, and perhaps that which you so eagerly seek will be better revealed to you as our discourse proceeds. Tell me now——

S. Y. Tell you what?

STR. Something which I think you have often heard mentioned. I know of course that you have never yourself seen fish reared on the banks of the Nile or in the stews of the Persian king; but you have perhaps seen them reared in fountains.

S. Y. Certainly, I have seen the latter and have often heard about the others.

STR. So too with flocks of geese and cranes; you have never yourself travelled in the Plain of Thessaly, but you must have heard that such flocks *are* reared, and you believe it.

S. Y. What are you getting at?

STR. I ask you all these questions because some of the animals thus reared collectively are aquatic and others terrestrial.

S. Y. Quite.

STR. Do you not then agree with me that we should make a two-fold division of the science of collective rearing and apply to each of these groups that branch of the science which concerns it, calling one 'wet rearing' and the other 'dry rearing'?

S. Y. Yes, I agree.

STR. In that case we shall not inquire to which of these two arts the kingly function belongs, for it is perfectly obvious.

S. Y. Indeed it is.

STR. Again, anyone could subdivide that branch of the rearing of flocks and herds which we have called 'dry rearing'.

S. Y. How would he do it?

STR. By distinguishing creatures that fly from those that walk.

S. Y. Quite true.

STR. Well then, need we ask ourselves whether the Statesman is to be sought among those that walk; or will you agree that the veriest simpleton, so to speak, knows the answer?

S. Y. I am sure he does.

STR. We must next show that this art of rearing creatures that walk is (like numbers, which we mentioned earlier) itself capable of being divided into two.

S. Y. Evidently.

STR. [265] Now, as I see it, there are two paths leading to the goal of our inquiry: the first is shorter and divides by contrasting a small part with a large one; the other is longer, but it follows more closely our recent advice to make an equal division so far as that is possible. We may choose whichever of these paths we like.

S. Y. Can't we take them both?

STR. Good heavens! not at the same time; one after the other, obviously yes.

S. Y. Well, I choose both—one after the other.

STR. That is easy, considering the little we still have to do; at the beginning, and even in the middle of our journey, it would have been difficult to oblige. But as things are, since that is the way you feel, let us take the longer path: being still fresh, we shall cover it the more easily. Observe now the method of division.

S. Y. Go ahead.

STR. Of tame animals that walk, those that live in flocks or herds are naturally divisible into two kinds.

S. Y. How so?

STR. Some are born without and others with horns.

S. Y. Clearly.

STR. Now when you divide the art of rearing animals that walk, confine yourself in each case to a bare statement of characteristics. To try and give each branch a name would complicate the task unnecessarily.

S. Y. What then are we to say?

STR. We are to say that, having divided into two the science of rearing animals that walk, we apply one branch to the horned kind, and the other to that kind which has no horns.

S. Y. That way of expressing it is most satisfactory; it is as clear as one could wish.

STR. Now as regards the King, it is perfectly clear that his charges will be found in the flock without horns.

S. Y. Undoubtedly.

STR. Let us then split up this flock and try to assign him the particular kind that is his own.

S. Y. By all means.

STR. On what basis would you like to make this division—according as the hoof is cloven or uncloven, or according as the breed will or will not cross? I am sure you understand what I mean by this latter alternative.

S. Y. What do you mean?

STR. I mean that horses and asses can unite to produce young.

S. Y. Yes.

STR. Whereas all other members of the gentle class of tame animals are naturally incapable of so doing.

S. Y. That is a well-known fact.

STR. Good. Now do you think the Statesman has care of the breed that will or that will not cross?

S. Y. Clearly, of the one that will not cross.

STR. Well, this also must apparently be likewise divided into two.

S. Y. Certainly it must.

STR. [266] Down to this point we already have a complete division and subdivision of the whole body of tame animals that live in flocks and herds. For one can scarcely reckon dogs among beasts that are reared collectively.

S. Y. Certainly not. But according to what principle shall we make the next division?

STR. According to a principle well worthy of guiding all divisions made by students of geometry like Theaitetos and yourself.

S. Y. What is that?

STR. Why, the diagonal of course, and then the square constructed on that diagonal.

S. Y. What do you mean?

STR. Well, is the nature possessed by us humans equipped for walking otherwise than is expressed by the diagonal of a square whose side measures one foot?

S. Y. No.

STR. And the mode of walking that characterizes the other kind is expressed by the square constructed on our own diagonal: nature has given it twice two feet.

S. Y. Of course. I'm beginning to see what you're driving at.

STR. Is it not also clear, Socrates, that our process of division has led us into doing something rather absurd?

S. Y. What is that?

STR. Matching mankind against the noblest and also the most indolent kind of beings.

S. Y. Yes. I see that; it is a fantastic state of affairs.

STR. Is it not probable that the slowest will come in last?

S. Y. Assuredly.

STR. And do we not see that the King will appear even more ridiculous, competing with his own flock and running against the man best trained to an indolent life?

S. Y. Definitely.

STR. Now, Socrates, we understand better what was said during our hunt for the Sophist.

S. Y. You mean——?

STR. That our method of discourse was no more closely concerned with a lofty theme than with another, that it paid no more regard to small things than to great, and that it pursued its search for truth relying solely upon itself.

S. Y. Apparently.

STR. And now, in order to prevent you forestalling me by asking what is that shorter road to a definition of the King, may I come straight to the point myself?

S. Y. By all means do.

STR. I say that we must straightway divide the walking kind by contrasting bipeds with quadrupeds; then, seeing that the human race is thus actually lumped together with winged creatures, we have in turn to divide the bipeds into naked bipeds and feathered bipeds. Lastly, having thus brought the art of rearing human beings into the full light of day, we must place the Statesman or King in that setting and hand over to him the reins of state as belonging to him by right, since it is he who has this science.

S. Y. [267] There now, your explanation has paid me in full—with interest, in the form of a digression, for good measure.

STR. Well, let us go back to the beginning and trace once again the definition of the Statesman's art.

S. Y. Certainly.

STR. We began by distinguishing in theoretical science a directive part, and in the latter a branch which we called by analogy 'self-directive'. Next, the rearing of animals was recognized as a distinct and far from unimportant branch of the self-directive science. One branch of rearing animals is the rearing of flocks and herds; one subdivision of which is the rearing of animals that walk. Again, one (and indeed the principal) branch of rearing animals that walk is the rearing of those without horns. It is necessary to plait the most important branch of this from three strands, if we are to bring it under a single name: we shall call it 'rearing those kinds which will not cross', and it gives rise to the last remaining branch concerned with bipeds—the science of rearing men. Here precisely is the object of our search: it is called the art of kingship or statecraft.

S. Y. You are perfectly right.

STR. But have we, Socrates, really fulfilled our undertaking as perfectly as you say?

S. Y. What undertaking?

STR. Have we satisfactorily answered the question asked? Is not our inquiry defective particularly in that it reaches a definition, but one that is not altogether perfect.

S. Y. How do you mean?

STR. I am going to try, for my own benefit as well as yours, to explain my thought more clearly.

S. Y. Yes, I wish you would.

STR. Well, among the numerous forms assumed by the pastoral art we have reckoned statecraft and have assigned it its charge.

S. Y. We have.

STR. And our discourse has shown that the science of collective rearing is concerned with men rather than with horses or other brute beasts.

S. Y. Exactly.

STR. Let us see then how kings differ from all other pastors.

S. Y. Yes, how do they?

STR. We must ask ourselves whether anyone professing another art could lay claim to being just as much shepherd of the human flock as is a king or statesman.

S. Y. What do you mean?

STR. Are you aware, for example, that all merchants, farmers and bakers, as well as athletes and the whole medical profession, might very well present themselves [268] before these pastors of men, whom we call kings or statesmen, arguing one and all that it is *their* job to care for men—not only those who are members of the flock, but their rulers also?

S. Y. And would they not be right?

STR. Perhaps; we shall consider that point. But this we do know, that there are certain titles which no one can claim as against the herdsman. He is the one who rears the herd; he it is who pastures the kine. He is their doctor; he is, so to speak, their matchmaker; and he alone knows how to act as midwife to the young when they are born no less than to the mothers who give them birth. Moreover the same is true as regards games and music, in so far as those under his care are by nature accessible thereto: no one knows better than he how to console them and to charm their savage breasts; whether by the use of instruments or with his voice alone, he produces to perfection the melodies best adapted to his herd. Does not the same apply to other pastors in their respective fields?

S. Y. Perfectly true.

STR. How then can we discover the correct and precise definition of the King, we who, in order to establish him as pastor or nurse of the human flock, have preferred him without further consideration to thousands and thousands of competitors?

S. Y. We certainly cannot.

STR. Were we not then justified, a little while ago, in feeling uneasy when we began to suspect that, although we might draw a rough sketch of the King or Statesman, we cannot work it up into a really faithful portrait of him until we have isolated him from all those who surge around him and claim a share in his rights as pastor, in other words, until we have distinguished him from his rivals in such a way as to reveal him alone in all his purity?

S. Y. We were indeed justified.

STR. There then, Socrates, is our remaining task, unless we are willing to bring the discussion to an untimely end.

S. Y. On no account must we do that.

STR. Then we must make a new beginning and follow a different road.

S. Y. How?

STR. By discussing something that might be described as virtually mere entertainment, inasmuch as we shall have to make extensive use of a great myth. Afterwards we shall resume and complete our former journey, continually dividing and subdividing until we reach the very goal of our search. That is what we must do, is it not?

S. Y. Exactly.

STR. Good. Now pay close attention to what I am going to say, like children do to a storyteller. After all, it is not so very long ago that you were a child.

S. Y. Go ahead.

STR. One of many ancient myths that used to be told, and will be told again, is that of an incident connected with the celebrated quarrel between Atreus and Thyestes. No doubt you have heard and still remember what is said to have happened.

S. Y. You mean perhaps the prodigy of the golden lamb.

STR. [269] Certainly not; I mean the reversal of the rising and setting of the sun and other stars, which now rise in the quarter where they used at that time to set, and vice versa. It was on this occasion, in order to testify in favour of Atreus, that the god reversed their course and introduced the present order.

S. Y. Yes, that is another episode in the story.

STR. There is also the myth of the reign of Cronos, which is the subject of many tales.

S. Y. Yes, of very many.

STR. And yet another which relates how, in that bygone age, men were born from the earth instead of procreating among themselves.

S. Y. That too is found among the old legends.

STR. All these marvels, and very many others still more wonderful, can be traced to the same phenomenon; but in the course of ages some of them have disappeared while others have been made into a number of independent tales. As for the phenomenon which produced them all, no one has mentioned it, and it is now time to make it known, for it will help us to establish the nature of the King.

S. Y. Excellent. Go on then, and leave nothing out.

STR. Listen now. At certain times God himself guides the progress of this world and presides over its revolution. At other times, when the periods assigned to it have run their course, he leaves it alone; and then, of its own accord, it begins to travel on its circular course *in the opposite direction*, by virtue of the life which animates it and the intelligence wherewith its framer has endowed it from the beginning. Now this disposition to retrograde movement is necessarily innate, for the following reason.

S. Y. What is this reason?

STR. Always to preserve the same state, the same modes of being, and to remain for ever identical, belongs only to that which is pre-eminently divine; and the corporeal nature is not of this order. That which we call 'the Heavens' or 'the World', though richly endowed by its maker with glorious qualities, nevertheless partakes of corporality, and therefore cannot be wholly exempt from change. On the other hand it moves in the same place with an identical and simple motion, so far as its nature allows; hence it shares in circular retrogradation, which, of all forms of movement, causes it to depart least from its original motion. Nothing, however, can for ever be the author of its own rotation, except that which carries with it all things that are moved; nor may this latter move now in one direction and now in another. For all these reasons we cannot say either that the world is the continual author of its own rotation, nor that some god leads entirely and uninterruptedly in these alternating and contrary revolutions, [270] or, again, that these revolutions are due to a pair of gods whose wills are opposed to one another. As I was saying just now, the only remaining solution is that (a) the world is sometimes governed by some external and divine action and, taking on a new life, it also receives from its author a restored immortality; and that (b) at other times, left to itself, it moves with its own motion and that consequently, from the very moment that it is thus abandoned, it travels a retrograde circuit through thousands upon thousands of ages, because its enormous mass turns in perfect equilibrium on an extremely small pivot.

S. Y. All that you have said sounds highly probable.

STR. Following this line of thought let us see what is the phenomenon which, we say, is the cause of so many prodigies. It consists precisely in this——

S. Y. In what?

STR. In this alternation of the world, which revolves now in one direction and now in the opposite.

S. Y. How do you mean?

STR. Of all the upheavals to which the world is subject this change of direction must be considered the greatest and most complete.

S. Y. Fair enough.

STR. We must believe then that at this moment also there are produced those changes which are most important for us who dwell within the world.

S. Y. That too seems probable.

STR. But we are surely aware that the animal nature cannot easily endure a concurrence of major changes, both numerous and varied.

S. Y. That is a well-known fact.

STR. Inevitably then death takes its greatest toll among animals in general, and the human race in particular is reduced to a very small number of survivors. These moreover undergo all sorts of strange and unusual experiences, of which the most serious is due to the Universe changing direction, when the existing state of affairs goes into reverse.

S. Y. What is this experience?

STR. To begin with the age of every living creature came to a halt; everything mortal ceased to present the spectacle of gradual ageing. From that moment there was progress in the opposite direction—they began to advance in youth and freshness. The white hairs of old age began to blacken; the sprouting beard gave place to smooth cheeks; and every creature returned to the springtime of its youth. The bodies of the young became day by day slimmer and more supple, returning eventually to the condition of new-born babes; and their souls followed the example of their bodies; after which a steady decline ended in their total disappearance. As for those who died a violent death at this time, their corpses passed through [271] the same series of transformations with such speed that within a few days nothing remained of them.

S. Y. Tell me, sir, how were living things born at that time? What means had they of procreation?

STR. Clearly, Socrates, procreation was impossible in nature as it then was. Those were the days of the legendary autochthones, when men sprang from the bosom of the earth; the memory of it was handed down by our first parents, who lived in the times immediately following the ancient cycle, i.e. who were born at the very beginning of the present one. They, in fact, are our authority for these traditions which many people today, and for no good reason, disbelieve.

For here, I think, is the conclusion to which we are forced: from the moment when greybeards turned back towards infancy, the dead, lying in the ground, must inevitably then and there have put off their state of dissolution and come back to life in obedience to that turn of the tide which reversed the laws of generation and decay. Thus they necessarily sprang from the bosom of earth; whence the name 'autochthones' and the legend applied to those of them who were not doomed by a god to some other fate.

S. Y. The result is beyond doubt. But are we to assign the kind of life which you say prevailed in the reign of Cronos to the earlier cycle or to that which is now running its course? For clearly the reversal of the sun and stars occurs in both.

STR. You have followed the argument well. The state of affairs to which you refer, in which everything sprang to life of its own accord for the use of man, does not belong to the present cycle; it too belonged to the preceding one. The government and providence of the god was exercised then, as it is now, over the circular motion as a whole; and the same providence was exercised locally, all parts of the world being distributed among the several gods entrusted with their government. Moreover the animals themselves had been allotted, by kinds and herds, to the pastoral care of divinities, each of whom himself provided fully for all the requirements of his charges. And so well did these divinities fulfil their task that there was no such thing as a wild animal, no animal preyed upon another, nor indeed was there war or any kind of hostility throughout the animal kingdom. Such a state of affairs brought in its train innumerable other benefits. Returning, however, to mankind, here is the explanation of their effortless life. They were watched over and tended by the god himself, [272] just as other kinds of animals are looked after by human beings, who are a more god-like race and superior to them. Under his rule there were no systems of government, and no possession of wives or children; all sprang to life from the bosom of the earth, retaining no memory of their previous existence. Instead they had abundance of those fruits which grow on trees and of other vegetable products, without having to till the soil which yielded them of its own accord. Without clothing or bedding men lived mainly in the open air; for the climate was then so mild that it could do them no harm, and they lay upon the soft grass that grew in profusion from the earth. Such, Socrates, was life under Cronos. You have direct experience of that which now prevails in the so-called reign of Zeus. Do you feel able and willing to judge which of them was the happier?

S. Y. I certainly do not.

STR. Would you like me then to try and make the choice for you?

S. Y. Please do, by all means.

STR. Well, if the nurslings of Cronos, having so much leisure and so many facilities for getting together not only with men but also with brute beasts, used all these advantages for the purpose of philosophy, conversing with the beasts as well as among themselves, and interrogating all creatures in order to

learn whether there existed one capable of enriching the
common store of knowledge with some original discovery;
then, I say, it is easy to see that the men of those times were
infinitely more fortunate than those of today. If, on the other
hand, preoccupied with the pleasures of food and drink, they
were able to exchange among themselves and with the beasts
only such tales as are now told about them, in that case (at
least in my opinion) the answer is again not far to seek. However, let us leave this question until such time as we may meet
with someone capable of telling us in what spirit men in those
days approached the sciences and the interchange of thought.
As to our purpose in recalling this legend, now is the time to
state it if we are to bring our discourse to a successful conclusion.

When the time allotted to all these events was fulfilled,
when the change was due to take place and the whole earth-
born race had disappeared, every soul having accomplished
its appointed number of rebirths and returned as often to the
earth as seed, then the helmsman of the world, abandoning
control of the rudder, so to speak, withdrew to his look-out
post, while the universe was turned back in the opposite
direction by its destiny and natural tendency. All the local
deities, who assisted the supreme divinity in his rule, recognizing at once what was happening, likewise abandoned the
parts of the world entrusted to their care. [273] Turning this
somersault, which involved a complete reversal of its direction,
the world produced within itself a mighty upheaval, which
once again destroyed animals of every kind. Later on, after
the passage of sufficient time, when this cataclysmic upheaval
had ceased, the universe followed its normal and appointed
course, watching over and controlling both itself and all that
it contained, remembering as best it could the instructions of
its author and father. At first it managed to carry out those
instructions exactly; but towards the end its fallibility
gradually increased owing to the corporeal principles of its
constitution and to the inherited characteristics of its primitive
nature, which included a large element of disorder before
attaining the present cosmic order. From its maker it received
all that it has of beauty; but all the ills and evils of the world
flow from its former state, whence it receives them and

whereby it produces them in living beings. In so far, therefore, as it enjoyed the aid of its helmsman in nourishing the living creatures it contains, it engendered (with few exceptions) nothing but great good. Once separated from him, on the other hand, it begins by still doing all for the best; but as time goes on and it becomes subject to forgetfulness, so do the remnants of its primitive chaos gradually regain control, until at length confusion bursts into full flower. Then indeed benefits are few and far between, and so numerous are the evils of which it is compounded that it is in danger of destroying itself together with all that it contains. Wherefore the god who organized it, seeing its perilous situation, begins to fear lest it break up amid the waves that buffet it, and sink in the bottomless ocean of dissemblance. So he takes his place once more at the helm: regrouping the parts that have been damaged or dislodged in the cycle just completed, he puts it in order and restores it in such a way as to render it immortal and imperishable.

So ends the myth. In order to make it serve our theory of the King we have only to link the discussion with what has gone before. When, as a result of a new reversal, the world returned to that path which led to the present mode of generation, the progress of age was again halted and set out in a direction opposite to that which it had followed hitherto. Living things, whose decrease had reduced them almost to nothing, started to increase once more; their bodies, lately sprung from the earth, having grown grey, began to perish and return to the earth. [274] Everything else underwent the same change, imitating and following the new condition of the universe. In particular, the processes of gestation, parturition and nurture inevitably adapted themselves to the general trend. It was no longer possible that an animal should be born, in the bosom of earth, from a concourse of diverse elements; just as the world had been ordered to govern its own progress, its parts also had by a similar law to conceive, bear and nourish their young of their own accord so far as they were able. And this brings us to the point to which our whole discussion was directed. As regards the brute beasts, it would be a long and laborious business to describe the condition of every species at that time, and by what influences each was modified; but so far as concerns man, such an account will be both shorter and more to the point. Abandoned by that god who possessed and protected us, surrounded moreover by beasts the majority of which (by nature wild) had become completely savage, man, weak and unprotected, became their prey. At this early period he was without industry or art, so that, when nourishment ceased to supply him of its own accord, he did not know how to procure it, having never until then been obliged to do so. For all these reasons he was in terrible straits. Hence those gifts which tradition says we received, together with necessary teaching and instruction, from the gods: fire from Prometheus; arts from Hephaistos and the goddess who shares his skill; finally, seeds and plants from other deities. All that goes to make up human life proceeded from these first beginnings, once man, deprived as I have just said, of divine providence, had to guide and watch over himself—as indeed had the universe in general, which we do but imitate and follow, throughout eternity, by alternating between those two contrasted modes of birth and life. So much then for the myth. We shall find it useful in showing how we erred in defining the King or Statesman earlier in our discussion.

S. Y. What was this error to which you refer, and what is its importance?

STR. In one respect it was comparatively slight; but in another it was very considerable—far more momentous and more far-reaching.

S. Y. How do you mean?

STR. When asked for the King or Statesman of the *present* cycle and method of generation, we made a great mistake by pointing to the shepherd who ruled the human flock in the *opposite* period—at that time no man, but a god. [275] On the other hand when we presented him as head of the entire state, but without explaining *how*, we were uttering a truth, but not the whole nor the manifest truth. Thus our latter fault was less than the former.

S. Y. Quite so.

STR. It seems that if we wish to flatter ourselves upon having given a perfect definition of the Statesman, we must now determine what kind of authority he exercises over the state.

S. Y. Agreed.

STR. Well, it was for that very purpose that we introduced the myth. We not only sought thereby to show that the person on whose track we were had an indefinite number of rivals who could equally well claim to be rearing the flock; we wished also to get a clearer view of one who alone undertakes to rear the human flock in the same way as do shepherds and herdsmen their respective charges, and is therefore alone worthy to be recognized as such.

S. Y. Quite right.

STR. But, Socrates, to my way of thinking this image of the divine pastor is still too lofty for a king; our modern statesmen, who are by nature far more like their subjects, are likewise more closely akin to them on the score of their education and training.

S. Y. That is all quite true.

STR. They will not, however, require our study, either more or less, whatever their nature may be.

S. Y. Of course not.

STR. Let us then retrace our steps. This art which we have described as having a self-directive authority over animals, and as taking care of them collectively rather than individually, we have also described without hesitation as 'the art of rearing flocks and herds'. Do you remember?

S. Y. Yes.

STR. Well now, it is just there that we must have gone astray. For we have neither laid hands on the Statesman nor given him a name: he gave us the slip just as we thought to name him.

S. Y. How do you mean?

STR. It is the job of all pastors to nourish their respective flocks and herds, but the Statesman had no right to the name we gave him; and yet some name was required that might be applied to all of them.

S. Y. True enough—if there is such a name.

STR. Surely the act of 'minding' is common to them all, provided we do not restrict the sense of minding either to rearing or to any other distinctive branch of minding. In speaking of the art concerned with flocks and herds, which minds them or has the care of them, there we have a term which describes the function of them all and includes the Statesman together with all his rivals, which was the exact purpose of our inquiry.

S. Y. [276] Quite, but how shall we set about the subsequent division?

STR. As we did earlier, when we divided the art of rearing flocks and herds by distinguishing animals that walk and do not fly, animals that do not cross, animals without horns. Proceeding by means of analogous divisions, we were able to make a single notion cover the present-day art of minding flocks and herds as well as that which was practised in the reign of Cronos.

S. Y. That is clear; but what came next, please?

STR. Obviously with such a way of characterizing the art concerned with flocks and herds, we should never have heard certain people deny the very existence of any sort of minding, whereas it was possible to maintain just now that we possess no art that could properly be called rearing, or that if one *did* exist, it could be claimed by many men more readily and more justly than by any king.

S. Y. True.

STR. Well, as regards minding human society as a whole, the kingly art, above all others, will most promptly and most justly claim to exercise that function and to constitute a science of ruling mankind in general.

S. Y. You are right.

STR. But, Socrates, do we not find after all that on the very brink of our conclusion we have made a serious mistake?

S. Y. What mistake?

STR. I will explain. Even if we had been absolutely convinced that there is an art of rearing the whole class of bipeds, we should have had no right on that account to think we had reached our goal, and to declare forthwith that this art is the art of the King or Statesman.

S. Y. What are we to do then?

STR. Well, the first thing to do, as I was saying, is to recast the name, approximating it rather to the idea of 'minding' than to that of 'rearing', and then to subdivide this idea, which will be found to contain some clear-cut lines of demarcation.

S. Y. What are they?

STR. First, that which leads us to distinguish the divine shepherd from the human minder.

S. Y. Good.

STR. Next, having separated this art of minding, we have to divide it into two parts.

S. Y. How?

STR. By contrasting what is imposed by force with what is voluntarily accepted.

S. Y. So——?

STR. Yes, it was our failure to do this that led us into the absurd error of confusing the King or Statesman and the tyrant, whereas they are so unlike both in themselves and in their methods of government.

S. Y. True.

STR. We shall correct ourselves, as I said, by dividing into two the human art of guardianship, according as this guardianship is imposed by force or voluntarily accepted. Do you agree?

S. Y. Certainly.

STR. And may we call it tyrannical when it is wielded by force, and political or statesmanlike when its care is freely offered and freely accepted by bipeds? Shall we not in this latter case declare that he who practises this art of guardianship is in very truth King or Statesman?

S. Y. We shall indeed. [277] And it looks, sir, very much as if we have completed our demonstration as regards the Statesman.

STR. That would be splendid, Socrates; but it is not good enough that you alone should be convinced. No, we must both be in agreement. Now, to *my* way of thinking, our portrait of the King is as yet imperfect. Just as some over-zealous sculptors delay the completion of their works by piling on too much ornament, so we, anxious to show up at once and in grand style the error of our previous exposition, thought it unfitting to construct any but large-scale models of the King and thus loaded ourselves with so enormous an amount of myth that we could not avoid using too much of it. Thus we have prolonged the demonstration and failed after all to round off the myth. On the contrary, our discussion may be said to resemble a portrait sufficiently well sketched in outline but lacking the refinement given by paint and by the harmony of colours. But verbal description is more likely than pictorial or any other kind of manual representation to reveal a living subject to those who can understand; others derive more profit from material images.

S. Y. Quite so; but please explain in what respect you maintain that we have not yet said enough.

STR. My good friend, it is hard to deal with any subject of importance unless one has recourse to some illustration. One might almost say that each one of us knows everything as it were in a dream and finds that he knows nothing when awake.

S. Y. What do you mean?

STR. Here, oddly enough, I seem to have touched upon the phenomenon of human knowledge.

S. Y. I don't follow you.

STR. A paradigm, my dear fellow; I need one to explain even that.

S. Y. Oh, do carry on; don't hesitate on my account.

STR. I will, since you are prepared to follow me. We know of course that children, when they first make acquaintance with writing——

S. Y. Yes?

STR. They can distinguish well enough each letter of the shortest and easiest syllables, and are able to give a truthful account of them.

S. Y. [278] Undoubtedly.

STR. But they no longer recognize the letters in other syllables, thus forming an erroneous judgment and giving an erroneous account.

S. Y. Certainly.

STR. Well, I think you'll agree that the method I am going to describe is the easiest and surest way of leading them to what as yet they do not know.

S. Y. What method is that?

STR. First, to bring them back to the syllables whose letters they have interpreted correctly; then to confront them with syllables with which they are as yet unfamiliar, and make them compare the two sets of combinations to see what they have in common with one another. At last, by dint of showing them those groups which they recognize side by side with those that baffle them, the former, displayed thus in parallel columns, will serve them as paradigms which will help them (no matter what the letter in no matter what syllable) to spell differently those which are different from the others, but always in the same invariable manner those which are the same.

S. Y. Quite.

STR. So what constitutes a paradigm is the fact that a given letter, being found again in a new and absolutely distinct syllable, is interpreted correctly there also, and, having been identified in both groups, makes it possible to embody the two of them in a single and accurate idea. I think we've shown that to be the case, what?

S. Y. Definitely.

STR. Should we be surprised then if the human soul is by nature subject to the same variations with regard to the elements of the universe—sometimes firmly grounded in truth as to every element of certain composites, sometimes in doubt as to all the elements of certain others, and though just able to interpret correctly particular elements of these combinations, incapable of recognizing them when they have been transposed into the more complex and difficult 'syllables' of reality?

S. Y. It is not at all surprising.

STR. How, my friend, is it possible for a man who starts from a false opinion to attain even to the slightest degree of truth and thus to acquire wisdom.

S. Y. It is scarcely possible at all.

STR. That being so, it will not be out of place if, having attempted to find in a common or garden example the nature of a paradigm in general, you and I now undertake to raise this same procedure, which we have employed on humble objects, to its highest or kingly form, in order to attempt by using a different paradigm to discover step by step in what the care of a state consists, and so to pass from dreamland to wakening.

S. Y. A very good idea.

STR. [279] Let us then go back to the point where we agreed that, since innumerable rivals claim an equal hand in the care lavished by the kingly tribe upon states, it is necessary to separate them from that tribe in order to isolate the latter; and it is precisely for this purpose that I said we needed a paradigm.

S. Y. Exactly.

STR. Well, what paradigm, having the same functions as state-craft and although in itself quite familiar, will enable us to find what we are looking for? If there is no other to hand, will you agree that we may take weaving? I don't think we want the whole art of weaving: the weaving of wools will probably be sufficient, inasmuch as that branch of the art alone is likely to provide us with the evidence we require.

S. Y. I am quite agreeable.

STR. Having, earlier on in this discussion, used the method of dividing and subdividing the branches of various arts, why not do the same now with weaving? Why not try to explore the whole of this art by as rapid a survey as possible and so return quickly to that which is of present use?

S. Y. How do you mean?

STR. I will answer you by going right ahead.

S. Y. Splendid!

STR. Well now, all that we make or acquire serves us either as a means to some action or as a preservative against some form of suffering. These preservatives are themselves either antidotes (divine or human) or safeguards. Some safeguards are weapons of war, others are coverings. Coverings are either curtains or protections against heat and cold. Some of the latter are roofing materials, others fabrics; and fabrics are made to be spread underfoot or to be worn. Those which are worn are made of a single piece or of several. When of several pieces, they are either perforated or put together without perforation. The non-perforated kind are made either of plant fibres or of hairs; and those that are made of hairs are either cemented together with earth and water, or are simply bound together, thread by thread. Now the name 'clothes' is given to those preservatives which take the form of fabrics made of threads. As for the sort which is especially concerned with clothes, since we have called the man who has care of the state a states-man, let us do the same with this next art and call it [280] after its object, 'the clothing art'. Shall we not then say that weaving, because it is the most important stage in the making of clothes, is identical, except in name, with 'the clothing art' itself, just as the kingly art differs only in name from the art of statesmanship?

S. Y. That would be perfectly fair.

STR. In which case one might reckon that the art of weaving clothes had been thus sufficiently explained, but for the realization that it has not been distinguished from allied and auxiliary arts, although it has been marked off from several others which are akin to it.

S. Y. How do you mean akin?

STR. It looks as though you have not followed what I have been saying, so we must retrace our steps, beginning at the end. If you know anything about kinship, there is one art which we have just separated from the weaving of clothes, when we set aside the making of carpets, that is, when we distinguished what is worn from what is spread under foot.

S. Y. I understand.

STR. Again, we excluded the manufacture of everything that is made from flax, esparto and plant fibres generally. We have likewise relegated the art of felt-making; also that of putting together with punch and thread, of which the main branch is shoemaking.

S. Y. Certainly.

STR. Then there is the art of tanning, which prepares materials made of a single piece; there is the manufacture of roofing for houses or other buildings, or, in other arts, for covering of streams. All these we have set aside, together with the arts that provide us with means of protection against theft and other acts of violence, in other words, those arts which make shutters and fix doors, and which are special branches of the art of joinery. We have also struck out the making of arms, which is only part of the large and complex industry of defence; and indeed of magic that is concerned with antidotes, thus leaving, as it seems, only that art for which we were looking—that, namely, which protects us against heat and cold by making defences of wool, and which is called weaving.

S. Y. That would seem to be the case.

STR. But we have not reached the end of our account, young man. For as we take the first step towards making clothes [281] we are evidently doing something quite different from weaving.

S. Y. What?

STR. Weaving may be described, in a word, as interlacing.

S. Y. Yes.

STR. But I am talking about a process which disentangles what was compressed and matted together.

S. Y. To what exactly do you refer?

STR. To the function of the carder's art, unless we are going to call carding weaving, and say that the carder is actually a weaver?

S. Y. We must not do that.

STR. The same applies of course to the art which makes the warp and woof: to call it weaving would be an absurd lie.

S. Y. Indeed it would.

STR. Then again, shall we decide that mending, as well as the several stages of fulling, play no part in the production of a garment; or shall we say that they are all a part of weaving?

S. Y. By no means.

STR. And yet all these arts will deny that weaving alone is concerned in the business of producing clothes. While conceding the lion's share to weaving they will nevertheless claim a large part as their own.

S. Y. Certainly they will.

STR. It is highly probable that, besides them, those arts which make the tools employed in weaving will claim to be at least joint producers of every woven article.

S. Y. Too true.

STR. Then shall we provide a sufficient account of this our chosen branch of weaving if we give it pride of place as the fairest and most important of all processes having to do with clothes? Or would that, however truthful, be an obscure and inconclusive statement inasmuch as we should not have eliminated all those rivals?

S. Y. It would indeed.

STR. Is not now the time to do so, if we wish to make headway with our discussion?

S. Y. Undoubtedly.

STR. Well, first let us consider that every product is the result of two arts.

S. Y. What are they?

STR. One is a mere auxiliary cause of the effect, the other is its proper cause.

S. Y. What does that mean?

STR. Those causes are auxiliary which do not fashion the object but merely supply those which do so with the instruments necessary for carrying out their task.

S. Y. A very sound distinction.

STR. Accordingly we shall describe as auxiliary those which provide the spindles, shuttles and other instruments which help towards the production of clothes, reserving the term 'proper causes' for those which function directly therein.

S. Y. Quite right.

STR. [282] Now since there are so many stages in the preparation of cloth, it will be most convenient to treat certain of these proper causes (washing, mending, etc.) as a single part thereof, and call it by the general name of 'the fuller's art'.

S. Y. Agreed.

STR. But the arts of carding, spinning and all such operations as enter into what we call the direct manufacture of clothing —all these form a single and universally recognized art: the art of working wool.

S. Y. Undoubtedly.

STR. There are two branches of the art of working wool, and each of them results from the union of two arts.

S. Y. How so?

STR. Carding, half of that done by the shuttle, and those operations whose purpose is to separate what was inter-mingled—all these, taken together, belong to the working of wool properly so called, and we recognize an overall distinction of two great arts: that of assembling and that of separating.

S. Y. Yes.

STR. Now the art of separating includes carding and all those other processes just enumerated; for the work of separating the hairs or strands of the wool (the former by hand, the latter by means of the shuttle) are called by the names I mentioned just now.

S. Y. Quite so.

STR. Now let us turn to the art of assembling and take a branch of it which belongs also to the working of wool; and let us leave aside all those branches of the separative art belonging thereto, thus dividing the working of wool into its two sections: that which separates and that which assembles.

S. Y. Very well.

STR. And now, Socrates, if we desire fully to understand the said art of weaving, we must subdivide this part of assemblage which is included in the working of wool.

S. Y. Yes, we must.

STR. Indeed yes, and we shall say that its function is either to twist or to interlace.

S. Y. Do I understand you? It seems to me that when speaking of twisting you have in mind the preparation of thread for the warp.

STR. Not only for the warp, but also for the woof. Or shall we find a means of preparing the latter without twisting?

S. Y. Certainly not.

STR. Well, analyse each of these operations: from doing so you may derive some timely assistance.

S. Y. Analyse it how?

STR. I will tell you. Among the products of carding there is one that has length and breadth, and we call it yarn.

S. Y. Yes.

STR. When this is wound on to the spindle so as to form a solid thread, there you have the material of the warp, and the art which directs this operation is the art of making the warp.

S. Y. Quite.

STR. And all those strands which form fluffy threads, and which have just the requisite softness and tensile strength to interlace with the warp, may be described as strands of the woof, and we may say that the art which handles their arrangement is directed to the manufacture of the woof.

S. Y. [283] Exactly.

STR. Now at last we are perfectly clear as to the branch of weaving with which we are concerned. When that process of assembling which is a branch of the working of wool has casued the warp and woof to intersect, so as to produce a web, we call the whole web a woollen garment and the art which produces it weaving.

S. Y. Certainly.

STR. Come though, why did we not go straight to the point and reply: 'Weaving is the art of interlacing warp and woof', instead of running round in circles and making a heap of useless distinctions?

S. Y. Well, sir, I personally see nothing useless in what we have said.

STR. That does not surprise me, but you may perhaps do so later on. As a precaution against the likely event of your being overtaken by such a disease—an event that would not be surprising—listen to these considerations that apply in all questions of this sort.

S. Y. Go ahead.

STR. First let us consider excess and defect in general; we shall then have a standard according to which we may praise or blame unnecessary prolixity and its opposite in discussions such as ours.

S. Y. Yes, let us do that.

STR. Those, I think, are the very things to which it would be right to apply the considerations of which I spoke.

S. Y. To what things?

STR. To length, to brevity and to all that is excess or defect; for, as we know, it is with all such that the art of measurement is concerned.

S. Y. Yes.

STR. Now let us divide this art into two parts, as our present purpose requires.

S. Y. What kind of a division do you mean?

STR. On the one hand according to the mutual relationship of great and small, and on the other according to the law of all creation.

S. Y. I don't follow.

STR. Do you not agree that the greatest cannot in any circumstances be so called but by comparison with the smallest, and vice versa?

S. Y. I do.

STR. Very well then, may we not say that what exceeds or falls below the level of moderation, either in word or deed, constitutes the most fundamental difference between good and bad?

S. Y. Manifestly.

STR. We are therefore obliged to recognize in the great and the small two modes of existence and two standards of measurement. We must not, as we were doing a little while ago, confine ourselves to their mutual relationship, but rather distinguish as we are doing now, (a) the relations they bear to one another and (b) their relationship to the mean. Shall I tell you why?

S. Y. Please do.

STR. [284] If one claims that the nature of the greatest is unrelated to anything except the nature of the smallest, there will be no relationship between it and the mean, will there?

S. Y. No.

STR. By such a claim, in fact, we destroy the arts and all their products, including, note, the art of statement, which we are trying to define, and the art of weaving which we have just been studying. For all these arts seek to exclude from their products anything that is in excess of or that falls short of the mean, not as something non-existent but as an undesirable reality. It is by preserving the mean that they ensure the goodness and beauty of their works.

S. Y. Of course.

STR. To do away with statecraft is surely to put an end to our search for the kingly science.

S. Y. Certainly.

STR. Are we then to do now what we did in the case of the Sophist, when we decided that the non-existent must exist because its existence was our only refuge? Are we, I mean, to decide that the more and the less are commensurable, not only with one another but also with the production of the mean. For unless we agree to do so it is quite impossible to establish beyond doubt the existence of the Statesman or of any competence whatever in the realm of action.

S. Y. We must do the same again in this case, as far as possible.

STR. It will be more difficult this time, Socrates—you will remember how long it took us on the previous occasion—but here is something of which it is only fair that we should take note in this connection.

S. Y. What is that?

STR. A day will come when we shall need all the time at our disposal for a closely reasoned demonstration. But confining ourselves to what has been well and sufficiently demonstrated for our present purpose, we find, I think, strong support in the argument both (a) that all the arts are realities and (b) that the great and the small are estimated not only with reference to their mutual relationship, but also with reference to their producing the mean. For if this last relationship exists, the arts also exist, and vice versa; but do away with one of these existences, and the other becomes impossible.

S. Y. Exactly; but where do we go from there?

STR. Clearly, in order to divide the science of measurement on the foregoing lines we have only to distinguish the following branches. We shall set on one side all the arts which measure number, length, depth, breadth and density by their opposites; on the other side we shall set all those which refer to the mean, to that which is seemly, opportune and desirable, to that which stands midway between extremes.

S. Y. There indeed we have two enormous branches which differ considerably from one another.

STR. [285] As a matter of fact, Socrates, what I have just said happens to be exactly what many learned men like to give out as a profound truth, namely that the science of measurement is concerned with everything that comes into being. All works of art share one way or another in measurement. Men, however, are unaccustomed to study things by distinguishing their several kinds; and so, notwithstanding the great difference between these two sorts of measurement, they forthwith identify them, thinking them alike; and they do the opposite with other things, because they do not distinguish their several parts. The correct procedure requires (a) that having observed that a certain number of things have something in common, one should not leave them before one has seen therein all the differences which constitute the several kinds; and (b) that when one has reckoned up all the variations in a certain number of things, one should be unable to relax one's concentration upon them until one has found a single mark of similarity to cover all those elements of relationship which they conceal, and thus include them in the essence of some one kind. But enough of this, and of excess and defect: we need only observe that we have found them subject to two sorts of measurement, and bear in mind the nature we have attributed to each.

S. Y. We shall remember that.

STR. Next let us deal with another question which affects not only the present inquiry but all matters to which this kind of discussion gives rise.

S. Y. What is that?

STR. Suppose we ask ourselves this question: When we ask someone in a reading class to tell us what letters form such and such a word, are we inviting him to do so merely in order to solve this particular problem, or rather to train him with a view to resolving all possible problems of grammar.

S. Y. Clearly, the latter.

STR. Then what about our inquiry as to the Statesman? Have we undertaken it with an eye to him alone, or rather with a view to becoming better dialecticians on all possible subjects.

S. Y. Again, the latter.

STR. Likewise of course no sensible man would be prepared to hunt for a definition of weaving merely because he was interested in weaving. But there is, I believe, one thing of which most people are unaware: the natural resemblance of certain objects resides in physical qualities which can be easily recognized and which are not difficult to describe to someone who asks for an account of that resemblance, if we desire to answer him simply and without elaborate explanation; but there is no created image whereby to convey a clear idea of the highest and most important realities, no image, I mean, which one who desired to quench another's intellectual thirst could adapt to any of the senses and hold up with a view to that other's complete satisfaction. It is necessary, therefore, to train oneself both to give and to understand a rational account of everything; for these incorporeal realities [286] which are the greatest and grandest can be clearly demonstrated by reason alone and in no other way. Such are the realities with which our present discussion has to deal. Now it is easier, no matter what the subject, to gain experience from small-scale rather than from large-scale exercises.

S. Y. That is perfectly true.

STR. Let us then recall why we have spent so much time discussing these matters.

S. Y. Why?

STR. Mainly because of the tedium engendered by those long and exhausting disquisitions on weaving, on the retrograde motion of the universe, and on the existence of non-being (in the *Sophist*). We felt that these had been too protracted, and therefore reproached ourselves with fear and trembling lest they should turn out to have been a series of lengthy digressions. Please understand then that it was in order not to expose ourselves in future to scruples of this kind that we have made the foregoing remarks.

S. Y. I understand. Do go on.

STR. My point is that you and I will do well to recall those observations when we come to praise or blame the length or brevity of our discourse upon any subject, so as not to estimate lengths by their mutual relations, but by that branch of the art of measurement which we said must be kept in mind—in other words, by what is fitting.

S. Y. Granted.

STR. At the same time, let us not subject everything to this rule. We shall not have to worry about proportion because of any need to give pleasure, except indirectly; and as for the solution of our problem, to find it in the easiest and quickest way should be only a secondary and not a primary concern. Reason tells us as much, bidding us give pride of place to the method whereby we are taught to distinguish kind from kind, and to pursue our way resolutely through any argument, however long it may be (provided it is calculated to enlighten the listener), without troubling any more today about its length than we should at another time about its brevity. Furthermore, as regards the critic who deplores prolixity in this sort of discussion and will not allow circuitous digressions, reason tells us likewise that we must not let him go scot free the moment he has made the bare statement [287] that we have talked too much: no, we must also challenge him to prove that if our discourse had been curtailed it would have made our hearers better dialecticians and better able to recognize those arguments which reveal the truth. As for any praise or blame directed at other aspects of our method, we should completely ignore it and not even appear to have heard such criticism. But enough of that; may I suggest that we return to the Statesman and apply to him our paradigm of weaving?

S. Y. I agree. Let us do as you say.

STR. Well, we have separated the King from all those arts which function in the same sphere of activity, and particularly those concerned with flocks and herds. There remain, within the state itself, the auxiliary and the immediately productive arts, which we must first distinguish from one another.

S. Y. Quite.

STR. You must realize that they are scarcely susceptible of a two-fold division; I think we shall see more clearly why as we go along.

S. Y. Then let us do so.

STR. Since twofold division is impossible we shall divide them limb by limb, as is done with a sacrificial victim. For we must always divide into the nearest possible number.

S. Y. How shall we set about it in this case?

STR. As we did earlier on. We have, in fact, included among the auxiliary arts all those which supply the tools of weaving.

S. Y. Yes.

STR. Very well then, we must do the same thing now, but on a more extensive scale. In any state, all those arts which manu-facture an instrument, great or small, must be ranked as auxiliary. Without them of course there could exist neither state nor statesman; but we cannot attribute to them any function of the kingly art.

S. Y. No.

STR. Actually we have undertaken a difficult task in trying to distinguish this class from the others, for there is nothing which we cannot with some semblance of truth describe as an instrument of something or other. There is, however, among the possessions of a state, one class of things which must be otherwise described.

S. Y. What is that?

STR. Its properties are different. For it was not made as an instrument to be used for the production of something, but to preserve something already produced.

S. Y. You mean——?

STR. I am referring to that miscellaneous class of things made (with or without fire) to hold wet or dry substances, and to which we give the generic name 'container'. [288] It is cer-tainly a very comprehensive class, and one which, in my opinion, belongs in no way to the science now under dis-cussion.

S. Y. That is perfectly true.

STR. Let us now take a look at a third class of objects, quite different from the others: they are made for use on land or water, are movable or immovable, and may be of precious material or otherwise; but we give them a single name because they are made exclusively to provide a *basis* and invariably serve to *support* something.

S. Y. What name do you mean?

STR. We call them 'vehicles'; they are not the work of a statesman, but of a carpenter, a potter or a smith.

S. Y. I understand.

STR. Now for a fourth class. Surely one must distinguish from the foregoing that which includes the majority of objects mentioned some time ago—clothing, arms and armour, walls, enclosures of earth or stone and a host of other such things. And since this whole group of objects is made to afford shelter, it is fair to give them the general name of 'covering'. Most of them belong not so much to the Statesman's art as to that of the architect.

S. Y. I quite agree.

STR. Do not let us hesitate then to recognize a fifth class as consisting of ornamentation, painting and whatever (by means of the foregoing or of music) serves to produce works whose sole purpose is to afford us pleasure and which can fairly be included under a single name.

S. Y. Under what name?

STR. 'Amusement', surely.

S. Y. Why, yes.

STR. It is the one name that will cover them all as a general term; for none of them has a serious aim—all are practised simply as forms of entertainment.

S. Y. I can understand that well enough.

STR. May we not reckon as a sixth class the materials employed for the purposes I have just enumerated? By 'materials' I mean that miscellaneous group of objects (itself the result of many different arts) from which and in which those arts to which I have just referred fashion their products.

S. Y. What do you mean?

STR. Gold, silver, all substances derived from mines, and timber or sticks for use respectively in carpentry or basket-making; then there are the raw materials of more complex products, raw materials furnished by the barking of trees, by the skinning of animal carcasses and kindred skills, as well as by the preparation of cork, papyrus and coral. We shall make one group of these and call it man's first acquisition, non-composite and by no means the product of the kingly art.

S. Y. Agreed.

STR. As for sustenance, all that has power to maintain the parts of our bodies by mingling its own parts therwith, we must recognize it as a seventh class [289], which, for want of a better word, we shall call collectively our 'nutriment'; and we shall be nearer the truth in crediting it all to the sciences of agriculture, hunting, gymnastics, medicine and cookery than in making it the work of statecraft.

S. Y. Undoubtedly.

STR. Under these seven headings we have, with the exception of domestic animals, enumerated all types of possessable goods; note, however, that they should really have been placed in the following order: 'Man's first acquisition', 'Instrument', 'Container', 'Vehicle', 'Covering', 'Amusement', 'Nutriment'. We are leaving out something which we may have overlooked as being quite unimportant and which can be assigned to one or other of the seven classes already mentioned: e.g. anything like money, a seal or a stamp. For these objects represent no class comparable with the others; on the contrary, some of them can be counted as ornaments, others as instruments—not very easily, I grant, but with an effort they can just be made to fit. As for domestic animals, slaves excepted, they clearly belong to an art already analysed, I mean the art of rearing flocks and herds.

S. Y. Certainly.

STR. There remain slaves and all kinds of servants, among whom I guess we shall find those who contend with the King as weavers of the web, in the same way as we found the spinners, carders and other such workers disputing with the weavers. All others have been described as auxiliaries, dismissed with the professions already listed, and separated from the function of the King or Statesman.

S. Y. Yes, I believe they have.

STR. Come then, let us take a closer look at the remainder, so as to obtain a more precise idea of them.

S. Y. Yes, we must do that.

STR. Looking from here at those who are servants *par excellence* we find them to possess a function and a character contrary to those we had expected.

S. Y. Who are they?

STR. Those who are bought or acquired in any such way. We must undoubtedly call them slaves, who have no share whatsoever in the kingly art.

S. Y. We must indeed.

STR. Now here is a question. Consider those freemen who voluntarily place themselves at the service of those to whom we referred just now, acting as middlemen between agriculture and the other arts, sometimes in the markets of one state and sometimes moving from one state to another by land or sea, exchanging money for commodities or money for money, [290] whether they be called money-changers, merchants, shipmasters or retailers. I ask you, have these persons any claim to statecraft?

S. Y. Perhaps they have—to commercial statecraft at least.

STR. Anyway, as regards the people whom we see offering their services to all comers in return for pay, there is little likelihood that we shall find them with any share in the kingly function.

S. Y. Oh no.

STR. What shall we say of those who constantly minister to our needs?

S. Y. To whom and what are you referring?

STR. I mean, what shall we call such persons as heralds, those whose frequent service makes them expert writers, and certain others whose high qualifications fit them for the manifold duties of government administration?

S. Y. As you said earlier: servants, and not independent rulers in their states.

STR. I don't think I was dreaming when I said it was from this quarter that the most determined pretenders to statecraft would arise. All the same, it would appear very odd to have to look for them among the servant class.

S. Y. It most certainly would.

STR. Well, let us come to closer grips with those who have not yet passed the test. They are, first, those who practise divination, itself a form of service inasmuch as they are thought to interpret the divine will to men.

S. Y. Yes.

STR. Again, the priestly caste, according to common belief, understands the business of offering to the gods those sacrifices which they require of us, and of praying to them on our behalf for their favours. Both functions are, I imagine, forms of ministration.

S. Y. Apparently.

STR. And now at last, I think, we are on the trail that will lead us to our goal. For priests and diviners undoubtedly command great respect. Their prestige is proportionate to the eminence of their duties, so much so that in Egypt no king may reign unless he has the sacerdotal dignity; and if he has been forcibly raised to the throne from an inferior station, he must afterwards obtain admission to the priestly caste. In Greece also one often finds the duty of offering the most important sacrifice assigned to the highest magistrates. This last statement is illustrated particularly well here in Athens, where we see the most solemn of the ancient sacrifices—those most hallowed by tradition—entrusted to the magistrate chosen by lot as King Archon.

S. Y. Certainly.

STR. [291] Well, let us examine these elected priest-kings, together with their servants, and also another large body of persons who have only just come into view now that we have eliminated the earlier claimants.

S. Y. Whom do you mean?

STR. Some very strange folk.

S. Y. Yes, but who are they?

STR. At first sight they are a race consisting of numerous tribes. Many of its members are like lions, centaurs and other such creatures. Even more of them resemble satyrs, beasts that have little strength but a great deal of cunning; and they quickly exchange outward appearances and inward characteristics. Yes, Socrates, I think that at last I know what those persons are.

S. Y. Explain what you mean; you appear to have made a strange discovery.

STR. Yes, for strangeness is in every case the fruit of ignorance. That is, in fact, what has just happened to me; I dared not believe that I had suddenly come face to face with that chorus that concerns itself with the affairs of states.

S. Y. Who are they?

STR. The greatest magicians of all the sophists, the most skilled in this art, men whom it is very hard to distinguish from true statesmen and kings, but whom we must nevertheless distinguish if we want a clear idea of the object of our search.

S. Y. We must not relax our efforts in that direction.

STR. I agree. Tell me this, then.

S. Y. Tell you what?

STR. Is not monarchy one of the recognized forms of government?

S. Y. Yes.

STR. After monarchy, I imagine, one would place government by the few.

S. Y. Undoubtedly.

STR. Is not the third form of constitution government by the many, which is known as democracy?

S. Y. Indeed yes.

STR. Do not these three really amount to five by producing from among themselves two further denominations?

S. Y. What denominations?

STR. With an eye to the contrasts presented by compulsion and willing acceptance, poverty and wealth, legality and illegality, one makes a twofold division of the first two. Monarchy, being of two kinds, is called by two names—tyranny and kingship.

S. Y. Exactly.

STR. States governed by a minority are called aristocracies or oligarchies.

S. Y. They are.

STR. [292] As for democracy, the name is unvaried, whether the rule of the masses is imposed by force or voluntarily accepted by the wealthy, and whether or not it functions in strict obedience to the laws.

S. Y. True.

STR. But do we really suppose that any of these forms of government is sound once it has been brought within the limits of such terms as few or many, wealth or poverty, constraint or voluntary acceptance, the possession of written laws or the complete absence of laws?

S. Y. Why should we not?

STR. Take a closer look from this point of view.

S. Y. What point of view?

STR. Do we adhere to what we said at the outset or are we not in agreement?

S. Y. What did we say?

STR. Did we not state that kingly government is one of the sciences?

S. Y. Yes.

STR. And not just any science, but a critical and directive science rather than any other.

S. Y. Yes.

STR. And within this directive science we have distinguished the direction of inanimate creatures from that of living beings, and thus by a process of subdivision we have reached our present position, without indeed having lost sight of the science, but as yet unable to define it with sufficient accuracy.

S. Y. That is so.

STR. Well, do we see that, if we are to remain true to our principles, the character that must serve to distinguish these constitutions is neither 'few' nor 'many', neither voluntary acceptance nor constraint, neither poverty nor wealth, but the presence of a science?

S. Y. Oh, we must be true to our principles at all costs.

STR. The inevitable question now arises: In which of these constitutions is the science of human government realized, the most difficult, one may say, and the greatest which it is possible to acquire? For we must consider this science in order to find out what competitors we should distinguish from the enlightened King, competitors who pretend to be, and convince many that they are, statesmen, whereas they are nothing of the kind.

S. Y. Yes, our discussion has shown we must do that.

STR. Well now, do you suppose that in any state the masses are capable of acquiring this science?

S. Y. That is out of the question.

STR. Do you think that in a state of ten thousand souls one hundred or even fifty persons could manage to become proficient therein?

S. Y. If that were so, statecraft would be the easiest of all arts. We know that among any ten thousand men in the whole

Greek world we should never find a hundred or even fifty champion chess players, let alone that number of kings. For remember, we have said anyone who possesses the kingly science must be [293] given the royal title, whether or not he occupies a throne.

STR. You did well to remind me. I imagine we must infer from this that wherever the right form of government occurs we shall find it in the hands of one, or two, or at the most a few persons.

S. Y. Yes indeed.

STR. But whether these persons govern with or without the consent of their subjects, whether or not they observe written laws, whether they are rich or poor, they must, as we now think, be considered rulers, provided they govern according to an art, regardless of the form their authority may assume. In the same way doctors are so called whether they cure us by using the knife, the cautery or any other painful treatment, whether they follow written rules or ignore them. No, we have no hesitation in calling them doctors provided they work according to the medical art, and provided that, whether they reduce our girth (by purgatives or other means) or even help us to put on weight, they do it for the good of the body, improve its condition and one and all preserve the health of those entrusted to their care. It is along those lines, I think, and only along those lines, that we must look for the correct definition of medicine and of every other art.

S. Y. Certainly.

STR. It seems obvious then that among the various forms of government the principal and indeed unique right form will be that in which one can find rulers who not only seem to have but really are possessed of a science. Whether they govern according to written laws or dispense with them, whether they govern willing or unwilling subjects, and whether they are rich or poor—these considerations have nothing whatever to do with the rightness or otherwise of a constitution.

S. Y. Granted.

STR. And whether the rulers put to death or banish certain individuals in order to purge the state, whether they send out colonies like swarms of bees to decrease the population, or increase it by introducing foreigners and creating new citizens, provided they govern in accordance with science and justice so as to preserve the state and improve it to the best of their ability, then and on these grounds we must recognize the constitution as the only right or genuine form. As for the others we have mentioned, they must be described as neither legitimate nor even true constitutions. They are mere imitations; those of them that have good laws and those that have not model themselves respectively upon the good and the inferior characteristics of the right constitution.

S. Y. Most of your observations, sir, appear to me very reasonable; but it is painful to hear you say that one should govern without laws.

STR. You are a step ahead of me there, Socrates. [294] For I was going to ask you whether you agreed with all I have said or whether there was anything of which you disapproved. It is now clear that we shall wish to debate the rightness of government without laws.

S. Y. Certainly we shall.

STR. In a way of course legislation is a kingly function; but it is best to strengthen not the laws but the kingly man endowed with practical wisdom. Do you know why?

S. Y. Why?

STR. Because law can never comprehend what is both best and most equitable for all men, and thus be able to enact the most useful regulations. For the differences between men and deeds, and the fact that no human affairs are ever, as it were, static, allow no room in any art or other form of activity for an absolute standard applicable at all times and in every case. I think we are agreed as to that.

S. Y. Certainly.

STR. Now it is, in short, after just such an absolute norm that we find law striving, like a man self-assured but ignorant, who will allow no one to do anything contrary to his own instructions and will tolerate no suggestion, even in presence of a new situation, better than his own arrangements have foreseen.

S. Y. True; the law acts, in regard to each one of us, exactly as you have just said.

STR. Surely, then, what is always absolute can never adapt itself to what is never so?

S. Y. Very likely.

STR. Why, in that case, is it necessary to make laws, since law is not a perfect instrument? We must discover the reason.

S. Y. Naturally.

STR. Have not you Athenians, like other states, certain communal exercises in which your races and other forms of competition are inspired by the spirit of emulation?

S. Y. Yes, we certainly have, and many of them.

STR. Very well, let us recall the rules laid down for the regulation of these exercises by the trainers who organize them according to scientific principles.

S. Y. What rules?

STR. They see no reason to waste time on individuals by drawing up separate rules for each and every trainee; on the contrary, trusting to a more inclusive view, with an eye to their pupils as a whole, they draw up rules which will benefit the body in general.

S. Y. Agreed.

STR. That, in fact, is why they subject a whole group of trainees to the same regime, making them begin and cease together, be it running, wrestling or any other physical exercise.

S. Y. That is so.

STR. Well, let us think of the legislator in the same way. Having to instruct his charges in their duties of [295] justice and mutual contract, he will never be able, while enacting regulations for the whole group, to provide each individual with the precise rule suitable to him in particular.

S. Y. Likely enough.

STR. Rather, I think, he will lay down what is best in the majority of cases and for the majority of individuals. And in this way I suggest he will legislate for each of his subjects by legislating for them as a whole, either by drawing up a written code of laws or by giving the force of law to traditional and unwritten custom. Am I right?

S. Y. You are.

STR. Of course I am, Socrates. How could a man spend his whole life sitting, so to speak, at the bedside of every individual, prescribing down to the last detail what was good for him? In my opinion, if anyone truly possessing the kingly art were capable of doing that, he would scarcely trouble to tie his own hands by writing these so-called laws.

S. Y. Certainly, sir, at least according to what we have just said.

STR. And even more certainly, my dear fellow, in the light of what we are now going to say.

S. Y. What is that?

STR. I will tell you. Suppose a doctor or a gymnastic trainer were about to go on a journey which would separate him from his charges for some considerable time: surely such a one, convinced that his pupils or (in the case of a doctor) his patients would forget his instructions, would decide to leave them written memoranda.

S. Y. Yes.

STR. But what if he came back after a shorter absence than he had anticipated? Would the doctor hesitate to substitute new rules for those memoranda if he found that conditions had altered in his patients' favour, owing to the wind or to some other unexpected change of celestial phenomena? Or would he stubbornly determine that the earlier instructions, once laid down, were on that account inviolable, that he must prescribe nothing new, and that his patient must not presume to do anything contrary to the written rules, on the ground that these alone proceeded from the healing art of medicine whereas all others were founded upon ignorance and therefore dangerous? Would not all such behaviour invariably be regarded in the light of science or true art as the most ridiculous way of making laws?

S. Y. It certainly would.

STR. Suppose someone has laid down (in writing or otherwise) what is just and unjust, right and wrong, good and evil, in the case of one or another of those human flocks who dwell in scattered states under the laws of their respective legislators; and then suppose that the legislator himself, [296] or someone equally well qualified, turns up. Is he to be debarred from making new and different laws? Would not such a prohibition in this latter case appear just as absurd as in the former?

S. Y. Yes indeed.

STR. Do you know what most people say in this connection?

S. Y. I'm not sure at the moment.

STR. It is very much to the point. They say that if anyone knows of better laws than those laid down by his ancestors, he has no right to promulgate them for his own state unless and until he has obtained the consent of every citizen.

S. Y. Well, are they not right?

STR. Perhaps. Anyway, suppose someone imposes innovation by force, without obtaining that consent, what will that act of force be called? But wait, let us go back to the previous examples.

S. Y. What do you mean?

STR. Suppose a doctor cannot persuade a child, a man or a woman to undergo a course of beneficial treatment, but, being a master of his art, obliges the patient to accept that treatment in defiance of written rules. What will this constraint be called? Surely not a sin against medical science and a pernicious error? And the very last thing the patient will have a right to say is that he has been the victim of harmful and unskilled treatment on the part of the doctor who applied it without his consent.

S. Y. That is absolutely true.

STR. And now what do we call a violation of the Statesman's art? Do we not describe it as shameful, wicked and unjust?

S. Y. Certainly.

STR. Can it possibly be that violence is just if its author is rich, unjust if he is poor? Should we not rather say that whether or not a ruler employs persuasion, whether he is rich or poor, whether or not he abides by written laws, provided that he governs advantageously, there we must recognize the true formula of the right administration of a state, a formula according to which the wise and good man will govern in the interests of his subjects? [297] A sea captain looks after the safety of his passengers and crew by concentrating always upon the welfare of his ship and those who sail in her, using no written code, but treating his own science as law; so also a ruler capable of acting on these principles will achieve the right constitution, providing that he rules by means of his art rather than by means of the laws. What say you to that? And is it not true that intelligent rulers can do all things without risk of error, so long as they observe this one paramount rule: always administer perfect justice to the citizens, justice endowed with knowledge and understanding, and thus manage not only to preserve them, but even to improve them as far as that may be?

S. Y. These last remarks, at any rate, are incontestable.

STR. But so are the next ones.

S. Y. What are they?

STR. A large body of persons, whoever they may be, will never be able to acquire such a science sufficiently well to be capable of administering a state with intelligence; it is to a small number, to two or three, and even to a single individual that one must look for the only right constitution, of which other forms of government must be regarded as mere imitations, which, as we said just now, sometimes reproduce the nobler features of the true constitution, and sometimes shamefully disfigure it.

S. Y. What do you mean by that? Even when you spoke of these 'imitations' a little while ago, I did not understand you.

STR. All the same, it would be a serious matter to put forward a proposition of this kind, only to reject it out of hand instead of following it up by showing the error now in process of arising on this point.

S. Y. What error?

STR. Here at any rate is what we have to look for, although it is far from familiar and easy to discover. Let us, however, try to lay hands on it. Listen now. Since we recognize only one right constitution, which we have already described, do you know that the others, in order to survive, must borrow from it their written laws, thus doing what is nowadays approved, although it is not perfectly right?

S. Y. What is that?

STR. Forbidding any member of the state to do anything contrary to the laws, and punishing anyone who ventures to do so with torture and death. There you have the second most just and noblest principle, after the first, which we just now described. What we have to do now is to explain how this 'second' principle arises. Do you agree?

S. Y. Absolutely.

STR. Let us go back then to the images that one cannot avoid if one wishes to describe kingly rulers.

S. Y. What images?

STR. Those of the good captain and the doctor 'who is worth many others'. Let us take a look at the imaginary setting in which we think of them.

S. Y. What setting?

STR. I will tell you. [298] Suppose we all take it into our heads to complain how terribly we suffer at their hands. If the doctors wish to cure one of us, cure that one they do; if they wish to ill-treat him, they will do so by means of the knife, fire and extortionate fees, none of which, or only a very small fraction, is spent for the patient's benefit, most of it going for the maintenance of themselves and their families; and lastly, worst of all, they are bribed to kill off the patient by his relatives and other enemies. Now for the sea captains. They commit a thousand crimes of the same nature, cunningly abandon you on a desert island, handle their ships in such a way that you are pitched overboard in mid ocean, and devise many other treacherous schemes. Suppose now that, telling ourselves all this, we put our heads together and come to the following decision. We will no longer permit either of these two arts to lord it over anyone whomsoever, slave or freeman; we will summon an assembly, either of the whole people or of the rich alone, and there any ignoramus from any walk of life shall be entitled to advise upon navigation and sickness, to say how remedies should be applied and surgical instruments used, how ships and their equipment should be handled, whether for sailing, for escaping the perils of wind and wave or pirates during the voyage, or for fighting naval craft. The decisions taken by the masses in this connection, whether on the advice of doctors, sea captains or simple laymen, shall be engraved on columns and stelae, or, instead of putting them in writing, we will give them the force of national customs, and thenceforward for a time navigation and care of the sick shall abide by them.

S. Y. Why, what an utterly fantastic idea!

STR. Yes, and we shall place the rank and file of the state under magistrates chosen annually by lot, either from the rich or from the whole people, and these magistrates shall function according to written rules, whether their business is to handle ships or to heal the sick.

S. Y. That would be even more unsuitable.

STR. But see what follows. When these officials end their year of office, we shall have to establish a tribunal of judges chosen by lot either from a list of the wealthy, [299] drawn up in advance, or directly from the whole people. The outgoing officials will be summoned to appear before this tribunal and render an account of their administration, and anyone who so wishes will have the right to accuse them of having failed during their year of office to govern their ships in accordance with written law or ancestral custom. The same right will be allowed in respect of those who heal the sick, and the same court will impose the fine or other penalty on those who are condemned.

S. Y. All I can say is that anyone who willingly accepted office in such circumstances would richly deserve the penalty, whatever it was.

STR. Yes, but that is not the end of the story. It will also be necessary to make the following law: Anyone found guilty of studying the art of navigation, the rules of health or the medical effects of winds, heat and cold elsewhere than in written sources and of posing as an expert in such matters, shall, in the first place, be declared no doctor or sea captain but a mere weather-merchant or inexperienced sophist; and then the first comer of those who have the right shall denounce him in open court as a corrupter of youth on the grounds that he persuades young men to devote themselves to nautical or medical science independently of the statute book, as self-appointed governors of the sick and of our ships. If he is found guilty of instructing young or old in defiance of the laws he shall suffer capital punishment. For one never has a right to be wiser than the laws, since no one need be ignorant of medicine, hygiene, pilotage or navigation, seeing that anyone who so wishes may learn the written law and national customs. If this is to be the rule, Socrates, for strategy and every other form of the chase, for painting and every other form of the imitative art, for designing and every other form of decoration, for agriculture and every other form of growing plants; if a written code is to regulate horse breeding and every other form of rearing animals, divination and every other form of interpretation, counting and the science of numbers in general, whether pure or applied to two or three dimensions or to movement; what, I ask, will be the fate of all these things if controlled by written rules instead of by theory?

S. Y. Obviously, we shall find that all the arts completely

disappear without hope of recovery, ousted by this law forbidding all experiment; and life, which is always hard enough,
[300] will become absolutely insufferable.

STR. And what then? Having subjected the practice of all these
arts to written laws, and imposed this method of government
on a ruler chosen either by vote or by lot, let us suppose that
he disregards it, led by motives of gain or personal caprice to
act in defiance of its provisions, although he is ignorant of all
that concerns his duty. Will not that situation be worse than
the last?

S. Y. Indeed it will.

STR. Yes; it seems to me that anyone presuming to set aside
laws which are the fruit of long experience, and whose every
clause has been accepted by the legislature on the advice and
recommendation of experts, would commit a much worse
fault and stifle all activity far more surely than does the letter
of the law.

S. Y. Undoubtedly he would.

STR. It follows, therefore, that wherever we establish a written
code of laws we must never allow an individual or a group to
do anything that might nullify their provisions.

S. Y. Quite.

STR. In every field of activity then such codes will be imitations
of truth, drafted as perfectly as may be under the inspiration
of those who know the truth?

S. Y. Certainly.

STR. And yet we agreed, if I am not mistaken, that he who
knows the truth, the real statesman, will in practice often rely
upon his art, regardless of the written law, if he finds that a
new way of acting is more profitable than the regulations
drawn up by himself and promulgated for the duration of his
absence.

S. Y. Yes, that is what we said.

STR. Yet when any individual or group of persons, possessing
a body of laws, attempts to act in defiance of its regulations,
are they not doing, so far as in them lies, the same as our 'real
statesman?'

S. Y. Of course they are.

STR. Do you agree that if ignorant persons adopt such a course
they will make a very poor job of imitating the truth, but that

in the case of those with the requisite knowledge there will be
no mere imitation but the full reality itself?

S. Y. I do.

STR. But we agreed, earlier on, that a large number of people
can never acquire any art.

S. Y. We did.

STR. So if there is such a thing as the kingly art, neither the rich
as a body nor the masses as a whole will ever attain to the
science of statecraft.

S. Y. Most definitely not.

STR. It follows then that if these apparent constitutions are to
imitate perfectly the true (ideal) constitution—I mean [301]
government by one competent individual—they must be
careful, once their laws are established, never to do anything
contrary to the written code and national custom.

S. Y. Granted.

STR. Now when the rich imitate the true constitution the resulting form of government is called an aristocracy, but when they
disregard the laws it is known as an oligarchy.

S. Y. Yes, I think so.

STR. And again, when an individual governs according to laws,
imitating the one competent ruler, we call him King, regardless of whether such a monarch is guided by knowledge or
opinion.

S. Y. That would seem to be the case.

STR. Nor again, if government is in the hands of an individual
who is himself really competent, shall we hesitate to call
him a King. Hence the number of constitutions reckoned
nowadays does not exceed five.

S. Y. Apparently.

STR. What about a single ruler who takes no account of law or
established custom, but counterfeits the genuine ruler by
pretending that the greatest good demands a violation of the
written code, whereas he is actually inspired by passion and
ignorance. Does not such a ruler, always and everywhere,
deserve the name of tyrant?

S. Y. Most certainly he does.

STR. We may say, then, that the tyrant, the king, oligarchy,
aristocracy and democracy arise from man's natural dislike of
a single monarch. They refuse to believe that anyone can ever

be so worthy of such authority as to be able and willing to govern with virtue and knowledge, dispensing justice and equity impartially to all, and not to insult, ill-treat, or put to death whomsoever and whensoever he pleases. A real monarch such as we have described would be acclaimed as controlling and administering the one and only perfectly right constitution.

S. Y. Of course.

STR. But since in fact, as we are agreed, kings are not produced in states like queen bees in hives, unique both in body and in soul, it seems that we must get together and compile legal codes as near as possible according to the pattern of the truest form of government.

S. Y. Apparently we must.

STR. Well then, Socrates, can we wonder at the many evils that arise and will continue to arise in such constitutions, founded as they are on this basis of subjecting their activity to written rules and custom instead of to science, an arrangement which destroys the fruits of activity in every other field? [302] Ought we not rather to be surprised at the innate power of resistance belonging to a state? For notwithstanding this evil to which states have been liable from time out of mind, some of them have avoided disaster and remained stable, although of course, from time to time, many have perished like doomed vessels. This still happens and will continue to do so, thanks to the wickedness of their pilots and crews, who, though they know nothing of the art of statesmanship, imagine themselves more learned in all the details thereof than anyone else, and are thus guilty of the most disastrous ignorance in matters of the greatest moment.

S. Y. That is perfectly true.

STR. And now let us ask which of all these imperfect constitutions renders life least difficult (for it is difficult in any case), and which is the most intolerable. We need an answer to this question; it may be of secondary importance as compared with the subject of our present inquiry, but when all is said and done I think it likely that this problem dominates our every action as human beings.

S. Y. Yes, we must inquire into that; it cannot be avoided.

STR. Very well, you must admit that one of three is the hardest and one the easiest to endure.

S. Y. What do you mean?

STR. Well, government by an individual, by the few and by the many are the three main constitutions of which we spoke at the beginning of this long discussion.

S. Y. True.

STR. Let us now divide each of them into two and make six, setting aside the ideal constitution as a seventh.

S. Y. How?

STR. We have seen that monarchy includes kingship and tyranny; government by a few gives us what is appropriately called aristocracy and oligarchy; government by the many has already yielded something which we called just now by the single name of democracy, but which we must now recognize as twofold.

S. Y. How so; what is to be our line of division?

STR. The same as we used for the other types of constitution, although in this case there is no second name; for democracy, like them, can govern in conformity with or contrary to the laws.

S. Y. I understand.

STR. Now, when looking for the right constitution this division was unnecessary, as we showed earlier on. But once we have set aside this perfect form of government and recognized the others as inevitable, legality and illegality are in each case a principle of dichotomy.

S. Y. Yes, according to that explanation.

STR. Monarchy, when tied down by written regulations which we call laws, is the best of the six constitutions, but without laws it is the one that renders life most difficult and unendurable.

S. Y. [303] I am afraid so.

STR. Since 'few' is the mean between one and many, we must consider government by the few as intermediate between the other two. As for government by the many, it is feeble in every respect, without much strength either for good or ill in comparison with other forms, because its powers are distributed among too many people. Moreover, when these imperfect constitutions are subject to laws, democracy is the worst of all, but when they violate the laws it is the best. When all are in confusion life is best under a democracy, but if all are well regulated democracy is the last under which one would choose to live; monarchy is from this point of view far and away the best, excepting always the perfect constitution, which must be set apart from all others as if it were a god among men.

S. Y. Apparently that is so, and we must do as you say.

STR. Consequently all those who play a part in these constitutions, excepting that which rests upon science, must be rejected as no statesmen but raisers of sedition, creators of the worst illusions, nay themselves illusions, mountebanks and charlatans.

S. Y. That remark seems to bring us back to the subject of bogus statesmen.

STR. Very good, we may consider ourselves as at the end of a drama. We spoke some while ago of a troupe of centaurs and satyrs, whom we had to separate from statecraft, and now we have succeeded in doing so, though with great difficulty.

S. Y. Surely we have.

STR. But there is another troupe, harder to distinguish because closely related to the kingly race, and not so easy to detect. Here, I think, we are rather like men purifying gold.

S. Y. How so?

STR. Those engaged in such work begin by getting rid of earth, stones and many other impurities; after which there remain those valuable metals that are mingled with and akin to the gold, from which they cannot be separated except by fire. This laborious separation of bronze, silver and sometimes even of adamant, by means of fire yields in its free state what we call pure gold.

S. Y. Yes, that is what is said to happen.

STR. Well, we appear to have followed the same procedure in separating from the science of statecraft all that differs from it, all that is alien and hostile thereto, and retaining only the precious sciences related to it. These latter include the military and the judicial science, as well as the whole art of rhetoric (that ally of the kingly science), [304] which lends persuasive force to justice and thereby helps to control all activity within the boundaries of a state. What then will be the surest means of separating these sciences, and thus providing us with the object of our search, naked and unalloyed?

S. Y. Clearly we must try to do that by some means or another.
STR. We shall find a way if we only try. Consider music now and tell me something.
S. Y. Tell you what?
STR. Does not music, like (*a*) all sciences requiring manual skill, need to be learnt?
S. Y. Yes.
STR. Next, tell me whether or not we shall describe as a science (*b*) that which determines whether or not we should learn one or another of the sciences included under (*a*) above.
S. Y. Yes, we shall.
STR. And shall we not agree that it is distinct from them?
S. Y. Yes.
STR. Shall we maintain (1) that none should control the others, or (2) that (*a*) should govern (*b*), or (3) that to (*b*) belongs the right to control and government in general.
S. Y. The third proposition is the correct answer.
STR. You say then that as between the science that determines whether or not we should learn and that which learns and teaches, the former has the right of control?
S. Y. Definitely.
STR. And likewise as between that which determines whether or not we should persuade and that which knows how to persuade?
S. Y. Of course.
STR. Very well, to what science shall we attribute the power of swaying the masses by means of fables rather than by instruction?
S. Y. Why, surely that is the business of rhetoric.
STR. But what science is to determine whether force or persuasion, or neither, should be applied to given persons in given circumstances?
S. Y. To that which governs the art of persuasive speaking.
STR. And that, I think, is none other than statecraft.
S. Y. Undoubtedly.
STR. Thus then it seems we have quickly distinguished proud rhetoric from statecraft; it belongs to another and subordinate class of sciences.
S. Y. Yes.
STR. But what about this other faculty?

S. Y. Which one?

STR. That of knowing how to fight those upon whom we have declared war: shall we say that it belongs to an art or that it has nothing whatever to do with art?

S. Y. How can we set it down as divorced from art when it is the product of strategy and military practice in general?

STR. Shall we distinguish from this the faculty of deciding whether to make war or deal peacefully, or shall we reckon it the same?

S. Y. We shall have to distinguish it, if we are going to be consistent with ourselves.

STR. [305] Must we then declare that it governs the other, if we wish to stand by our previous assertion?

S. Y. I think we must.

STR. Considering how pre-eminent and comprehensive is the art of war, to what science could we ever say it is subject, except to the true science of kingship?

S. Y. To none other indeed.

STR. So we shall not rank military science with statecraft, of which it is only the handmaid.

S. Y. No indeed.

STR. Come now, and consider the judicial function when it is properly exercised.

S. Y. Certainly.

STR. I think you will agree that it does no more than view contracts in the light of those many legal provisions it has received from the kingly lawgiver, and decide what acts are classified as just and unjust; and in accordance with the character of judicial virtue no form of bribery, fear, pity, hate or love can induce a judge willingly to violate the principles established by the legislator for deciding as between the claims of plaintiff and defendant.

S. Y. True; the judicial function does no more than you say.

STR. Which is proof that the authority of a judge does not amount to kingly power, but is only the guardian of laws and the handmaid of that power.

S. Y. Apparently.

STR. Having therefore considered these various sciences, we have to acknowledge that none of them appears to be the science of statecraft. The true kingly science has in fact no practical task: on the contrary, it governs those which are intended for such tasks, knowing what occasions will be favourable and unfavourable for a state to initiate or pursue important undertakings, whereas the others have only to carry out its orders.

S. Y. That's right.

STR. Thus, although none of the sciences we have just reviewed is mistress of the others, to each of them there belongs a certain kind of activity all its own, from which it derives its particular name.

S. Y. Fair enough.

STR. But as regards that which governs them all, which supervises the laws and all affairs of the state, and which weaves everything into a perfect tissue, we shall, I think, be doing no more than justice in choosing a name sufficiently wide to cover the universal scope of its function, and calling it statecraft.

S. Y. I entirely agree.

STR. Now that we have a clear view of all the different functions in the state, it may be a good thing to return to our illustration from the art of weaving, in order to throw light upon the science of statecraft.

S. Y. Undoubtedly.

STR. [306] What we have to explain, it seems, is the nature of this kingly function, how it interlaces the various strands, and the quality of its finished product.

S. Y. Evidently.

STR. I believe we have committed ourselves to a very difficult task.

S. Y. All the same, we must go through with it.

STR. Popular opinions being what they are, argumentative folk batten on the fact that one part of virtue is in a sense different from another part of virtue.

S. Y. I don't understand.

STR. Let me put it another way. I think you will agree that courage is a part of virtue.

S. Y. Indeed I do.

STR. And yet wisdom is something other than courage, although this latter is itself a part of virtue.

S. Y. Yes.

STR. Good; then we must venture to say something remarkable about these two parts of virtue.

S. Y. What is that?

STR. That they are, in a sense, fiercely hostile to one another and form opposing factions among many of the subjects in which they reside.

S. Y. What do you mean?

STR. Something different from what is commonly believed by those who maintain that there is a natural harmony between all the parts of virtue.

S. Y. Yes, that is the common view.

STR. Well, let us examine the matter closely and see whether there is really such a perfect harmony as is generally supposed, whether there is not far more often strife between one part and another.

S. Y. Yes, but please explain how we are to conduct this inquiry.

STR. We must search in every field of reality for those things which we call admirable but which we classify under two opposite headings.

S. Y. Please be a little more explicit.

STR. Have you yourself ever admired, or been present when someone else has admired, promptness and speed of body, soul or voice, whether in the domain of reality or among representations created by the imitative skill of painters or musicians?

S. Y. What if I have?

STR. Do you remember what form such praise invariably assumed?

S. Y. No, I don't.

STR. I wonder if I can find words to explain what I have in mind.

S. Y. Why not?

STR. You seem to imagine it an easy thing to do. Anyway, let us look at the facts in two classes of things that are opposed to one another. Often, in many forms of activity, we are impressed by the speed, force and vivacity of a mind, a body or a voice; and at such times our admiration expresses itself in the one word 'vigour'.

S. Y. How so?

STR. We say, for example, that one thing is lively and vigorous, another quick and vigorous, another forceful and vigorous, and so on. In short, we praise those qualities (liveliness, speed, etc.) by applying to them the above-mentioned epithet.

S. Y. Yes.

Str. Again, do we not often, in many other forms of activity, [307] praise the tranquil manner in which things take place?

S. Y. Certainly we do.

Str. And in speaking of them do we not use expressions contrary to the others?

S. Y. How?

Str. Whenever we apply the words 'peaceful' and 'wise' to thoughts or actions whose slowness or gentleness we admire, or to smooth and solemn sounds, or again to any rhythmic movement and any work of art which is marked by appropriate gravity, we no longer in such cases speak of 'vigour' but of 'reserve' or 'moderation'.

S. Y. That is very true.

Str. On the other hand, if one or other of these opposite qualities is found to be out of place we change our tune, and express our disapproval by means of epithets which signify the very opposite.

S. Y. How?

Str. If those things of which we were speaking appear too lively, too rapid or too harsh, we call them 'violent', 'extravagant'; if too solemn, too slow or too soft, we call them 'slack', 'lazy'. And we nearly always find that these qualities, as well as the opposite qualities of moderation and vigour, are characteristics which happen to constitute two hostile factions, incapable as they are of mixing together in the acts in which they occur; and we shall also find similar conflicts between the minds in which they reside, if we follow those minds closely.

S. Y. Follow them where?

Str. Into all the circumstances we have just mentioned and of course into many others as well. For according to the affinity which they have with one or the other tendency, they praise that which seems to reflect their own nature and blame that which they feel to be alien to themselves. Hence endless hatred towards innumerable objects.

S. Y. That would seem to be the case.

Str. Now the mere conflict of characteristics is insignificant. But in matters of great consequence it becomes the most terrible disease with which a state can be afflicted.

S. Y. In what sort of matters do you mean?

STR. Why, in those which concern the organization of life. There are, you know, persons of a most retiring disposition; ever anxious to lead a quiet life, they keep to themselves and mind their own business. This temperament pervades the whole of their domestic life, and even extends to their attitude towards foreign states, with whom they are always ready to live at peace somehow or other. As a result of this untimely love, while living as they wish, they unconsciously lose all aptitude for war, bring up their sons to be similarly incompetent and place themselves at the mercy of anyone who chooses to attack them. Thus, within a very few years they find [308] themselves, their children and the whole state sliding insensibly from freedom into slavery.

S. Y. A hard and terrible fate!

STR. But what about the more vigorous sort? Are they not for ever trying to commit the state to some new war, as a result of their consuming passion for this kind of life, exposing their country to so much powerful hatred that they bring her to complete ruin or subject her to slavery beneath an enemy yoke?

S. Y. That again is true.

STR. Surely then we must recognize here a source of continual and profound discord between these two kinds of mind.

S. Y. Impossible to do otherwise.

STR. Have we not thus completed the first part of our inquiry by discovering that certain highly important parts of virtue are naturally opposed to one another and engender the same opposition between those minds in which they reside?

S. Y. It would seem so.

STR. Then let us take the next point.

S. Y. What is that?

STR. Whether any of the combinative sciences is prepared to use bad as well as good elements in producing any of its works, however lowly, or whether the aim of every science, in every field of activity, is not rather to eliminate bad elements as far as possible, to preserve the good elements, and to combine these latter (whether similar or dissimilar) into a unity perfect both in its properties and in its structure.

S. Y. What is the answer to that?

STR. Statecraft as we conceive it, in true conformity with nature, will never choose to weld good and bad elements into a state. Clearly it will first have its subjects taught how to play, after which it will turn them over to competent persons qualified to educate them, itself, however, retaining control and direction. Just so does the weaver's science with regard to the wool-carders and other auxiliaries who provide it with the materials it will employ, governing and directing their every movement, and assigning to each the tasks it considers will advance its own work of weaving.

S. Y. Exactly.

STR. Well, that is how I think the kingly science treats all those who dispense instruction and education within the framework of the laws, reserving to itself directive authority, not allowing them to impose any form of exercise which does not tend to further its own work of synthesis, and obliging them to confine their methods within these limits. Those whom it is impossible to endow with energy, temperance and other virtuous tendencies, and who are driven by a flaw of character [309] to atheism, overweening pride and injustice, it removes by a sentence of death or exile and other severe penalties.

S. Y. That, at any rate, is more or less the usual teaching.

STR. And upon those who wallow in ignorance and abjection it lays the yoke of slavery.

S. Y. Quite right.

STR. As for the remainder, who are by nature capable of being trained in virtue and fused by art into a whole, if they tend towards vigour it regards the toughness of their character as showing that they belong to the warp; if they incline rather to moderation it views them (to continue with our metaphor) as the supple and soft material of the woof, and it endeavours to knit these opposite tendencies in a certain way.

S. Y. In what way?

STR. First, it binds together the eternal part of the soul with a divine thread and afterwards the animal part with human strands.

S. Y. What do you mean by that?

STR. If a soul is endowed with a really true and firm idea of the beautiful, the good, the just, and their contraries, then, I say, something godlike has been accomplished in an inspired race of beings.

S. Y. That is a fair statement.

STR. Now do we not know that the Statesman or wise lawgiver alone enjoys the privilege of being able, helped by the muse of kingly science, to implant such an idea in minds that have been formed by the good education of which we spoke just now?

S. Y. Likely enough.

STR. So let us never, Socrates, call a man a statesman or wise lawgiver unless he has this power.

S. Y. I quite agree.

STR. Very well, does not a vigorous soul become more sober when permeated with this truth; will it not then more willingly embrace ideas of justice, whereas in other circumstances it inclines rather to almost bestial violence?

S. Y. Undoubtedly.

STR. And now what about the naturally moderate man? Do not such ideas render him truly temperate and wise, at least to the extent required by membership of a state? But if he is without these lights does he not rightly incur a reputation of miserable faint-heartedness?

S. Y. Certainly.

STR. Must we not then assert that this divine thread will never permanently interweave either the bad themselves or the bad and the good, and that no science will ever seriously contemplate using it for such purposes?

S. Y. That is unthinkable.

STR. [310] It is only among characters of innate nobility which has been fostered by education that the laws will be able to accomplish such a task; for them alone art has devised this remedy which is, as we were saying, the truly divine thread that binds together the several parts of virtue, no matter how dissimilar by nature they may be, and no matter to what opposite extremes they may tend.

S. Y. Perfectly true.

STR. As for those other, merely human strands, it is not difficult, once the divine link has been created, to see what they are and then to give them reality.

S. Y. How so, and to what 'strands' do you refer?

STR. To those created between states by the marriages which they authorize and the exchange of their children, and in particular to the daughters whom they settle and the marriages they arrange for them. Now most of these alliances are contracted upon conditions that do not favour the procreation of children.

S. Y. How is that?

STR. Marriages brought about with a view to the acquisition of money or power are not worthy even of criticism, are they?

S. Y. Certainly not.

STR. We shall do better to discuss those persons who have the welfare of the race at heart although their conduct is faulty.

S. Y. Yes indeed.

STR. Well, they behave quite unreasonably inasmuch as they consider only their immediate comfort, allying themselves with those of their own type, detesting everyone else, and allowing themselves to be guided for the most part by their antipathies.

S. Y. How?

STR. Moderate characters look for persons of their own disposition, and choose their wives as far as possible from the women of that class, into which they eventually remarry their own daughters. The vigorous type does the same kind of thing, looking for someone of their own sort, whereas each group ought to do the exact opposite.

S. Y. How, and why?

STR. Because if vigour remains for several generations unmixed with the moderate character, it tends by nature to expend all its brilliance at the beginning and ends by lapsing into the most absurd follies.

S. Y. That is the probable result.

STR. On the other hand, a soul too full of reserve, which, instead of allying itself with strenuous daring, goes on reproducing itself through several generations, inevitably becomes utterly careless and finishes in a state of hopeless incompetence.

S. Y. That again is probable.

STR. There then are the strands of which I said that they will not be hard to fashion provided only that the two types of person take the same view of good and evil. For herein lies the whole kingly art of weaving: never to allow a divorce of the moderate from the vigorous character, but to bind them together by means of common opinions, honours and glories, as well as by mutual exchange of undertakings, so as to produce a supple and, as we say, a close knit web, and always to treat [311] both characters alike when distributing the offices of state.

S. Y. How treat them alike?

STR. When a single ruler is required, a man should be chosen who has this twofold character; when there is need of several, the various offices should be distributed equally between men of each kind. For rulers of temperate disposition are very prudent, just and take no risks; but they lack the audacity and determination which get things done.

S. Y. That also would appear to be the case.

STR. Vigorous rulers, on the other hand, are somewhat lacking in justice and circumspection, but when it comes to getting things done they have more resolution than anyone else. It is in fact impossible for the state as a whole or for its individual members to prosper unless those two characteristics are combined.

S. Y. Evidently.

STR. Let us say, then, that we have completed a well woven material and produced statesmanship when that kingly science brings together men both of vigorous and of temperate character, unites their two lives in concord and friendship; when it fashions the best and most magnificent of all materials, incorporates therein the whole population (slave and free) of every state, holds them all together in this single tissue and governs in such a way as to make sure that the state enjoys to the full the happiness of which it is capable.

Soc. Sir, your account of the kingly man or Statesman[1] has given us another fine portrait.

---

[1] The projected dialogue on the Philosopher was never written.

EVERYMAN'S LIBRARY: A Selected List

This List covers a selection of volumes available in Everyman's Library. Those volumes marked with a ★ indicate that a paperback edition of this title is also available. Numbers only of hardback editions are given.

BIOGRAPHY

Brontë, Charlotte (1816–55). LIFE, 1857. By *Mrs Gaskell*.   318
Byron, Lord (1788–1824). LETTERS. Edited by *R. G. Howarth*, B.LITT.   931
Cellini, Benvenuto (1500–71). ★THE LIFE OF BENVENUTO CELLINI, written by himself. 51
Evelyn, John (1620–1706). DIARY. Edited by *William Bray*, 1819.   2 vols. 220–1
Franklin, Benjamin (1706–90). AUTOBIOGRAPHY, 1817.   316
Goethe, Johann Wolfgang von (1749–1832). LIFE, 1855. By *G. H. Lewes*, 1817–78. 269
Hudson, William Henry (1841–1922). FAR AWAY AND LONG AGO, 1918.   956
Johnson, Dr Samuel (1709–84). LIVES OF THE ENGLISH POETS, 1781. 2 vols. 770–1.
  ★BOSWELL'S LIFE OF JOHNSON, 1791. 2 vols. 1–2.
Keats, John (1795–1821). LIFE AND LETTERS, 1848. By *Lord Houghton* (1809–85). 801
Nelson, Horatio, Viscount (1758–1805). LIFE, 1813. By *Robert Southey* (1774–1843). 52
Pepys, Samuel (1633–1703). DIARY. Newly edited (1953), with modernized spelling.
  3 vols. 53–5
Plutarch (46?–120). LIVES OF THE NOBLE GREEKS AND ROMANS. Dryden's edition,
  1683–6. Revised by *A. H. Clough*, 1819–61.   3 vols. 407–9
Rousseau, Jean Jacques (1712–78). CONFESSIONS, 1782. Complete and unabridged.
  2 vols. 859–60
Scott, Sir Walter (1771–1832). LOCKHART'S LIFE OF SCOTT. An abridgment from the
  seven-volume work by *J. G. Lockhart* himself.   39
Sévigné, Marie de Rabutin-Chantal, Marquise de (1626–96). SELECTED LETTERS.   98
Vasari, Giorgio (1511–74). LIVES OF THE PAINTERS, SCULPTORS AND ARCHITECTS.
  Edited by *William Gaunt*.   4 vols. 784–7
Walpole, Horace (1717–97). SELECTED LETTERS. Edited, with an Introduction, by
  W. Hadley, M.A.   775

ESSAYS AND CRITICISM

An Everyman Anthology. Over a hundred authors from Everyman's Library
  represented.   663
Bacon, Francis, Lord Verulam (1561–1626). ★ESSAYS. 1597–1626.   10
Belloc, Hilaire (1870–1953). ★STORIES, ESSAYS AND POEMS.   948
Burke, Edmund (1729–97). REFLECTIONS ON THE FRENCH REVOLUTION, 1790.   460
Carlyle, Thomas (1795–1881). ESSAYS. Introduction by *J. R. Lowell*. Essays on men
  and affairs. 2 vols. 703–4. PAST AND PRESENT, 1843. 608. SARTOR RESARTUS,
  1838; and HEROES AND HERO-WORSHIP, 1841. 278
Castiglioni, Baldassare (1478–1529). THE BOOK OF THE COURTIER, 1528. *Sir Thomas
  Hoby's* translation, 1561.   807
Century. ★A CENTURY OF ENGLISH ESSAYS FROM CAXTON TO BELLOC.   653
Chesterfield, Earl of (1694–1773). LETTERS TO HIS SON; AND OTHERS.   823
Chesterton, Gilbert Keith (1874–1936). ★STORIES, ESSAYS AND POEMS.   913
Coleridge, Samuel Taylor (1772–1834). BIOGRAPHIA LITERARIA, 1817. 11. SHAKE-
  SPEAREAN CRITICISM, 1849. Edited by *Prof. T. M. Raysor* (1960). 2 vols. 162, 183.
De Quincey, Thomas (1785–1859). ★CONFESSIONS OF AN ENGLISH OPIUM-EATER, 1822.
  223. THE ENGLISH MAIL-COACH AND OTHER WRITINGS. 609. REMINISCENCES
  OF THE ENGLISH LAKE POETS. 163. All edited by *Prof. John E. Jordan*.
Dryden, John (1631–1700). OF DRAMATIC POESY AND OTHER CRITICAL ESSAYS. The
  whole of Dryden's critical writings.   2 vols. 568–9
Elyot, Sir Thomas (1490?–1546). THE GOVERNOR, 1531. Edited by *S. E. Lehmberg*. 227
Emerson, Ralph Waldo (1803–82). ESSAYS, 1841–4.   12
Gray, Thomas (1716–71). ESSAYS. (*See* Poetry and Drama Section.)
Hamilton, Alexander (1757–1804), and Others. THE FEDERALIST, 1787–8.   519
Hazlitt, William (1778–1830). LECTURES ON THE ENGLISH COMIC WRITERS, 1819; and
  FUGITIVE WRITINGS. 411. LECTURES ON THE ENGLISH POETS, 1818; and THE
  SPIRIT OF THE AGE, 1825. 459. THE ROUND TABLE AND CHARACTERS OF SHAKE-
  SPEAR'S PLAYS, 1817–18. 65. TABLE TALK, 1821–2, 1824. 321
Holmes, Oliver Wendell (1809–94). THE AUTOCRAT OF THE BREAKFAST-TABLE, 1858. 66

1

FICTION

3

SCIENCE

TRAVEL AND TOPOGRAPHY